Christina Rossetti's Faithful Imagination

Christina Rossetti's Faithful Imagination

The Devotional Poetry and Prose

Dinah Roe

First published 2006 by
PALGRAVE MACMILLAN
Houndmills, Basingstoke, Hampshire RG21 6XS and
175 Fifth Avenue, New York, N.Y. 10010
Companies and representatives throughout the world

PALGRAVE MACMILLAN is the global academic imprint of the Palgrave
Macmillan division of St. Martin's Press, LLC and of Palgrave Macmillan Ltd.
Macmillan® is a registered trademark in the United States, United Kingdom
and other countries. Palgrave is a registered trademark in the European
Union and other countries.

ISBN-13: 978-0-230-00507-5   hardback
ISBN-10: 0-230-00507-1   hardback

This book is printed on paper suitable for recycling and made from fully
managed and sustained forest sources.

A catalogue record for this book is available from the British Library.

A catalog record for this book is available from the Library of Congress.

10   9   8   7   6   5   4   3   2
15   14   13   12   11   10   09   08

Printed and bound in Great Britain by
Antony Rowe Ltd, Chippenham and Eastbourne

For Charlotte Roe
We don't have to sneak into lectures anymore.

Contents

Abbreviations

Note: Unless otherwise indicated, references to Christina Rossetti's poems are to *The Complete Poems of Christina Rossetti*, ed. Rebecca Crump, 3 Vols., Baton Rouge: Louisiana State University Press, 1979.

ACR   Kent, David A., ed. *The Achievement of Christina
            Rossetti* (Ithaca and London: Cornell University Press,
            1987)

CGR   Christina Georgina Rossetti

CR   Diane D'Amico, *Christina Rossetti: Faith, Gender, and
            Time* (Baton Rouge: Louisiana State University Press,
            1999)

DGR   Dante Gabriel Rossetti

FD   Christina Rossetti, *The Face of the Deep: A Devotional
            Commentary on the Apocalypse* (London: SPCK, 1892)

JK Letters *The Letters of John Keats*. Edited by Hyder Edward
            Rollins, 2 Vols. (Cambridge: Cambridge University
            Press, 1958)

KCP   Keats, John. *Complete Poems*. Edited by Jack Stillinger
            (London: Belknap Press, 1982)

LB   Jan Marsh, *Christina Rossetti: A Literary Biography*
            (London: Jonathan Cape, 1994)

Letters   *The Letters of Christina Rossetti*. Edited by Antony
            H. Harrison, 4 Vols. (Charlottesville: University Press
            of Virginia, 1997–2005)

LS   *Letter and Spirit: Notes on the Commandments* (London:
            SPCK, 1883)

Memoir   William Michael Rossetti, 'Memoir' in *The Poetical
            Works of Christina Georgina Rossetti* (London:
            Macmillan and Co., Limited, 1904)

PRB   Pre-Raphaelite Brotherhood

SF   Christina Rossetti, *Seek and Find: A Double Series of
            Short Studies of the Benedicte.* London: SPCK, 1879

TF   *Time Flies: A Reading Diary* (London: SPCK, 1885)

TP   Tennyson, Alfred. *The Poems of Tennyson*, 2nd edn.,
            ed. Christopher Ricks (3 Vols. London: Longman,
            1987)

VDP   G. B. Tennyson, *Victorian Devotional Poetry: The
            Tractaria Mode* (Cambridge and London Harvard
            University Press, 1981)

WMR   William Michael Rossetti

Acknowledgments

My gratitude is owed first and foremost to other Rossetti scholars who have set the bar so very high, particularly Diane D'Amico, Antony Harrison, David A. Kent, Jan Marsh, Jerome McGann and Mary Arseneau. Their work never forgets to inspire as well as instruct.

This book might not have come about without the generous encouragement and sound advice of Margaret Reynolds. For her help, freely and graciously given, I thank her. I also value tremendously the editorial eagle eye of Danny Karlin, which has roved critically over many of this book's pages. Thanks are also due to Mary Arseneau for her close reading and insightful comments on this book when it was still in proposal form. For their sage counsel in the early stages of this project, I thank Sharon Ruston and Jerome DeGroot. Their patience and diligence makes them a credit to their profession.

My gratitude is owed to my parents, without whose example I never would have dared to attempt this project. Their continued emotional and financial support amounts to more than I can ever repay, but I will do my best.

I should also thank James Kidd for his unflagging support. His assistance on the poetry and letters of Keats was invaluable. That he was willing to share a living space with me during this project also testifies to his mental strength and his good heart.

David Shelley has been an incredible source of support from the beginning when I was a stranger to London, and I am honored that he counts me as a friend.

Darren Cohen's technical advice was most helpful, particularly on the topic of polo match etiquette.

I would like to give special thanks to Paul Lancaster, one of the dearest people I have ever met, whose kindness toward me was more appreciated than he will ever know.

The British Library, Senate House Library, and in particular the wondrous London Library, were very generous in allowing me access to the best resources and most helpful staff that London has to offer.

Introduction

Virginia Woolf once wrote that if she were to put God on trial, she would summon Christina Rossetti as a witness.[1] If Rossetti's devotional work were submitted into evidence, this case would almost certainly result in a hung jury, if not an outright acquittal. Woolf's indictment of God comes up hard against the same problem that faces all of Rossetti's critics: a long and diverse career which takes our 'witness', and her beliefs and influences, from novice to authority. Rossetti's poetic imagination was shaped by her faith, and her faith by her poetic imagination, in a symbiotic relationship that intensified over her half-century of writing. As critics are beginning to observe, it is a mistake to think, as Woolf does, that 'years of traffic with men and books did not affect [Rossetti] in the least'.[2] The development of her faithful imagination is so subtle and slow that it is all too easy to miss, especially if there is an attempt to force a clear distinction, as Germaine Greer does, between 'the poems of Rossetti's rebellion and self-assertion' and 'those of her resignation and self-denial'.

The evidence of Rossetti's literary life supports neither Woolf's case against God nor Greer's charge that the poet's 'religion is a matter of devout sentiment'.[3] Religious faith provided Rossetti with the two things every poet needs along with money and a room of her own: inspiration and a muse. It also gave her a text. The Authorized Version of the Bible is easily Rossetti's greatest literary influence, yet a curiously neglected source in the criticism of her work. Betty S. Flowers notes this oversight in the most recent edition of the complete poems. She argues that Rossetti would have expected her audience to be familiar with 'biblical characters and voices, and the stories in which they are embedded', and that 'her poems often depend on this knowledge for their effectiveness'.[4]

Critics like Diane D'Amico, Lynda Palazzo and Mary Arseneau have recently made great strides in the rediscovery and rehabilitation of Rossetti's devotional work. They have called for further investigation of the role of religious faith, and specifically Rossetti's reading of the Bible, in the career of this devout poet. The purpose of my project is to demonstrate the effects of religious reading (both the reading of religious texts, and the religious reading of texts) to Rossetti's poetry and thought. Rossetti's lifelong practice of religious reading significantly affected her own writing, and the way she responded to the literature of the past and of her own time. Dante and Keats were as important to her as to her brother Dante Gabriel, but she brought to her reading of both a different sensibility, an active devotional aesthetic which, though clearly influenced by the Tractarian movement, was never subordinated to it.

I place a strong emphasis on Rossetti's devotional prose as an intrinsic part of her achievement as a writer. Although she wrote five books of devotional prose in all, I concentrate on *Time Flies* and *The Face of the Deep* because they present a strong challenge to the characterization of Rossetti as an 'over-scrupulous' Christian writer.[5] *Time Flies* is a 'Reading Diary' whose intimate, almost chatty tone, good humor, and lightness of touch counters lingering notions that Rossetti's daily life unfolded in 'dreary days of unremitting self-denial' (Greer, 376). Rossetti's seriousness and rigor as a religious thinker are confirmed by her very last work, *The Face of the Deep*, a meditation on the Book of Revelation. Its probing biblical exegesis, intense feeling, and imaginative flair are qualities which readers of Rossetti's poetry will recognize.

Both these books, moreover, weave verse into their prose fabric. Although Rossetti herself collected the poems written for her prose-works in a separate volume (*Verses*, 1893) there is much to be gained from reading them in context. The ideology and aesthetics of these poems are often explained and contextualized by the prose passages following or preceding them. Through the movement between prose and poetry, we catch a glimpse of the poet's mind at work; as Rossetti modestly puts it to Theodore Watts in a letter of 22 November 1886, during the composition of *The Face of the Deep*: 'I work at prose, and help myself forward with little bits of verse' (*Letters* 3: 346).

In associating 'work' with 'prose' and 'help' with 'verse', Rossetti seems to substantiate her brother William Michael's judgment that her 'habits' of poetic composition 'were eminently of the spontaneous kind'.[6] Her prose struggles, at times, to balance the scholarly with the devout; in verse she is more open to uncertainty and ambiguity. Yet the two are not separate, but parts of a single enterprise. And as Lynda Palazzo and Mary Arseneau have recently argued, the prose, like the poetry, reveals a mind more alert and less limited by Christian doctrine than that with which her freethinking brother cared to credit her.

Although the Bible was always a 'primary' influence on Rossetti, its literary and doctrinal treatment by Anglo-Catholic writers of her own time (Isaac Williams, John Henry Newman, John Keble) can be traced in her awareness of the formal and thematic differences between poetry and prose, as well as her interest in the suitability of each medium for serving God, man, woman, and writer. The extent of these Victorian influences on her mind and her work does not begin to be fully represented by the poetry alone.

This is not to suggest that these High Church influences are not identifiable in her poetry — on the contrary, a Tractarian philosophy, particularly in regard to the doctrines of analogy and reserve, often operates within both the form and the content of Rossetti's poems. The work of Anthony Harrison and G. B. Tennyson has revealed how an understanding of the Anglican theology behind her devotional poems enriches our understanding of author, text, and era. Recently, the Tractarian connection has come under scrutiny with Lynda Palazzo's contention that Rossetti's devotional work offers 'a revolutionary rejection of the dominant atonement theology of the Tractarians'.[7] Palazzo is right to identify Rossetti as an active and critical reader of the Tractarians, but I argue that Rossetti was more receptive to the dominant themes of Tractarianism than Palazzo allows.

The criticism of Rossetti's substantial body of devotional work has historically been hampered by a discomfort about treating religious writings, particularly by a middle-class, nineteenth-century, single woman, as works of literature. The literary merit of Rossetti's devotional works was as much an issue in her own time as it is in ours, as twentieth-century critic Colleen Hobbs observes:

> The reception this work has experienced may be determined less by artistic merit than by critical presuppositions regarding popular religious texts by women writers. In 1897, for instance, the *Dictionary of National Biography* unselfconsciously revealed its bias against Rossetti's successful devotional books when it described them as 'religious edification, meritorious in their way, but scarcely affecting to be literature'.[8]

Although 'poetess' was an acceptable designation for a middle-class woman (provided her status was amateur or semi-professional), 'Christian theologian' was not. During the Victorian era, women's religious texts were often treated, Robert M. Kachur observes, as 'practical and unremarkable echoes of men's exegetical texts'.[9] The limited availability of Rossetti's devotional prose-works impedes the modern critic from challenging, updating, or even simply considering this Victorian evaluation. The argument becomes circular: lack of critical attention contributes to the impression that these writings are of little interest, which in turn discourages critical attention.

A question mark still hangs over the literary merit of Rossetti's devotional writing, with many choosing to 'treat the prose as an interruption of her stronger work' (Hobbs, 410), and to dismiss her religious poetry as reflective of 'a natural theology without concrete dogmas or concrete problems'.[10] The persistence of this view is evidenced by the fact that no complete edition of her prose has been published, and none is currently planned.

The reluctance to engage with Rossetti as a serious devotional commentator is also reflected in the continuing investment in her earlier, more secular poems. Though a recent anthology gives Rossetti pride of place, along with Tennyson and Browning, as one of the three most important Victorian poets, there remains a critical and popular lack of interest in the poetry that postdates 1865, when she was only 35 years old.[11] Although she wrote prolifically until her death in 1894 at age 64, in the popular and critical imagination both Rossetti and the concerns of her work remain forever youthful. The evaluations of Edmund Gosse who wrote in 1893 that 'metrically her work was better in her youth than it has been since',[12] Mary F. Sandars who wrote in 1930 that 'never again does anything equal the beautiful peach-like bloom of the first-fruits of her genius',[13] Curran who wrote in 1970 that her 'best poetry was written before she was twenty', (Curran, 288), and McGann, who concludes in the 1980s that 'most of Rossetti's greatest verse was written before 1865',[14] have contributed to the neglect of Rossetti's later work. The critical consensus that Rossetti's increasingly devotional post-1865 work is somehow second-rate, artificially halts this poet's progress, freezing her in a post-Romantic / Pre-Raphaelite moment, when in fact an examination of the poetry of this period already forecasts the rejection of the Pre-Raphaelite aesthetic. That these poems are excellent and thoroughly deserving of analysis and attention is undeniable, but their status as entirely representative of her philosophy, theology, and poetic art is limiting to the serious study of Rossetti's life and work.

The early poetry was also the focus of the feminist recovery of Rossetti in the 1980s, as these earlier works were viewed as more in sympathy with its aims, rather than later works with their discomforting praise of patriarchal Christianity. Gilbert and Gubar's study points to a complex politics of renunciation and protest in Rossetti's early work, particularly *Goblin Market*. Germaine Greer singles out *'Goblin Market* and the poems leading up to it' as particularly important to feminist readers, while deeming Rossetti 'incorrigibly minor' as a 'religious poet' (359) largely because 'she used the aspiration of piety as a metaphor for her own frustrated sexuality' (360). This view of the poet dooms her to an existence in which her true instinct for unfettered self-expression is continuously suppressed, both by Victorian convention and her own piety. Reacting to this legacy, Dolores Rosenblum sees Rossetti's 'renunciatory aesthetic' as a liberating influence which offered her an alternative way of thinking about her position as a Victorian woman poet. However, as Linda E. Marshall notes, 'Both [Rosenblum] and Gilbert would have Rossetti wring her art from deprivation'.[15]

The recent work of Leighton, Lootens, and D'Amico has qualified and in some cases challenged such readings, on the grounds that their historical and psychological approaches do not take into account, on the one hand the playful aspects of Rossetti's art, and on the other hand its grounding in religious conviction. Palazzo points out that a 'critical preference ... for the negative values of renunciation', has been 'a stumbling block in the appreciation of Rossetti's devotional texts' (140) Arseneau goes further, arguing that the poet's 'most assertive, most feminist, most political, and most egalitarian statements are formulated not in resistance to her religion, but rather are firmly grounded in it'.[16]

My work is a response to these recent calls for a critical intervention in the feminist construction of Rossetti. While feminist scholarship has done much to revive the flagging poetic reputation of Rossetti, it has also established her in the modern imagination as a woman whose faith, gender, and creativity were incompatible impulses whose conflict made her miserable. This view confuses the poetic *persona* with the poet, and overlooks the centrally important fact that making conflict into art is not a miserable act, but a redemptive one.

I agree that there is more work to be done on Rossetti's connection to her faith and that this is a job for feminist criticism, given its interest in female agency and attention to historical context. Yet we should take care not to be so tantalized by Rossetti as a woman, or indeed as a Christian, that we forget about her as an artist. Exclusive concentration on the devotional works' challenge to patriarchy can have the undesired effect of obscuring its other achievements. Feminist evaluations which insist on Rossetti's outsider status and subversive aims miss opportunities to examine how the poet works within the boundaries of middle-class Christian Victorian society.

William Michael's famous lament of his sister's refusal 'to ponder for herself whether a thing was true or not', and her dependence on 'whether or not it conformed to the Bible', is, in a sense, true enough (*Memoir*, lxviii). Rossetti's religious faith, especially in later years, is absolute. Neither poetry nor prose is interested in challenging or questioning the existence of God, or the authority of his Book. The great question for Rossetti was not one of God's existence or his right to judge humanity, but rather of the relationship of God to nature, to humankind, and to poetry itself. Rossetti's flights of political or social fancy always 'take off' from Christian theology, and always acknowledge — even in their most wayward maneuvers — its necessary guidance. Feminist criticism, in particular, would benefit by starting from this principle rather than trying to ignore or undermine it.

Rossetti's biography, and her own self-mythologizing, have also contributed to the critical focus on her youthful poetry, and consequent neglect of her devotional work. She remains a figure best known for her unknowability, notorious for reserve both in poetry and in her private life. On 28 April 1849, the 17-year-old Rossetti writes to William Michael that it would be 'intolerable ... to have [her] verses regarded as outpourings of a wounded spirit', communicating her fear that her poems might be interpreted as 'love personals', a horror attributable not only to her Victorian modesty but also to her burgeoning sense of herself as a true poet (*Letters* 1: 16).

Her poems, characterized by mystery and ambiguity, seem to dare biographers to uncover, in the words of *Maude*'s narrator, her 'secret source of uneasiness'.[17] The 'source' has been assumed to be sexual, and a number of theories have been explored, ranging from a secret affair with William Bell Scott to closeted lesbianism to sexual abuse by her father or Dante Gabriel. These theories rely exclusively on biographical interpretations of her early work, and are silent on how later devotional writings might fit into their postulations. G. B. Tennyson has attributed this critical trend to 'the strange, modern view that all longing must be sexual, especially if it is the longing of an unmarried Victorian woman'.[18] What is always omitted from the love story, as Tennyson implies, is Rossetti's longing for God, which, if it is mentioned, is usually regarded as a pose or a blind, under cover of whose conventions

Rossetti is free to fantasize about sexual love or political freedom. Such disproportionate attention has been given to what is withheld in Rossetti's work that very few have taken on the more obvious task of interpreting what is actually present. Though any true-life object of Rossetti's affection is always cloaked in her amatory poems, much of the time, and particularly in her later work, he is entirely revealed as Jesus Christ. Although the identity of this love-object is no mystery at all in Rossetti's devotional works, the poet's lifelong relationship with Christ generally is underexplored biographically and critically.

Although my focus is on the religious in Rossetti's work, and on the Bible as her primary source material, I do not wish to suggest that her Christian beliefs make her devotional work antagonistic to other kinds of interpretation. On the contrary, Rossetti's own insistence, stylistically and theologically, on the slipperiness of meaning, the pitfalls of translation and interpretation, and the shortcomings of human understanding, encourages her readers to think and feel for themselves.

I argue that Rossetti is a major author precisely because of the ways in which her work skillfully synthesizes various influences, the devotional, the Romantic, the Pre-Raphaelite, the Tractarian, the Dantean, the Petrarchan, speaking not only to and about the experience of women, but the experience of art. Her claims for herself as an artist are by far the most radical, yet undervalued, aspect of her writing. That such claims are largely to be found in works of religious devotion makes their existence all the more intriguing. In her devotional prose and poetry, Rossetti invites her reader to engage with a sophisticated network of biblical allusion, in which Christian doctrine is re-thought and sometimes re-forged. Unless we take this invitation seriously, we will not take the true measure of Rossetti.

1
'Real Things Unseen': The Tractarian Influence

In his introduction to David A. Kent's *The Achievement of Christina Rossetti*, Jerome McGann writes about the language of revelation in the devotional poem 'Now They Desire':

> It does no good to reach back for original texts in Scripture or their exegetical and iconographical translations. Rossetti's poetry works precisely because it forces us to read everything *simply*, in literal ways; to seek and therefore not to find any human or worlded equivalents for what we read.[1]

McGann identifies reading 'simply' as an effective strategy for apprehending (or, indeed, not apprehending) Rossetti's poetry. He suggests that an appreciation of Rossetti's poetry is not helped by knowledge of the Bible; the poetry itself 'forces us' (willing or not) to read her words literally, simply. The problem with this approach is twofold. First, it does not address the question of Rossetti's intended audience, for whom at least the 'original texts', if not their 'exegetical and iconographical translations', would have had more resonance than for modern readers. What is conspicuously absent from twentieth-century criticism of Rossetti is any sort of exegetical approach, which underestimates the vital and immediate role religion played in the lives and consciousness of Rossetti's contemporaries. Literary criticism ignores what social history well knows. F. M. L. Thompson writes that during the Victorian era, 'Religion was at the centre of middle-class lifestyles', and that 'regular church- or chapel-going was universal among the middle-classes, often to two or three services each Sunday'. Even social life 'outside the home ... revolved round the church or chapel.'[2] Readers in the twenty-first century, unlike nineteenth-century readers, must 'reach back for original texts in Scripture', simply because such texts are unlikely to be as firmly established in their cultural frame of reference.

The second problem with McGann's argument against exegetical reading is that it overlooks the literary and philosophical implications of Rossetti's engagement with the Bible, arguably her primary lexicon. It could be said that Rossetti's poetry is in fact constituted by exegesis. She refers to the Bible, either by quotation or allusion, in nearly every poem, often recycling the same quotations and images in different poems. Read exegetically, her poems present complex theological arguments, not only about God's relationship to man, but also about the relationship of the Old Testament to the New, and the relationship of God, the ultimate Creator, to the poet, the human creator.

McGann adds that Rossetti uses a 'language of revelations' of 'portentous but obscure import'; he undermines any notion of the poet's deliberate and conscious process of selection and composition, making her sound something like a sibyl. He writes that 'Rossetti is not our authority ... since this language is entirely appropriated', reinforcing the idea of the poet as a sort of mouthpiece (8). Appropriation in Rossetti's devotional poetry, however, is an allusive act in itself, which reinforces rather than undermines Rossetti's 'authority.' Rossetti chooses certain biblical phrases which run like a refrain through many of her poems, in imitation of the books of the Bible in which various phrases turn up again and again to bridge the gap between different parts of the Old Testament, and between the Old Testament and the New. The significance of these phrases is unfixed, metamorphosing with each use, keeping the poet's meaning in motion. In the same way that it is difficult to find unity and consistency in the Bible, it is challenging to find unity among the mysteries and contradictions of Rossetti's poetry. Her devotional work, like the Bible, is meant for contemplation, not resolution. However, reading her poetry 'simply' and 'literally' by ignoring its theology does no justice to Rossetti's daring and imaginative agency. Her confident selection and re-imagining of biblical image and text challenges the passivity associated with simple appropriation.

For example, by using quotations from Revelation in 'Now They Desire', Rossetti places herself in the tradition of St. John, an inheritance not without its dangers, as Revelation makes clear:

> For I testify unto every man that heareth the words of the prophecy of this book, If any man shall add unto these things, God shall add unto him the plagues that are written in this book:

And if any man shall take away from the words of the book of this prophecy, God shall take away his part out of the book of life, and out of the holy city, and from the things which are written in this book. (Rev 22:18–19)

Revelation may have appealed to Rossetti as a book which is notably self-conscious about its own material existence. John is repeatedly exhorted to 'Write' its prophecies; prophecies which correspond in language and theme to earlier books of the Old and New Testaments. Rossetti's poem also brings together the Old and New Testaments by invoking 'the bride / in raiment white and clean', a figure who first appears in the Old Testament Song of Solomon and becomes in the New Testament a symbol of the Christian Church (3: 33–4).

McGann remains one of the best and most influential of Rossetti's critics, which is perhaps why his ideas on exegesis in the introduction to *The Achievement of Christina Rossetti* resurface in Tom Paulin's 2002 review of *The Complete Poems*: 'Although it is helpful to know the biblical sources of these lines, I do not think that they, and indeed most of Rossetti's poetry, are helped by that knowledge'.[3]

McGann's doubts about the usefulness of 'exegetical and iconographical translations' appear to have had a lasting impact, even though they are not reflected elsewhere in his work on Rossetti. For example, he has also written that 'to read Rossetti's religious poetry with understanding ... requires a more or less conscious investment in the *peculiarities* of its Christian orientation' (*The Beauty of Inflections*, 239).

One way of exploring these 'peculiarities' has been to view Rossetti's work in the religious context in which it was created, namely, the Anglo-Catholic revival. Yet interpreting and affirming biblical texts through a kind of poetical exegesis was not a new literary phenomenon of the late 1840s. Christian writers whom Rossetti admired greatly, from Dante to Herbert, built literary reputations on their interpretative use of biblical language and tradition. The textual history of the Bible itself contributed to this practice, as the New Testament, always looking over its shoulder, frequently appropriated phrases, stories, and ideologies from the Old Testament in order to legitimize and reinforce its Christian agenda. The Oxford Movement of the nineteenth century took self-conscious account of this relationship between the books of the Bible, developing an aesthetic whose influence pervades Rossetti's own poetics.

The history of the Oxford Movement, and the Tractarian poetics which were its lasting literary legacy, has been well documented, and its effects on Rossetti's poetry generally acknowledged: most notably in

G. B. Tennyson's *Victorian Devotional Poetry*, and later by Antony Harrison. The history of Tractarianism and its poetics is worth touching upon here, but not simply as a retread of what has become a commonplace of Rossetti studies. In fact, the position of Tractarianism is far from secure. The question of Rossetti's debt to the Tractarians has become a contentious issue in feminist readings of her poetry. Lynda Palazzo recently challenged the idea that Rossetti 'accepted the teaching of Pusey and other great Tractarians, writing poetry in the wake of Keble until finally consolidating an imitative Tractarian position in her devotional prose'.[4] Palazzo also contends that Rossetti's work critiques Anglo-Catholic sisterhoods on the grounds that they were 'an exploitation of women's spirituality' (6). Mary Arseneau has deftly sidestepped a confrontation with Palazzo on this issue:

> where Palazzo emphasizes the devotional prose of Rossetti's later years, its various departures from Tractarian theology, and its continuities with twentieth-century developments in feminist theology, I emphasize the early and middle phases of Rossetti's career, focusing on her poetry and poetics and attributing a formative influence to Tractarian theology, aesthetics, and worship.[5]

Despite the widespread acceptance of Tractarianism as a 'formative influence', the debate continues. Rossetti responds to this heritage not just as a woman and an Anglo-Catholic, but, primarily, as a poet. I agree with Tennyson and Harrison that the doctrines of reserve and analogy (of which more later) shape and inform her devotional writing. Yet as Palazzo's work suggests, a re-evaluation of Rossetti's response to Tractarian poetics remains invaluable to feminist critics who want to respond to a legacy of criticism which finds her work morbid, sexually repressed, simplistic, or unintellectual. Another look at how Tractarian poetics work in combination with other contemporary literary influences on Rossetti can expose the daring imaginative agency under the surface of work which is still too often dismissed as flatly dogmatic or pious.

Tractarian poetics grew out of the Oxford Movement (1833–41), which was begun by spiritual leaders at Oriel College, Oxford, when they published a series of pamphlets called 'Tracts for the Times,' advocating the restoration of religious rituals long abandoned by the Church of England. These pamphleteers became known as 'Tractarians,' a term which also refers to their literary style. Although the Oxford Movement itself was brief, it had a lasting impact on both the religious and literary practices of the Victorian High Church.

The High Church revival of the 1840s, in which the young Christina Rossetti, her mother, and her sister actively participated, was regarded as one of the more radical religious movements of its time. Its 'Romish' practices, such as confession, icons, and incense during church services, were considered highly suspect. That the establishment of 'Anglican Sisterhoods' caused a public outcry did not stop Rossetti's sister Maria from joining one in adulthood. Close relationships with High Church clergy remained central to Rossetti's life, from Dodsworth in her adolescence to Littledale and Canon Burrows in midlife to Gutch and Nash in her old age, to name a few.

But it was not only the religious practices of the High Church revival that inspired Rossetti. Her study of the Tractarian poets was informal, but was no less intense for that. Her well-thumbed and annotated copy of John Keble's *The Christian Year* (1827), as well as the pictures she drew to illustrate some of its poems, testifies to her deep engagement with the Tractarian preacher and poet.[6] Her admiration of the Tractarian leader John Henry Newman, even after his conversion to Catholicism, is made plain in a sonnet on his death ('Cardinal Newman' 5–6, 3:52), while her letters and later devotional prose works give evidence of her admiration for the devotional writing of Isaac Williams.

G. B. Tennyson writes, 'Like all Tractarians, [Rossetti] was receptive to nature as a vehicle of divine grace, and especially like Isaac Williams, she was willing to bring an intense personal response to nature as a religious experience' (*VDP* 202). Most importantly, Rossetti shared with the Tractarian poets the belief in poetry itself as a vehicle for the human expression of, and meditation on, divine truth. Readings of Rossetti's poetry which take into account the literary effects of both her relationship to the Bible and to Anglo-Catholicism reveal the development of a religious philosophy virtually inseparable from the poetic one.

For Rossetti, art and religion are closely related because both seek to describe the ineffable. The description of abstract religious concepts is necessarily difficult and not easily understood, not least because of the incapacity of the human mind to grasp fully the divine, while the necessary mediation of art (whether visual or linguistic) can further confuse the issue. Though Rossetti cannot solve this problem, she can make it bear fruit in her poems, which exemplify the need for meditation and contemplation to overcome the difficulties inherent in human representation of the abstract and the divine. The oft-cited secrecy and mystery of Rossetti's writings have less to do with her personal desire to be elusive than with her artistic desire to represent God and the sanctity of human emotion in a way which is mindful of the problematics of such a project. The religious philosophy of the Tractarians, with its reliance on tenets such as the doctrines of reserve and analogy, gave the poet a means with which to express this dilemma.

In brief, analogy, typology, and reserve are poetic means of talking about the divine, while acknowledging that direct communication with, or complete understanding of divinity is impossible. Keble, in Tract 89, writes about analogical interpretation as 'the way of regarding external things, either as fraught with imaginative associations, or as parabolic lessons of conduct, or as symbolic language in which God speaks to us of a world out of sight'.[7] Analogy is defined by John Henry Newman in his *Apologia* as 'the doctrine that material phenomena are both the types and the instruments of real things unseen'.[8] His use of the word 'type' here links analogy to the idea of typology, which also has a role to play in Tractarian poetics.

Practiced by Tractarians but in use since early Christianity, typological interpretation is when Old Testament events are seen as prefigurations of New Testament events. Thus the Old Testament can be interpreted as a spiritual anticipation of the New Testament without losing its literal status as its predecessor. The philosophies of both Testaments can be at odds, but the integrity of the entire biblical narrative can be maintained by typological exegesis. To give an example: the near-sacrifice of the Old Testament Isaac by his father Abraham would be seen as a kind of foreshadowing of the New Testament God's sacrifice of his son for mankind.

It is probable that Rossetti learned about the aesthetic possibilities of typology, and its outgrowth, analogy, from both religious and secular sources, and this aspect of her learning process is reflected in her poetry. Like the PRB, Rossetti believed that the expression of powerful feeling in poetry was an important part of its meaning. Yet for Rossetti's purposes, emotion was not expressed for its own sake, nor for art's, but for God's. She takes her cue not only from the Tractarians, but also from Ruskin, for whom, as Sussman writes, 'the aim of the artist is to imitate not only the Book of Nature but also the Book of God'.[9] In Tractarian poetics, the doctrine of reserve ensures that this form of imitation stays on the right side of flattery. Reserve is the idea that nature exists as a codified expression of a God too divine and powerful for human perception. Human beings cannot see God directly,[10] and so nature acts as a mediator between the earthly and the divine. Nature, taken as a whole, is confusing, vast, and incomprehensible, but viewed as the sum of its components, the function of its forms becomes clearer.

Analogy and reserve are useful to the devotional poet because they make possible the idea that divinity inheres in earthly design, that it coexists with the human. These doctrines, whose philosophy is dependent on the idea of coexistence, allow the poet to create space in her poetry for ambiguities and seeming paradoxes. Isaac Williams writes of the potential contradictions which can be thrown into relief by these doctrines.

> Things, therefore, so Divine and manifold are necessarily replete with what appear to man as contradictions ... invisible, and yet visible; a visible kingdom, yet seen only by faith, and not by sight ... it is the kingdom of heaven, yet in the world.[11]

Like the principles at the heart of analogy and reserve, like the books of the Old Testament and the New, Rossetti's devotional poetry often is created and sustained by seeming contradiction. The earthly and the spiritual are at odds, yet both come from God. Thus nature, earthly yet filled with spirit, becomes not only a metaphor for man but also an allegory of language. As man can seek to perceive the divine in nature, so too can he seek divine meaning in earthly words.

Rossetti's poetry is an open invitation to join the poet on her quest to reveal the divine expressed in the earthly. She makes this invitation explicit in her devotional prose work, *Seek and Find*:

> A work is less noble than its maker: he who makes a good thing is himself better than it: God excels the most excellent of his creatures. Matters of everyday occurrence illustrate our point: an artist may paint a lifelike picture, but he cannot endow it with life like his own ... Wise were the ancients who felt that all forms of beauty could be but partial expressions of beauty's very self: and who by clue of what they saw groped after Him they saw not. Beauty essential is the archetype of imparted beauty; Life essential, of imparted life ... but such objects, good, living, beautiful, as we now behold, are not that very Goodness, Life, Beauty, which ... we shall one day contemplate in beatific vision. (*SF* 14)

Here, the poet sees reserve, typology, and analogy as extensions of neo-Platonic ideals (essential beauty as the archetype of imparted beauty, essential life of imparted life), reminding the reader of the impossibility of fully comprehending the divine. Yet at the same time she does not discourage the effort. She draws a comparison between

God's relationship to creation, and the artist's to his art, suggesting that although God's creation is made in his image, this image is only a representation of the divine, and not the divine itself, just as an artist's painting is only a representation of a living thing, but not itself alive. She takes care, however, not to draw too close a parallel between the creative powers of God and Man. Because an artist cannot endow his creation 'with a life like his own', he is not entirely like God, but rather a 'less noble' imitation of Him. He cannot give life to his picture, therefore, the artist's earthly work is only a 'partial expression' of original divine beauty.

At the same time Rossetti praises the wisdom of the 'ancients' who trusted in their earthly vision, 'who by clue of what they saw groped after Him they saw not.' She suggests here that modes of perception can be spiritual as well as physical, that the unseen is as important as the seen, and that recognition of the unseen must take place in the mind rather than the eye. She quotes in *Time Flies*, '"Blessed are they that have not seen, and yet have believed"' (John 20:29). She continues, 'St. Paul declares: "We look not at the things which are seen, but at the things which are not seen: for the things which are seen are temporal; but the things which are not seen are eternal"' (*TF* 17). The biblical quotation from John refers to Christ's rebuke to Thomas, who does not believe in the fact of his messiah's return until he sees Christ for himself. Following the example of this New Testament parable of faith, Rossetti privileges the unseen in linking it to the eternal. She interrogates the link between sight and belief, suggesting that using the external senses to perceive things in an internal spiritualized way is the closest humanity can come to the divine. For Rossetti, the process of contemplation is not just a means to come to understanding, but is understanding itself.

Rossetti's obscurity, her secretive, mysterious tone, often leads to a misunderstanding of her poetry as a sort of riddle, a reading which the poet probably would resist. In *The Face of the Deep* she writes, 'I must beware of scrutinizing any text of Holy Scripture as if it were a puzzle or a riddle. I must beware of making guesses at what is withheld from me'. Later she adds, 'Whoever by loving submission turns intellectual poverty into voluntary spiritual poverty, has discovered a super-excellent philosopher's stone, apt to transmute ignorance into wisdom' (350). Here, 'what is withheld' takes on a sacred significance, which would be violated by making an intellectual guess at its nature. Obscurity in Rossetti is not only a stylistic but a moral choice, intimately linked to Tractarian belief in analogy and reserve.

Rossetti's devotional work is committed to trying to create spiritual feeling as well as thought. Or, to put it another way, the poet tries to make her point by illustration rather than explanation, to privilege intense feeling over literal significance. Understanding, in Rossetti's poetry and prose, has as much to do with emotional and imaginative perception as it does with intellectual prowess. The mysterious ('what is withheld') can only begin to be understood when the reader respects the unknowable by re-imagining his / her own 'intellectual poverty', as humble 'spiritual poverty'. This recognition of the limit of human thought paradoxically prompts the Socratic transmutation of ignorance into wisdom. In addition, for Rossetti, the fact that something cannot be understood is redemptive in itself because such a discovery proves that mystery exists. Through its allusive and elusive intensity, Rossetti's poetry attempts to express by indirection what cannot be directly known — the essence of divine meaning.

A Tractarian interest in divine mystery combined with a Ruskinian typological aesthetic dominates '"Consider the Lilies of the Field"' (1: 76). The doctrine of reserve is at play in the poem, as God is not addressed directly, but is a presence alluded to in an analogical description of nature. Rossetti encourages the reader not to see the flowers visually, but rather to envision them, as it is their essence and analogical meaning which concern her. She does not describe the texture and color of the lilies or violets, and although she does write of the 'scarlet head' of the poppy, the physical properties of the flowers are not as important as what they say. Rossetti's flowers speak: they 'preach' (1), the 'rose saith' (2), the 'poppy saith' (6), the lilies both 'say' (11) and 'preach' (12), the 'violets whisper' (13), and the 'lichen and moss and sturdy weed / tell' (21–2). The lessons of the flowers are learned not only from looking at them, but also from listening to them. Their meaning is inherent not only in their design, but in their relationship to one another and to their location in the totality of nature. This understanding of the flowers is not predicated on how they look, but on their interaction with God, nature, the reader, and the imagination. Their significance becomes clear, not in the eye of the reader, but in his / her mind. The poet here addresses the problem of what is lost, not only in the translation from an object to its visual representation, but also in the discrepancies of visual and verbal mimesis, by relocating vision in the mind's eye, the imagination. Only imagination can combine both the act of seeing and the act of thinking. Through such contemplation, the poet suggests, we can begin to perceive the ineffable, the indescribable, God. Focusing the reader's eye solely on the literal, earthly existence of the flowers would violate the doctrine of reserve, but presenting the flowers as a verbal analogue of God privileges the existence of their divine creator. These double modes of perception, visual and contemplative, suggest not only the sanctity of the divine, but relate also to the miracle of the relationship between the human mind and the power of the poet. The doctrines of reserve and analogy inform Rossetti's poetic strategy, but embedded in their use is another analogy about the poet-mind's ability to perceive and transcribe the connection between nature and divinity.

The poem begins assertively with the command in the title, "'Consider the Lilies of the Field'". The title appears in quotation marks, not only to let the reader know that it is appropriated from another source, but also to emphasize the verbal power of the command. The quotation marks let the reader hear a voice, though whether it is the poet's, God's, Matthew's or Luke's remains an open question.[12] The significance of the quotation marks points to the fact that this is a poem as much about voice as it is about vision. Divinity is speaking to the reader through nature.

'The light of the body is the eye', writes Matthew, 'if therefore thine eye be single, thy whole body shall be full of light' (6:22). Rossetti's poem explores Matthew's link between vision (visual and spiritual), goodness, and the body. The poem suggests that perceiving God's imprint in his works is the way to see with a 'single'[13] eye, and that the recognition of God will lead to the purification of the body and spirit. The poem engages also with the idea that spiritual vision is stimulated not only by seeing God in nature, but also by hearing His teachings. Just as Paul was converted by the voice of God, so too must humanity 'hear' His teachings in nature and not be distracted by earthly beauty.

'Flowers preach to us if we will hear', if we will 'consider' them, and so too does Rossetti's poem preach in the voices of saints, flowers, and a poet. However, the reader must read the poem closely and 'consider' its voices in order to understand its 'humble lessons' (17). Both kinds of perception, visual and aural, take place in the reader's imagination. The poet does not directly tell the reader how to interpret either the poem or God's message; her only command is that s / he 'consider.' Rossetti gives the reader certain images and voices, but she leaves it up to the reader to make associations and connections. In this way, Rossetti's poem itself enacts the very doctrine of reserve with which it is concerned.

In 'A Testimony' (1:77), Rossetti used Ecclesiastes and the gospels of Matthew and Luke to warn against vanity, but in "'Consider the Lilies of the Field"', she offers a positive solution. Instead of warning against human weakness, the poet celebrates the potential of the human mind to perceive goodness. Although she does write that 'Men ... / ... take no heed / Of humble lessons we would read', the poem itself is a lesson in how to 'read' nature's lessons correctly, demonstrating a certain amount of faith in the potential of man to understand the divine (15–17). Whereas 'A Testimony' speaks of vanity, decay, and punishment, '"Consider the Lilies of the Field"' speaks of the generative love which comes from God.

Both Matthew and Luke use the phrase 'consider the lilies':

> And why take ye thought for raiment? Consider the lilies of the field, how they grow; they toil not, neither do they spin:
> And yet I say unto you, That even Solomon in all his glory was not arrayed like one of these.
>
> (Matthew 6:28–9)

> Consider the lilies how they grow: they toil not, they spin not; and yet I say unto you, that Solomon in all his glory was not arrayed like one of these.
>
> (Luke 12:27)

Both are lessons about trusting in God and in His divine plan. Though antimaterialist ideology is at work here, so too is the positive alternative of asceticism. Matthew 6 records Christ's Sermon on the Mount, which advocates humility in alms-giving and prayer, contains the 'Our Father' prayer, and promotes a quiet faith in God. Earlier in his chapter, Matthew gives specific advice about charity and prayer, advising that both be done privately and without fanfare:

> That thine alms may be in secret: and thy Father which seeth in secret himself shall reward thee openly.
>
> (Matthew 6:4)

> But thou, when thou prayest, enter into thy closet, and when thou hast shut thy door, pray to thy Father which is in secret; and thy Father which seeth in secret shall reward thee openly.
>
> (Matthew 6:6)

Rossetti would have read this secrecy in relation to Tractarian ideas of reserve. She engages stylistically and formally with this idea of the secret as an indicator of sincerity in '"Consider the Lilies of the Field"'. The poem itself, through its contemplative air of mystery, enacts Christ's words about the true expression of faith in secrecy. Like Matthew 6, '"Consider the Lilies of the Field"' acts as a transcription of a sermon, albeit a sermon from nature rather than man. An explicit command is contained in the poem's title, but its quotation marks mediate what might have been too bold an assertion of authorial power, reminding the reader that the poet is aware not only of her source (God) but also of her duty to express His message about humility.

The familiar and the transfigured coexist in '"Consider the Lilies of the Field"'. In keeping with the title's instruction to contemplate, the poem's first line turns the responsibility for interpretation over to the reader: 'Flowers preach to us *if* we will hear' (1, emphasis mine). Rossetti's are secretive flowers, the efficacy of whose message depends upon man's willingness to 'consider' it. Their secrecy is linked to the doctrine of reserve, as each flower contains an allegorical lesson for man. The lovely bud of the rose camouflages the danger of a thorn, while the 'scarlet head' of the poppy holds the 'juice of subtle virtue' (7, 9). The 'language' of these flowers is as paradoxical as their appearance as the lilies 'preach without words', while the 'violets whisper' their 'humble lessons' (12, 13, 17). In order to understand their message, man must perceive the flowers with what Rossetti was later to call 'the spiritual eye'. In *The Face of the Deep*, Rossetti writes explicitly about spiritual vision and imagination: 'Whether natural or spiritual, eyes that look are the eyes likely to see. Meditation fixes the spiritual eye on matters worthy of insight: it sees something, it may gradually perceive more and more' (*FD* 267). '"Consider the Lilies of the Field"' is an appeal to the spiritual eye; while its words create a vision of the flowers, such a vision takes place in the mind, not in the eyes of the reader. Their spiritual beauty is given precedence through the 'spiritual eye' of the reader's imaginative vision. The imagination, therefore, becomes the fertile ground in which spiritual vision can grow.

'"Consider the Lilies of the Field"', like 'A Testimony', is engaged in presenting a unified vision of Old and New Testament text. Again, Rossetti uses a typological analysis of the figure of Solomon to bring together Old Testament and New Testament ideas, but this time the poet is more concerned with promoting wisdom than pointing out the pitfalls of human vanity.

Allusions to Solomon in this poem come not in the form of direct Old Testament quotations but are filtered through the New Testament interpretations of Matthew and Luke. The advantage of this strategy is that the poet is allowed more interpretive license as her language is freed from direct Old Testament quotation, while at the same time maintaining links to Old Testament ideology. Solomon is very much a part of '"Consider the Lilies of the Field"'. Although he makes no direct appearance in quotation or description, the poem itself can be read as a response to the ideology of Ecclesiastes. Like the lessons of the flowers, Solomon's presence is vague and intangible, and needs contemplation to perceive and understand.

Solomon is linked to the lily in several ways.[14] Matthew mentions Solomon in the verse immediately following 6:28, 'And yet I say unto you, That even Solomon in all his glory was not arrayed like one of these' (Matthew 6:29). In Matthew, the mention of Solomon takes place in a chapter devoted to the refutation of material, earthly things, concluding that mankind should 'seek ... first the kingdom of God, and his righteousness' (6:33). The implication here is that Solomon was distracted from God by his own tremendous material wealth, that in fact, his possessions became a burden to him, and an obstacle to his relationship with God. Christ draws an analogy between the lilies of the field and human beings, suggesting that if, like the lilies, they trust in God's love, they will want for nothing. The lilies of the field do not 'toil' or 'spin' to survive, but trust in God to provide for them.[15] The lilies symbolize Christ's people in another way because the lily is a flower native to Palestine.

An implied criticism of the vanity of Solomon's wisdom appears also in Matthew 6:27: 'Which of you by taking thought can add one cubit unto his stature?' Solomon was famous for his wisdom, his 'thought', but his wisdom ultimately would come to nothing before God because it was earthly rather than divine. 1 Kings 7 describes the carved lilies which decorate the Temple, providing another association between Solomon and lilies.[16] Despite the fact that Solomon has built the Temple of God and accomplished many great works, in Ecclesiastes he 'looked on all the works that my hands had wrought, and on the labour that I had laboured to do: and behold, all was vanity and vexation of spirit' (Ecclesiastes 2:11). The Gospel of Luke also speaks of the lilies of the field, but in this case, the reference to Solomon is contained in the same verse, literally bringing Solomon and the lilies closer together. Luke references Solomon in order to offer a critique of materialism and the vanity of wisdom, echoing Matthew 6:27.

The wisdom of which Ecclesiastes writes has less to do with a crisis of faith than with an existential anxiety about the purpose of life and the inevitability of death. In the first chapter he is concerned with being a wise king, using his wisdom to build houses, plant vineyards, and acquire treasures. He worries about dying, and about his kingdom being inherited by a fool, which causes his 'heart to despair' (2:20). However, once he begins to use the wisdom of his heart, he gains some contentment. In chapter 7 he writes, 'I applied mine heart to know, and to search, and to seek out wisdom and the reason of things', and it is the wisdom of his heart which leads him to advise that man try to please God (Ecclesiastes 7:25).[17] Once he '[applies] mine heart to know wisdom', he comes to terms with the difficulties and incongruities of life:

> a man cannot find out the work that is done under the sun: because though a man labour to seek it out, yet he shall not find it; yea farther; though a wise man think to know it, yet shall he not be able to find it.
>
> (8:17)

Ecclesiastes' wisdom gets reinterpreted by the gospels of the New Testament as Matthew and Luke suggest that the failure of Solomon's wealth and intelligence has directly to do with a lack of faith in God's providence. The Tractarians went further, treating Solomon's story as typological proof of the coming of Christ. Isaac Williams, in his *Characters of the Old Testament*, writes about the story of Solomon in relation to the New Testament:

> As St. Augustine has observed, the Jews were thus taught that this was not that true Son of David, that they might look forward to another Solomon in whom the promises were fulfilled, and something higher and better in the Heir of the Kingdom.[18]

Here, Williams interprets Solomon's failings as a sign of the world's need for Christ. He continues:

> Solomon was very highly favoured; he comes before us almost like one of the saints of God in his earlier years: but he needed the great mark of Christ ... There is a secret knowledge which is hid from the wise and revealed by the Father unto babes; and this is the mystery of the Cross; it is made known to Christ's little ones; of whom as clothed with His righteousness it may be said, that "Solomon in all his glory was not arrayed like one of these". (218)

According to Williams' typological reading, Solomon fails as a king not because of vanity or wisdom or idolatry, but because he lacks 'the great mark of Christ.' In his interpretation, the antimaterialist ethic of the gospels of Matthew and Luke is secondary in importance to the notion of an Old Testament king as a prefiguration of Christ. Matthew and Luke's lilies of the field are read as Christian children. In this way, Williams alludes again to Christ's power to make the word flesh (lilies = babes), to make the symbolic literal, in the same way that symbols in the Old Testament manifest themselves literally in the New Testament.

This typological reading is important to Rossetti because it reveals the Tractarian philosophy of the mutually reinforcing relationship between the Old and New Testaments. Williams's reading elides difference and inconsistency in the texts in order to create unity; an ambitious project in the case of Solomon because Ecclesiastes' writing is largely about man's struggle with the inconsistencies of life and worship. Rossetti's poetry accommodates such Old Testament and New Testament difference with a more abstract and conceptual, but no less typical approach, by introducing the unifying New Testament concept of love.

The title's quotation marks, as mentioned before, self-consciously reference other voices which have gone before Rossetti's (Solomon, Matthew, Luke, Christ) as she engages with the questions raised by Ecclesiastes. The first line, 'Flowers preach to us if we will hear', is another veiled allusion, as Ecclesiastes begins, 'The words of the preacher'. In keeping with the idea of reserve, when the lilies do preach, they say ambiguously, 'Behold how we / Preach without words of purity' (11–12). The line implies that though the lilies have no language, their physical purity is a lesson in itself.

Lilies mean different things to the Old and New Testaments, representing simultaneously the relationship of love between humans, God's love for Israel, divine love for the soul of man, Solomon's love for his kingdom, and Christ's love for the Church. Rossetti uses the analogy, reserve, and typology of Tractarian theology to create a discursive space where such diverse meanings can coexist. Rossetti's poem addresses the issue of conflicting meanings and incongruities: roses whose 'loveliness is born / Upon a thorn' (4–5), poppies 'held in scorn' (8) yet containing 'juice of subtle virtue' (9), lilies which 'Preach without words' (12) violets which whisper but are unheard. Ultimately, however, what these living things have in common, despite their internal incongruities, is something more powerful and significant than difference: they carry the imprint of God's love. In the final stanza, not only 'the fairest flowers' (18) but also 'merest grass' (19) and 'Lichen ... moss and sturdy weed' all 'Tell of His love who sends the dew' (21–22). Despite the ambiguities and impurities inherent in each, Rossetti's flowers and plants are all a testimony to God's love.

'"Consider the Lilies of the Field"' is also a poem about language, its inconsistencies, shortcomings, and failings, whose efforts mirror the struggle of Ecclesiastes in its search for wisdom and meaning. In imitation of Ecclesiastes, its deliberate ambiguity accommodates a multiplicity of conflicting meanings. The poem tries to describe the ineffable and to locate the hidden unity in conflicting testimonies by using multiple voices and styles. The purity of the living things of the earth, because they 'tell of his love who sends the dew', is recuperated by God's love. The redemptive power of divine love is more a New Testament idea than an Old Testament one, and has to do with a typical reading of Solomon as a king who failed because he was without the love of Christ. However, Rossetti views the failings of Solomon from a different perspective, one more interested in his struggle for loving wisdom than in the absence of Christ.

Ecclesiastes begins to realize in chapters 7 and 8 that it is the wisdom of the heart which leads man to '[discern] both time and judgement' (Ecclesiastes 8:5). Chapter 9 comes to a similar conclusion as '"Consider the Lilies of the Field"' about the connection of all living things to God:

> For all this I *considered in my heart* even to declare all this, that the righteous, and the wise, and their works, are in the hand of God: no man knoweth either love or hatred by all that is before them. (9: 1, emphasis mine)

Once Ecclesiastes uses the wisdom of his heart, he begins to understand better the workings of the divine and his place within the divine plan. When he '[applies his] heart to know wisdom' (8:16), he accepts that 'All things come alike to all: there is one event to the righteous, and to the wicked' (9:2) and that 'time and chance happeneth to them all' (9:11). The wisdom that comes from his heart seems 'great' (13) to him, and he discovers that 'wisdom is better than strength' (16). Thus, when he considers the matter in his heart, he realizes that God is more powerful than man, and writes that 'God shall bring every work into judgment, with every secret thing, whether it be good, or whether it be evil' (12:14).

The message of '"Consider the Lilies of the Field"' conflates New Testament redemptive promise and Ecclesiastes' wisdom. Rossetti, although undoubtedly aware of the typical reading of Solomon as representing the failure of a world without a messiah and at the same time

4 Christina Rossetti's Faithful Imagination

prefiguring Christ, chooses instead to address a different aspect of Solomon's incapacity. Ecclesiastes ends on a somber note about divine justice and mortality, while '"Consider the Lilies of the Field"' concludes with an image of dew, rain, and sunshine sent from God 'To nourish one small seed' (24). The dew, rain, and sunshine are all New Testament baptismal metaphors, but the idea of baptism is less important here than that of the natural life cycle and what man can learn from 'considering' it. This generative moment takes further Ecclesiastes' argument about the wisdom of the heart, suggesting that wisdom is not only about fearing God's judgement, but recognizing His love. God in '"Consider the Lilies of the Field"' is a supportive and nourishing New Testament God, full of love for his creation. The implicit suggestion that Rossetti makes about Solomon has to do not only with his inability to know / be Jesus Christ, but his ultimate failure to recognize God's love in addition to his judgment.

Rossetti revisits this theme ten years after '"Consider the Lilies of the Field"', in the 1863 poem 'Consider'. While '"Consider the Lilies of the Field"' with its multiple voices and instructions has more in common with a sermon, 'Consider' reads more like a parable. 'Consider' (1: 218) eliminates the voices of the flowers, replacing them with the voice of the poet and echoes of the voices of the biblical authors. No one directly speaks, preaches, or whispers in this poem, as did the flowers of '"Consider the Lilies of the Field"'. The flowers here are not given voices; rather, they allude to the voices of the past, like Isaiah, Matthew and Luke. The poem's vision of nature redeemed by God's love is communicated through echoes of voices, like Ecclesiastes' 'words of wise men ... heard in quiet' (Ecclesiastes 9:17). Nature in this poem becomes even more analogical than in '"Consider the Lilies of the Field"'; no longer preaching in language, but solely in allegory. The only preaching is done by the poet, who urges the reader to 'consider' the ways in which mankind, nature, and God, as well as the Old and New Testament, are intimately linked.

'Consider / The lilies of the field' comprises the first and second lines, but here the New Testament understanding of lilies as illustrative of God's care for humanity is tempered by an Old Testament comparison between decay in nature and mankind's inevitable decay.

> Consider
> The lilies of the field whose bloom is brief: —
> We are as they;
> Like them we fade away,
> As doth a leaf.

(ll. 1–5)

Here the poem is not considering how the lilies grow, but how they decline. The stanza's comparison between withering, fast-fading nature and human mortality alludes to Matthew 6:30: 'Wherefore, if God so clothe the grass of the field, which to day is, and to morrow is cast into the oven, shall he not much more clothe you, O ye of little faith?', and to Luke 12:28: 'If then God so clothe the grass, which is to day in the field, and to morrow is cast into the oven; how much more will he clothe you, O ye of little faith?'. This stanza reminds us that while God clothes humanity as he clothes both lilies and grass, his protection does not preclude eventual mortality for all. As God treats nature, so he treats his people.

The symbolic connection of grass with mankind has an Old Testament precedent in Psalm 90:5–6: 'Thou carriest them away as with a flood; they are as a sleep: in the morning they are like grass which groweth up. In the morning it flourisheth, and groweth up; in the evening it is cut down, and withereth'. Like Rossetti's 'lilies of the field whose bloom is brief', the grass has a limited lifespan determined by nature, whose ruler is God. The verses from Matthew 6 and Luke 12 also look back to Isaiah 40:6–7: 'The voice said, Cry. And he said, What shall I cry? All flesh is grass, and all the goodliness thereof is as the flower of the field: The grass withereth, the flower fadeth: because the spirit of the Lord bloweth upon it: surely the people is grass'. This is an especially important link because the verse from Isaiah is itself cited in another New Testament text, 1 Peter 1:24: 'For all flesh is as grass, and all the glory of man as the flower of grass. The grass withereth, and the flower thereof falleth away'.

Rossetti's layers of allusion draw together New Testament lilies of the field and Old Testament grass in an extended metaphor of decay. The stanza reconsiders the lilies through the perspective of the Old Testament, emphasizing not so much that they are looked after by God, but that they will die. The tone here echoes Ecclesiastes' somber musings on the inevitability of death, only hinting at Matthew and Luke's promise of salvation through Christ. It is as if Rossetti has sown the New Testament lilies in Old Testament ground, in a poetic re-imagining of a world not yet touched by the redemptive hand of Christ.

Her allusion to Isaiah has to do with the same kind of typological reading that allows the stanza to shuttle back and forth between the Old and New Testament understanding of mortality. Though Isaiah 40 asserts that 'all flesh is grass', it also promises that 'the word of our God shall stand forever' (40:8). The chapter goes on to foretell a time when 'the Lord God will come with a strong hand, and his arm shall rule for him: behold, his reward is with him, and his work before him'. Isaiah further predicts that God 'shall feed his flock like a shepherd: he shall gather the lambs with his arm, and carry them in his bosom, and shall gently lead those that are with young' (40:10–11). Here 'the Lord God' is a figure present in, and interacting directly with the world, like a shepherd leading his flock. Rossetti would have interpreted Isaiah typologically, as very strong evidence of the eventual coming of Christ. 1 Peter interprets Isaiah in this way also, borrowing not only from Isaiah 40:6–8, where the flesh is grass and 'the word of the Lord endureth for ever' (1 Peter 25), but giving Isaiah a New Testament twist in verse 23, when humanity can look forward to 'Being born again, not of corruptible seed, but of incorruptible, by the word of God, which liveth and abideth forever'. The rest of Psalm 90 informs Peter's reading of Isaiah, as well as Rossetti's, in that it anticipates the return of God to the world: 'Return, O Lord, how long? And let it repent thee concerning thy servants' (90:13).

The movement from the Old Testament world suffering the absence of God to the New Testament's relief in his return is illustrated in the remaining stanzas of 'Consider'. Its second stanza likens men to sparrows:

> Consider
> The sparrows of the air of small account:
>   Our God doth view
>   Whether they fall or mount, —
>   He guards us too.
>
> (6–10)

The stanza references Matthew 10:29: 'Are not two sparrows sold for a farthing? and one of them shall not fall on the ground without your Father', and Luke 12:6–7: 'Are not five sparrows sold for two farthings, and not one of them is forgotten before God? But even the very hairs of your head are numbered. Fear not therefore: ye are of more value than many sparrows'. Rossetti here reminds us of the analogical relationship among nature, man and God. The allusion to Matthew and Luke stresses that mankind is more valued by God than the other things of a temporary world, and so will be saved. Just as the return of Christ in the New Testament changes the significance of 'all flesh is grass' (because of the promise of human resurrection), the presence of a protective God in this second stanza marks a shift in tone from the somber Old Testament mood with which the poem began.

In the third stanza, the poet returns to the Matthew and Luke's lilies.

> Consider
> The lilies that do neither spin nor toil,
>   Yet are most fair: —
>   What profits all this care
> And all this coil?

(11–15)

The lilies are here returned to the redemptive aspect of their New Testament context, where they are a symbol of God's care for his people. Rossetti reiterates the New Testament philosophy of trust in a benevolent God; lines 14 and 15 are a rephrasing of Luke 12:29: 'And seek not ye what ye shall eat, or what ye shall drink, neither be ye of doubtful mind'. Now that God has entered the poem, care for the lilies (and by extension mankind) can be entrusted safely to him.

The final stanza reaffirms the New Testament trust in God's care.

> Consider
> The birds that have no barn nor harvest-weeks;
>   God gives them food: —
>   Much more our Father seeks
> To do us good.

(16–20)

Rossetti again makes use of Matthew and Luke: 'Behold the fowls of the air: for they sow not, neither do they reap, nor gather into barns; yet your heavenly Father feedeth them. Are ye not much better than they?' (Matthew 6:26); 'Consider the ravens: for they neither sow nor reap; which neither have storehouse nor barn; and God feedeth them: how much more are ye better than the fowls?' (Luke 12:24). Once again, nature provides man with a parable about trusting in God's love and in his special relationship with mankind. If God provides for the birds, who are less important to him than men, then surely he will give humanity 'Much more'.

The poem is a New Testament answer to Ecclesiastes' existential questions about the meaning of life, death, and wisdom. Like Ecclesiastes, Rossetti's poem considers the meaning of death, decay, and the purpose of labor both intellectual and manual ('What profits all this care / And all this coil?' 14–15). However, these lines allude also to Matthew and

Luke's view that the vanity of mankind's earthly struggle lies in a distrust in the benevolence of God. The conclusion the poet reaches is somewhat different from that of 'the preacher' because she reads Matthew, Luke, and Peter's faith in Christ's redemption of mankind as an extension of the Psalms and Isaiah's hope in God's return, and Ecclesiastes' resignation to His will.

In *Time Flies* (1885), Rossetti makes explicit her interpretation of Ecclesiastes. She is more sympathetic to Solomon than was Isaac Williams; she remarks on the success of his wisdom, 'Solomon, who discreetly choosing "a wise and understanding heart",[19] received it with the "riches and honour"[20] which he asked not' (*TF* 18). Her quotation of 1 Kings 3:12 is significant because the complete verse 12 resists the typical view of Solomon as a precursor to Christ when God tells him, 'there was none like thee before thee, neither after thee shall any arise like unto thee'. For Rossetti, Solomon was not the disappointment he was to Williams; rather, she praises him for the qualities of discretion, wisdom, and understanding, all of which belong to his heart. The heart of Solomon's wisdom is what interests the poet not only because she sees it as emblematic of divine love, but also because, like the 'spiritual eye', it is an organ not of physical, but of spiritual perception. His heart allows him 'to judge ... so great a people' fairly (1 Kings 3:9).

Rossetti compares Christ with Solomon again in '"Consider the Lilies of the Field"' (2: 325). Here, Solomon makes his first overt appearance, and is not criticized for his failure to be a Christ figure, but rather lauded for his wisdom. The poem begins, 'Solomon most glorious in array / Put not on his glories without care' (1–2). The poet writes against the idea of a vain Solomon, because although his clothes are 'most glorious', the 'glories', given him by God, presumably his wisdom, his heart, and his judgment, are put on with 'care'. The glory of his dress here does not detract from, but rather coexists with his internal glory. Solomon is then prefigured as Christ, as Rossetti offers a typological reading of the Song of Solomon, which Christianity read as a prefiguration of God's love for man and Christ's love for the Church. The poet addresses God, asking Him to 'Clothe us as Thy lilies of a day', personifying lilies as God's people (3). The lilies are of God's 'making' (5) and, just as importantly, 'of (His) love partaking' (6). As in '"Consider the Lilies of the Field"' of 1853, the metaphor of nature becomes useful in conveying what Rossetti sees as the cyclical relationship, created by God's love, between the earthly and the divine. The lilies, made and clothed by God's love, '[fill] with free fragrance earth and air', in a metaphor of prayer (7). The lilies become fully personified in the last line in the poem's request: 'Thou Who gatherest lilies, gather us and wear' (8). Here, Christ has clothed the lilies in love, and will in turn be clothed by the love he has created in them. The poem's last line also creates a parallel between Christ and Solomon, suggesting that both reap the benefits of their creation, though Solomon's glories are earthly and God's divine. Typologically, Solomon is a precursor to Christ, but Rossetti, in contrast to Williams, chooses to emphasize the king's success rather than his failure. Her poem is more interested in what the two figures have in common than in what makes them different.[21]

In '"Consider the Lilies of the Field"' 1892, Solomon, in all his glory, *is* arrayed like the lilies because the source of his 'glories', like theirs, is God. Divine love is the dominant theme and connecting force among all three 'Consider' poems, linking God and nature, God and man, and, implicitly, the Old Testament and the New. Rossetti elides difference by concentrating on the shared and the common. Things in conflict (life / death, God / man, riches / wisdom, Old Testament / New Testament) can coexist in Rossetti's conception because of the overriding, unifying force of God's love. The three poems stand as an example of how different voices, those of the gospels, of nature, and of the poet, can be reconciled by their common interest in the redemptive power of God's love. Imagination is also brought into play because the 'considering' of nature, man, and God occurs internally, in the imagination. The reader does not actually see the poems' flowers, but only their description in words. The words are translated into vision in the reader's imagination, where both object and meaning can exist simultaneously, where earthly objects can become divine. Thus the redemption of the human imagination is also at the heart of Rossetti's poetic project.

Isaac Williams wrote that in 'Nature and Providence ... we doubt not that there is the perfection of exquisite order and arrangement; but it may appear to us in many respects otherwise, because we cannot comprehend the whole design.'[22] Rossetti's poetry puts forth the imagination as a locus for the comprehension of 'the whole design', suggesting that the human powers of multiple perception which can occur in the imagination are powered by a divine source. The human imagination, though corrupt like the poppies of '"Consider the Lilies of the Field"' (1853), can also accommodate 'juice of subtle virtue', which can be activated and stimulated by the contemplation of God's love.[23]

2
'Decayed Branches from a Strong Stem': Rossetti's Keatsian Heritage

Pre-Raphaelite and Romantic tensions in Rossetti's early poetry

William Michael Rossetti writes of his younger sister, 'In poetry she was (need I say it?) capable of appreciating what is really good; and yet her affections, if not her perceptions, in poetry, were severely restricted' (*Memoir* lxix). For Christina Rossetti, the effect of 'what is really good' in Romantic poetry was allowed to germinate before the Pre-Raphaelite influence, and, arguably, before the Tractarian influence. Although Rossetti's religious feeling restricted her affections for certain poems, William Michael notes that her 'perceptions', that is, her critical faculties, remained intact. In other words, Rossetti was, despite her religious restrictions, capable of critically separating, to an extent, the issue of morality from artistic merit, as her response to the Romantics illustrates. The young Rossetti's discovery of Romantic poetry runs alongside her developing Anglo-Catholicism, while her writerly experiments take place within the nascent Pre-Raphaelite movement. Her work of this period struggles to extract a Tractarian 'subtle virtue' from a Romantic and Pre-Raphaelite 'cup of curious dyes'. Rossetti effects this alchemy by reading the Romantics through the Tractarians, whose poetry reworked the Romantic sense of nature's relationship to the human imagination to imbue it with transcendent, explicitly Christian meaning.[1] What Rossetti learned from the Romantics concerns the power of the imagination, its relationship to the self, and a sense of the vital and organic importance of poetry.

Rossetti's early poems chronicle the young poet's efforts both to establish a philosophy and to find a poetic voice during the confusion of a post-Romantic, Pre-Raphaelite, and, it is often forgotten, adolescent

moment. Like any teenage writer, Rossetti necessarily begins by experi-
menting with the structure and ideology of her literary forefathers and
contemporary 'brothers', then increasingly adapting them to create her
own. Striving to reinvest poetry with religious meaning, Rossetti confronted the singular problem of how to be a devotional poet in the
increasingly skeptical atmosphere of the post-Romantic age. Rossetti
was not helped by the poetic vacuum caused by the early deaths of all
three of her immediate predecessors: Keats, Shelley, and Byron. Instead
of ignoring this seemingly unfavorable literary inheritance, Rossetti
embraced the work of the Second Generation Romantics. Rather than
returning directly to the religious poets of the past, Rossetti combined
devotionalist ideology of the Tractarians with Romanticism's concentration on nature, the material, the imagination, and the self.

Passion for Romantic poets was quite literally in the Rossetti blood:
John Polidori, better known as Byron's physician and author of *The
Vampyre* (1819) was Rossetti's maternal uncle, whose portrait hung in
her house until her death.[2] Christina's mother, Frances, maintained the
Polidori tradition, keeping a Common-Place Book 'into which striking
and edifying passages were copied', Polidori's and Byron's included, and
'to which the children were in time encouraged to contribute' (*LB* 26).
William Michael tells us that his sister read and admired Romantic
poets. He singles out Shelley and Coleridge as standing 'highest in her
esteem', though 'certainly not Wordsworth, whom she read scantily'
(*Memoir* lxx).[3] Although Keats is not named here by William Michael,
his influence on Rossetti's work is as apparent as the work of those he
mentions. Rossetti was arguably the first of her siblings to encounter
Keats: she read his 'The Eve of St. Agnes' in William Hone's *Everyday
Book* at the age of nine. According to Mackenzie Bell, 'in the compila-
tion she first saw the name of Keats, and read extracts from "The Eve of
St. Agnes" which naturally impressed her'.[4]

Perhaps it is Rossetti's religious interpretation of Keats that explains
her relative obscurity in accounts of his commercial and literary resurrection in the middle of the nineteenth century. Her emphasis on the
spiritual also seems, for example, to confirm her place on the margins
of the Pre-Raphaelite Brotherhood, who did so much to establish Keats
'among the English Poets'.[5] Admiration 'for Keats was almost a badge of
membership' for this 'Fleshly School of Poetry'.[6] The PRB claimed that
he was the first of their number, counting him among its 'immortals'
and repeatedly painting characters from his poems, particularly 'La
Belle Dame Sans Merci', 'The Eve of St. Agnes', and 'Isabella and the Pot
of Basil'.[7] In addition to the poetry, the publication of Milnes's *Life and*

Letters of John Keats (1848) was congruent with the formation of the Brotherhood. These formative encounters with the work of Keats also made a strong impression upon Christina Rossetti's youthful poetry, and her developing poetic theory. Like the Brotherhood, she came to Keats through her own contemporaries and near-contemporaries, most notably Tennyson. Tennyson's membership in the Cambridge Apostles, along with Hallam and Milnes, contributed to the rehabilitation of Keats's poetry to the extent that by 1848, as G. M. Matthews notes, 'It was unusual for anyone interested in literature not to have read Keats.'[8]

The Pre-Raphaelites admired Tennyson's treatment of Keats's amatory medievalism, as evidenced by their many tributes to Tennyson in painting and poetry. But the conventions of Arthurian romance and the external trappings of medievalism which so enthralled the Brotherhood are treated with some skepticism by Christina Rossetti. For example, when Dante Gabriel suggests that she include a tournament in her poem, *The Prince's Progress* (1: 95–110), she demurs in a letter of 10 February, 1865:

> How shall I express my sentiments about the terrible tournament? Not a phrase to be relied on, not a correct knowledge on the subject, not the faintest impulse of inspiration, incites me to the tilt: and looming before me in horrible bugbeardom stand 2 tournaments in Tennyson's *Idylls*.
>
> (*Letters* 1: 225–6)

Although Rossetti is ostensibly wary of exposing a prospective literary 'tournament' to comparison with Tennyson's, she is also deliberately distancing herself, and *The Prince's Progress*, from a Pre-Raphaelite interpretation of the laureate's medievalism. Her Prince's progress is fatally impeded by Pre-Raphaelite medievalism; the sensual and picturesque distractions of his journey (an Alchemist, a milkmaid, dalliances with various women), cause him to arrive too late to save his Princess from death: 'His slackening steps pause at the gate — / Does she wake or sleep? ...' (457–8). Unlike the narrator of 'Ode to a Nightingale' to which this line alludes, Rossetti's princess is dead, rendering the Prince's Romantic speculation about her consciousness moot. This moment of irony sounds a sober warning about the dangers of Pre-Raphaelite nostalgia.

The work of the PRB looked longingly back toward the chivalric ideal of love in an idealized feudal England, which was enjoying a revival whose literary landmarks included Sir Walter Scott's 'medieval' novels, *Ivanhoe* (1820) and *The Talisman* (1825), and Thomas Carlyle's *Past and*

Present (1843). J. M. Bullen tells us how Ruskin, an enthusiastic patron of the Pre-Raphaelites, was inspired by Carlyle's medievalism to '[develop] an aesthetic in which the facts of nature, of history, even of contemporary life can become through the intensity of their representation, radiant with transcendent meaning'.[9] For the Pre-Raphaelite painters, this meant a wider choice of subject matter, as the 'intensity' of what was depicted became as important as what actually was depicted. Both manmade and natural objects, as well as heroic and everyday subjects, could be imbued by the artist with the transcendental power of an ideal, chivalric past, and in this way could be 'rescued' from base earthiness or vulgar modernity. However, the PRB's interest in the transcendent meaning of the everyday world was often regarded as potentially 'Romish' or Tractarian. Ruskin worried about this himself, assuring his readers that:

> If [the PRB's] sympathies with the early artists lead them into medievalism or Romanism, they will of course come to nothing. But I believe there is no danger of this, at least for the strongest among them. There may be some weak ones, whom the Tractarian heresies may touch; but if so, they will drop off like decayed branches from a strong stem.[10]

Christina Rossetti, too, falls under the spell of the medieval revival during her association with the Pre-Raphaelite Brotherhood, writing under the pseudonym 'Ellen Alleyn', in *The Germ*. However, as Jerome Bump observes, she diverges from Pre-Raphaelite medievalism by trying to '[extrapolate] Romantic medievalism to the point where the ascetic Christianity of the Middle Ages emerged as an antithesis to Romantic egoism'.[11] This may lie behind Ruskin's hostility to her work after he read *Goblin Market*, when he wrote to Dante Gabriel that his sister's poems were unpublishable simply on grounds of form:

> Irregular measure (introduced to my great regret, in its chief wilfulness by Coleridge) is the calamity of modern poetry. The *Iliad*, the *Divina Commedia*, the *Aeneid*, the whole of Spenser, Milton, Keats are written without taking a single licence or violating the common ear for metre; your sister should exercise herself in the severest commonplace of metre until she can write as the public like. Then if she puts in her observation and passion all will become precious. But she must have the Form first.[12]

Ruskin's vehemence suggests a different kind of unease. His critique is so unbalanced, with its uncharacteristic emphasis on what 'the public like', that it looks like a displacement of something else — perhaps the suspicion that Rossetti's 'observation and passion' reflected 'Tractarian heresies'. If so, the suspicions were well-founded, as Rossetti went on to become the 'decayed branch' that fell far from 'the strong stem' of romantic medievalism championed by the PRB. This break from Pre-Raphaelitism, and the subsequent re-writing of Romanticism is neither clean nor swift, but evolves over her poetic career. She gives Romantic melancholy a religious twist, combining what Bump calls 'the aristocratic Romantic theory of creativity' with a self-abnegating, Christian asceticism (Bump, 344). She also uses Romantic ideas about the power of the imagination in order to hold together conflicting elements in her theology and her poetry. Even in her later religious prose, the 'wilful' influence of Coleridge can still be seen, while an identifiably Keatsian nightingale's song echoes through her earlier poetry.

Rossetti's publications in the Pre-Raphaelite magazine, *The Germ*, mark the beginnings of what will become her critique of the Pre-Raphaelite movement. Though it is uncertain whether she had any influence in the layout, the placement of the poems also reveals, accidentally or intentionally, the emerging critical differences between Rossetti and her 'brothers'. *The Germ*, subtitled, *Thoughts Towards Nature in Poetry, Literature, and Art*, begins on a deliberately 'medieval' note, its first issue of January 1850 containing poems entitled 'My Beautiful Lady', 'Of My Lady in Death', 'The Love of Beauty'. But Rossetti's notably darker contribution, 'Repining', investigates the spiritual aspects of the medieval revival. As James W. Hood reminds us, 'Victorian medievalism extended further than the Gothic architectural revival and mock tournaments. Tennyson's poems tap the old tradition of metaphorical linkage between spiritual and erotic devotion.'[13] 'Repining' is clearly influenced by Keats's 'The Eve of St. Agnes', yet Rossetti's religious treatment of its medievalism also has a distinctly Tennysonian flavor. Rossetti's early poetry may be populated by Keatsian belle-dames, nightingales, medieval surroundings, and altered states of consciousness, but her imagination, like Tennyson's, does not neglect the ascetic presence of the beadsman in Keats's 'The Eve of St. Agnes' who 'all night kept awake, for sinner's sake to grieve' (*KCP* l. 27, 229). Keats's beadsman, whose 'frosted breath, / Like pious incense from a censer old / Seem'd taking flight for heaven ...' (6–8), is given tribute in Tennyson's own 'St. Agnes' Eve': 'My breath to heaven like vapour goes: / May my soul follow soon!' (*TP* ll. 3–4, 1: 606).

Rossetti's poem is more interested in the ironies presented by Keats's juxtaposition of pagan ritual with Christian rite, and its subsequent confusion of earthly yearning and divine inclination, than with its love story. Rossetti's Madeline-like figure, rather than being awakened sexually, is awakened spiritually; unlike the women in Tennyson's 'St. Agnes' Eve', she is not granted a visionary ascension, but a sober return to her sole self.

'Repining' (1847) begins on a satirical note, its first four lines recalling Tennysonian heroines like Mariana and the Lady of Shalott, the title itself emphasizing the redundancy of such heroines' 're'-peated pining:

> She sat alway thro' the long day
> Spinning the weary thread away;
> And ever said in undertone:
> "Come; that I be no more alone."
>
> (ll. 1–4, 3: 17)

Unlike Tennyson's Lady, who initially enjoys her work, weaving with 'little other care' ('The Lady of Shalott', *TP* l. 44, 1: 390), Rossetti's female figure is oppressed by her spinning from the outset, her inherent dissatisfaction being ever-expressed in undertones borrowed from the refrain of Tennyson's 'Mariana in the South' (1832): 'And "Ah," she sang, "to be all alone, / To live forgotten, and love forlorn"' (ll. 11–12, 1: 397). The grief-stricken refrain of Tennyson's other 'Mariana' (1830) expresses a death wish:

> She only said, 'My life is dreary,
>   He cometh not', she said;
> She said, 'I am aweary, aweary,
>   I would that I were dead!'
>
> (ll. 9–12, 1: 207)

The woman of 'Repining', by contrast, seems less suicidal than terminally bored. Her refrain, '"Come; that I be no more alone"' (4), with its repetition in 'undertone' (3), suggests pent-up frustration along with expressed sadness. The woman's refrain does not have the rhythmic beauty of 'Mariana'; it is monotonous and sullen. The word 'Come' is poised between a plea and a command. Rossetti's woman is fed up with her house and her work, not because it is a poor substitute for an absent lover or because she longs particularly to join the outside world, but because it is an endless chore: 'Working, her task was still undone; / And the long thread seemed to increase / Even while she spun and did not cease' (6–8). Boredom shifts to self-pity as contemplation of turtledoves and swallows outside her window leads her to the conclusion that 'None lived alone, save only she' (15). Her crisis is one of almost adolescent *ennui*, caused, not by a real traumatic event, but by the absence of events, traumatic or otherwise. It is no real lover for whom Rossetti's woman pines; 'she sighed / For love' (19–20) to alleviate the tedium of 'the long day' (1). In this, her dilemma resembles that of Keats's Madeline, 'Whose heart had brooded, all that wintry day, / On love', who fasts and prays, impatient for bedtime and its promised dream of erotic fantasy ('The Eve of St. Agnes', ll. 43–4).

Like Keats's Madeline, the woman in 'Repining' longs for earthly satisfaction from a fantasy lover. Though Madeline offers rituals and prayers to St. Agnes, these acts are more pagan than Christian, as they are rites meant to secure 'Agnes' dreams, the sweetest of the year' ('The Eve of St. Agnes', 63). Her praying, too, is ironized by the voyeurism of Porphyro, and by the possibility of collusion from 'so pure a thing, so free from mortal taint' (225). Rossetti's woman, like Madeline, is both innocent and knowing. Although technically inexperienced in love, she longs for it obsessively, and, when a male figure appears in her room at night, she extends a clumsy erotic invitation:

> "Now thou art come I prithee stay,
> "That I may see thee in the day,
> "And learn to know thy voice, and hear
> "It evermore calling me near."
>
> (45–8)

The male figure, no Porphyro after all, tells her "'Rise and follow me'" (49). Undaunted, the woman tries again: "'And whither would'st thou go friend? Stay / Until the dawning of the day'" (50–2).

With the Christ-figure's next refusal, the tone shifts from satirical to polemical. This shift is forecast with his entrance, which occurs simultaneously with the silencing of a nightingale's song:

> She heard, what ne'er she heard before,
> A steady hand undo the door.
> The nightingale since set of sun
> Her throbbing music had not done,
> And she had listened silently;
> But now the wind had changed, and she
> Heard the sweet song no more ...
>
> (23–9)

This moment echoes Madeline's inarticulacy upon entering her bedroom:

> She clos'd the door, she panted, all akin
> To spirits of the air, and visions wide:
> No uttered syllable, or, woe betide!
> But to her heart, her heart was voluble,
> Paining with eloquence her balmy side;
> As though a tongueless nightingale should swell
> Her throat in vain, and die, heart-stifled, in her dell.

('The Eve of St. Agnes', ll. 201–7)

In Rossetti's poem, the nightingale's silence foreshadows the silencing of the erotic in the poem, prefiguring the Christ-figure's silencing of the woman's sexual invitation. The 'wind had changed', both literally and symbolically, blowing away the nightingale's song and the woman's lament, ushering in a devotional parable to destabilize the poem's amatory medievalism.

Unlike Porphyro, this male stranger brings dreams not erotic, but divine. While Keats's references to the divine are ironized by their context (Madeline's prayer as she undresses, Porphyro's plans to seduce his 'saint'), Rossetti reinscribes the divine in a Keatsian portrayal of the erotic. Her woman sees 'a dim glory like a veil' that 'Hovered about his head, and shone / Thro' the whole room till night was gone' (40–2), recalling Porphyro's awe when the moonlight falls on Madeline's hair, making her look 'like a saint' ('The Eve of St. Agnes', 222). Yet the halo around the male figure's head in 'Repining', although at first seeming to be a projection of the woman's sexual adoration, actually *is* a signifier of divinity. The male figure has materialized in direct response to the woman's plea, 'Come, that I be no more alone', quite literally as an answer to a prayer. The Christ-like figure firmly refuses to trade seductive metaphors with the woman, responding to her not with language, but with visions. The abrupt syntax, 'She bound her hair up from the floor, / And passed in silence from the door', marks the poem's departure from both Pre-Raphaelite medieval imagery and an exit from earthly Romantic yearning (55–6).

The couple in the poem proceed from the point where Keats's depart, 'away into the storm' ('The Eve of St. Agnes', 371). Rossetti takes her cue from the more religious tone of Tennyson's treatment of the legend, in which the woman's prayer to St. Agnes is answered with a visionary ascension. Rossetti's woman, however, remains on earth, with the Christ-figure now her guide, and at the poem's end, she does not ascend with him to heaven as his happy bride, but requests to be returned home. The outdoors into which the Christ-figure leads her is an inversion of an Edenic landscape, as she is taken on a walking tour of human suffering. What she sees borrows from the darker side of Wordsworthian imaginative experience, as nature here is sinister and forbidding, its only lesson mortality.

Rossetti's Romantic landscape is haunted, crawling with 'slimy things and slow' (111), the climate forebodingly inclement. As the Christ-figure shows her a village decimated by an avalanche, a ship sinking at sea, a city destroyed by fire, and men killed in war, she protests at the futility of life on earth. The woman, having abandoned her seduction of the stranger, becomes a mouthpiece for tortured humanity. Witnessing the burning of a city she says:

> "What is this thing, thus hurriedly
> "To pass into eternity?
> "To leave the earth so full of mirth?
> "To lose the profit of our birth?
> "To die and be no more? to cease,
> "Having numbness that is not peace?
>
> (197–202)

Here, Keatsian vocabulary is utilized in a Rossettian inversion of the death wish of 'Ode to a Nightingale'. Rossetti's language recalls lines 55–6 of Keats's poem: 'Now more than ever seems it rich to die, / To cease upon the midnight with no pain', and conjures the 'drowsy numbness' of its opening line, but Rossetti's speaker does not flirt with death; she is more horrified by, than 'half in love with' its mystery. The anguish here expressed stands in ironic a contrast to the self-obsession of the speaker's former lament: '"Come that I be no more alone"'. In a few stanzas she has progressed from envious contemplation of mating birds to asking fundamental questions about mortality. Her questions, however, go unanswered, the Christ-figure responding either with commands to follow, or with slightly impatient sighs.

In contrast to Rossetti's later work, the relationship of humanity to nature and to God in 'Repining' is a confused and doubting one. All Rossetti's heroine is offered in answer to her prayer is the nightmare vision of the guests in Keats's poem who dream 'Of witch, and demon, and large coffin worm' ('The Eve of St. Agnes', 374). What at first appears to be a romantic escape from a solitary life turns out to be an agony at the hands of nature (the avalanche and shipwreck) and human nature (the war), before a non-interventionist God.

The only thing the woman appears to learn is that a life lived outside her lonely walls is worse than a life within. It seems she will share the fate of Keats's beadsman, who 'after thousand aves told / For aye unsought for slept among his ashes cold' ('The Eve of St. Agnes', 377–8). In 'Repining' no peace or eternal reward is offered its subject; she is threatened rather than persuaded to abandon her sinful repining. Asceticism and detachment are the poem's uneasy solution, as the woman requests to go home: '"O Lord, it is enough"', she says, confessing, '"My heart's prayer putteth me to shame; / Let me return to whence I came"' (248–50). She feels ashamed of her craving for love, learned from her empathetic contemplation of the birds at the poem's beginning. Like the birds who are silenced by the larger horrors of the world, the woman is aggressively silenced by the unresponsive Christ-figure. From nature she has learned fear, and from God, shame.

At the same time, the woman has been given (and the poem records) an intense visionary experience which might be said to recuperate the Romanticism it disavows. It is significant that Rossetti's heroine, though she asks to be returned to her spinning, does not at all promise to cease pining for love. In fact, she defends herself by elevating the concept of love to a spiritual plane, suggesting divine love as both the motivation for Christ's admonition and the reason for His forgiveness. She says, '"Thou, who for love's sake didst reprove, / Forgive me, for the sake of love"' (251–2). The 'sake of love' in the poem's last line has a double meaning. The woman cites both Christ's capacity for love and the concept of love itself as reasons for forgiveness, implying His forgiveness will save both her and love itself. The word 'reprove' also is significant, echoing the poem's title in an attempt to draw God and the woman into an empathetic relation: as she re-pines, He re-proves. Here, the poet constructs the relationship of God to humanity as confrontational, beginning an argument with God using love as its primary defense.[14] Rossetti's defense of love at age 17 forecasts the development of the poet's theology, which will come to rely very much on the unifying power of love, both earthly and divine.

Barbara Fass's article discusses the influence of Keats's 'The Eve of St. Agnes' on Rossetti, but more from a biographical than a literary perspective:

> to think of Keats's poem in the context of the career of this lonely and repressed woman [Rossetti], whose entire life was a struggle to

negate passion, whose choices involved the chance to marry men she preferred not to wed, or to be a governess, a prospect she abhorred, is to discover the astonishing degree to which "The Eve of St. Agnes" spells out the plight of Victorian woman.[15]

Aside from the obvious critical problems inherent in what is meant by 'Victorian woman', at the time that this Victorian woman poet wrote 'Repining' (a poem on which Fass's article focuses) she had yet to have a context for her career or an 'entire life', nor was she lonely and repressed. On the contrary, she had just made a full recovery from the most intense period of depression of her life, was enjoying her grandfather Gaetano Polidori's private printing of her volume of juvenilia, *Verses*, and had not yet had 'the chance to marry' anyone. At 17, Rossetti was barely out of childhood herself, and it seems unlikely that she related to Keats's poem primarily in terms of 'the plight of Victorian woman'. This is not to suggest that Rossetti's treatment of the St. Agnes' Eve legend does not object to passive femininity, but, as 'Repining' itself does not present the active roles available to men as any improvement (indeed, the portrayal of active masculinity in the men at war is one of the poem's most horrifying), it is difficult to argue that 'Repining' is primarily a protest against gender division. Lynda Palazzo recently refined Fass's reading, viewing the poem as Rossetti's exposé of the 'Tractarian fervour' of 'young girls' who 'were caught ... in the grip of a religious extremism which not only deprived them of their natural vitality, keeping them docile and obedient ... but trapped them precisely through that which the poem defines as a feminine strength — spirituality'.[16]

Yet the spiritual dilemma of 'Repining' is not a uniquely feminine one. The crisis of the poem is as much metaphysical as it is gendered, pitting the safety of seclusion against the dangers of the world, and the desires of humanity against the natural and divine order, however painful and uncompromising. William Michael's 'Notes' on this poem in his edition of her *Poetical Works*, reveal that 'Repining is influenced by the eighteenth-century poet Thomas Parnell's 'The Hermit':

> The moral, however, is different. Parnell aims to show that the dispensations of Providence, though often mysterious, are just. Christina's thesis might be summarized thus: Solitude is dreary, yet the life of man among his fellows may easily be drearier; therefore let not the solitary rebel.
>
> (*Notes*, 460)

Like Fass, William does not identify the primary irony of this poem, which is the fact that its material existence subverts its heroine's (reluctant) capitulation. The absolute equation of Rossetti and the woman in 'Repining' obscures one of the truest havens for Rossetti, which quite plainly is her work as a poet. Though the woman in 'Repining' makes up her mind to return to her dreary, solitary life, the woman writing 'Repining' is published to critical acclaim in the Pre-Raphaelite magazine, beginning a long and distinguished public poetic career.

Rossetti's engagement with the eighteenth-century poetry of Parnell does, however, allow her to make a literary point about gender division. In 'Repining', it is a female hermit who goes on a journey with Christ, asking difficult metaphysical questions, offering qualified surrender and intellectual resistance. Rossetti's woman wishes to go out into the world because her curiosity about life and love has been piqued by glimpses of the world outside her window, much as the hermit's curiosity is aroused by outsiders' reports of the world: '(For yet by Swains alone the World he knew)'.[17] Both characters long to experience the world firsthand and unmediated, yet for both, the dream of the world outside their isolation, whether that isolation is masculine or feminine, turns out to be a nightmare.

Parnell's hermit leaves his life of 'serene Repose' (7) in order 'to clear this Doubt, to know the World by Sight' (21), while Rossetti's heroine, though initially searching for love, ends up on a similar quest to clear her doubts about human life on earth. The gender difference is that Rossetti's woman learns to name her existential doubt only after her journey begins, whereas the hermit, a scholar with access to books and limited company, sets out with his questions in place. Their different beginnings result in different endings, as Parnell's hermit 'gladly' returns with relief to 'his antient place', (248) while Rossetti's heroine 'in agony' begs to be returned 'to whence I came'. Yet, her heroine is now in a similar position to the hermit, in that, in the course of the poem, her painful refrain has turned into a series of questions, questions one imagines that she will continue to ponder on her return to isolation which will now resemble that of Parnell's hermit more than Tennyson's Mariana.

What Rossetti's poem does, in terms of gender, is to allow a woman to take part in a metaphysical debate, under the guise of Tennysonian melancholy and Keatsian dream-state. Rossetti challenges a male poetic vision of the 'woman in the tower' by allowing her woman not only to explore the surrounding world, but to engage in a theological argument with Christ himself, an argument in which the poet participates by proxy. Rossetti confidently contributes to a tradition defined by recent male predecessors like Coleridge, Keats, Tennyson, and the more distant Parnell. By conflating Parnell's hermit with Keats's Madeline and Tennyson's Bride of Christ, Rossetti creates a hybrid heroine through whom she can critique the eroticism of 'The Eve of St. Agnes', the passivity of 'The Lady of Shalott', and even the absolute trust in God of 'The Hermit'. The passionate and intellectually engaged treatment of such themes throughout her career, as well as the career of poetess itself, stand as strong evidence against Fass's conclusion that Rossetti's 'entire life was a struggle to negate passion'. Rossetti's career, it could be argued, is more of a struggle to *re-direct* passion to where she thought it belonged (with God and in heaven). That she chooses to do this through poetry presents problems in that poetry is an earthly pursuit. It is this conflict which increasingly becomes a focus of the adult Rossetti's work.

For the adolescent Rossetti, repining and reproving, it seems, lead to a kind of fatalistic stalemate between God and man, leaving the poet and her relationship to poetry in a state of confusion. Another offshoot of this opposition is the conflict between Romantic poetry and devotional aspiration, as nightingales must be silenced in order for God to be heard. The attempted conflation of the Metaphysical, the Romantic, and the Pre-Raphaelite results in erratic shifts in tone. 'Repining' jumps from the satirical to the bathetic to the polemical, giving the impression that its poet, like her heroine, is in search of a philosophy and a voice with which to express it. The nightingale's song has yet to be abandoned, and God's song yet to be fully embraced, but in 'Repining' the wind has changed.

Rossetti and melancholy

The success of Rossetti's famously melancholic poetry makes it easy to forget that melancholy is a stylistic choice. Her earlier works are self-consciously preoccupied by the connection between melancholy and poetic production, but her interest takes her poetry in a different direction to that of the Pre-Raphaelite Brotherhood. While Dante Gabriel was firmly in thrall to the tragic legend of Keats and Chatterton, Rossetti's relationship to melancholy was conflicted because of the suspicion of *vanitas* that Romantic melancholy carried with it.[18] In her *Germ* poems, Rossetti begins to articulate these conflicts, as she struggles to reconcile her desire for poetic distinction with her ascetic inclinations.

Unlike poets such as Wordsworth and Coleridge (and, indeed, unlike the heroine of 'Repining'), she does not set out to experience the full range of what life, or even nature has to offer. In reading her poetry, a large part of which is devoted to the natural world, it is hard to remember that she was an urban dweller who took rare trips to the country and sea-side. Jan Marsh notes that 'the Rossetti children heard real farmyard sounds only when staying with their grandparents in the country', and that Rossetti's childhood home 'had no garden, so the children played indoors' (*LB* 1, 4). Although visits to her grandparents' country home were a feature of her early childhood, in adulthood poor health kept her in London and indoors. Her sex, poor health, the urban landscape she inhabited, and her aesthetic and ascetic philosophy, meant that she, like Keats, wrote not about what she experienced day to day, but what she remembered or imagined.[19] Her relationship to nature is defined more by the intensity of her feelings about it than by daily experience, and perhaps she has a similar relationship to her poems' melancholy, which is height-ened and dramatized; it is a generalized and poetic emotion as much as a confessional or autobiographical one. This self-conscious melancholy appears in her early work, and its intensity becomes diluted, but never eclipsed, by the advocacy of faith and love in her later work.

Rossetti's early poems critique their own melancholy tendencies, and their narrator / speaker is often troubled by the lurking specter of vani-ty which might as easily appear in a life of public fame and glory as in a life of private renunciation and solitude. Such doubts arise not only from a religious understanding of *vanitas*, but also from a Keatsian lit-erary sensibility which cultivates melancholy and cherishes 'the wake-ful anguish of the soul' ('Ode on Melancholy', *KCP* 1. 10, 283). For Rossetti, melancholy is different to ordinary sadness or despondency, distinguished not only by its spiritual link to the suffering of humanity, but also by its literary connection with poetic production.

'Song' ('Oh roses for the flush of youth') written in February, 1849, and also published in *The Germ* (1850), is a short, deceptively simple poem which, veiled in the language of flowers, expresses these anxieties about the poetic vocation:

> Oh roses for the flush of youth,
>   And laurel for the perfect prime;
> But pluck an ivy branch for me
>   Grown old before my time.
>
> Oh violets for the grave of youth,
>   And bay for those dead in their prime;
> Give me the withered leaves I chose
>   Before in the old time.

(1: 40)

Though the self-reflexive manuscript title 'A Song in a Song', was shortened for publication, the sense that 'Song' is poetry about poetry remains. It is a poem which, by contrasting beautiful flowers and humble plants, constructs a commentary on the relationship of poetry and melancholy, youth and old age, fame and anonymity, ambition and resignation. Its flower imagery even points to the anxiety of influence, as its speaker, while recognizing the primary meanings ascribed to flowers, incorporates their secondary meanings as well. Gisela Hönnighausen remarks, '[Rossetti] deliberately turns away from accepted emblems and biblical parables ... Accordingly, she seldom uses traditional emblems ... and often prefers the humblest weed'.[20] The speaker of 'Song' insists on claiming the withered leaves and ivy as both symbols of resignation and asceticism, but also, in the context of the poem, as signifiers of endurance. While ivy, for instance, is associated with night, death, and the occult, it also symbolizes tenacity. Old age, for the speaker, is a double-edged sword, meaning on the one hand, life, and on the other, the prolonged suffering that living entails.

Read in its manuscript version, the poem's tone is generally mournful, but it is unclear for whom the speaker mourns: the dead woman or herself.[21] Rossetti chose only the last two stanzas for publication, and without any information about the poem's subject, their mournful mystery, overgrown with the language of flowers, is intensified. Antony Harrison mentions the manuscript poem's connection to Keats, with its speaker who 'loiters (like Keats's knight at arms) in expectation of his own death'. Its original title also alludes to the erotic and floral 'Song of Solomon' or 'Song of Songs'. However, in its final version, Rossetti's poem is 'reformed and refocused upon predominantly aesthetic issues rather than those of elegiac or courtly love poetry'.[22] This poem moves away from the romantic medievalism embraced by the PRB, both in its stated preference for sturdy ivy and dried leaves over colorful flowers, and in its treatment of death, not as a tragic end to a romance, but as a contemplation of the individual's relationship to her own mortality.

Rossetti's use of the language of flowers is significant here, not just in terms of decoding the poem, but in terms of the 'aesthetic issues' to which Harrison alludes. The language of flowers appealed to Rossetti's sense of the metaphorical, and, in later poems, the poet would increasingly use flowers as translations of the word and lessons of God. In 'Song', the flowers' metaphorical intensity refers as much to poetic design as it does grief. The idea of selection is emphasized as the speaker, despite noting the rose, laurel, violets, and bay, says, 'pluck an ivy branch for me' (3) and 'Give me the withered leaves I chose', mixing a note of assertion with the general tone of resignation (7). The poem's flower symbolism discourages simple decoding of its meaning by its sheer profusion and multiple meanings. Because Rossetti does not specify (as do language-of-flowers guides) what kind of rose, violet, bay, and ivy she presents, it is difficult to assign them one meaning. Yet inconsistent and even contradictory meanings are given space within the context of the poem; despite the speaker's renunciation of the rose, laurel, violet, and bay, the poem itself retains them.

For example, violets can signify innocence, hence their appropriateness on a 'grave of youth' (5), but they also mean modesty. Contrasted with the glory that the bay represents, they make an odd pairing, with the speaker renouncing both modesty / innocence and fame. In choosing neither glory nor modesty / innocence what is left? The speaker claims 'withered leaves', which, contrary to Diane D'Amico's assertion that they are 'not a part of the language of flowers', in fact officially symbolize melancholy. Though D'Amico reads them 'as the speaker's renunciation of love and fame', the withered leaves also resonate with the poetic (as in book leaves).[23] Modesty and innocence (violets) must be left on the grave of youth if good poetry is to be produced, but at the same time they should not be exchanged for the fame and glory of a poetic prime (bay). Rather than colorful thriving flowers (whose beauty, like youth, will fade), the speaker chooses hardier plants which signify unending fidelity (ivy) and plants already dead, signifying both melancholy itself, and the melancholy inherent in the poet's task of recording emotions already spent (withered leaves). Similarly, roses and laurel carry conflicting meanings, as roses can stand for love and beauty, but also pride and danger, while laurel, associated with poetry, can stand for ambition and glory, but also perfidy. The speaker renounces love, beauty and glory because she is aware of the potential threat that pride and vanity pose to creativity. What began as a poem about grief becomes, through Rossetti's floral 'arrangement', a parable about both the dangers and the excitement of the poet's creative art.

Just three days after composing 'Song', Rossetti re-arranges her flowers yet again for 'Sweet Death' (1: 74). Keatsian melancholy flavors this Tractarian lesson about the afterlife:

> The sweetest blossoms die.
>   And so it was that, going day by day
>   Unto the Church to praise and pray,
> And crossing the green churchyard thoughtfully,
>   I saw how on the graves the flowers

> Shed their fresh leaves in showers,
> And how their perfume rose up to the sky
> Before it passed away.
>
> (1–8)

This first stanza begins abruptly, 'The sweetest blossoms die' (1). But the poem shows the full stop at this sentence's end to be as false and impermanent a conclusion as death itself. 'Sweet Death' turns out to be a commentary on the illusion of absolute endings, as the fact of the blossom's death is the starting point for a meditation (itself cyclic by nature) on the cyclic nature of life and death. The interlinking rhyme pattern provides a formal echo of the poem's exploration of nature's cycles. Though joy's grape has burst, the poem suggests that a fine palate (a Christian palate) can appreciate its fleeting sweetness. The speaker's observations evolve over the calendar year (also a cyclic measurement of time) as 'going day by day / Unto the Church to praise and pray' (2–3) she sees 'how on the graves the flowers / Shed their fresh leaves in showers, / And how their perfume rose up to the sky / Before it passed away' (5–8). The sweetness of death here is characterized as the perfume that the dying flowers produce, which, like the speaker's prayers, rises to heaven. Communion with nature departs from a Romantic conception in that it helps the speaker come to terms with, not only this life, but death and afterlife. The second stanza echoes the abrupt beginning of the first:

> The youngest blossoms die.
> They die and fall and nourish the rich earth
> From which they lately had their birth;
> Sweet life, but sweeter death that passeth by
> And is as though is had not been: —
> All colours turn to green;
> The bright hues vanish and the odours fly,
> The grass hath lasting worth.
>
> (9–16)

'The youngest blossoms die' (9), yet their death is not an end, as they go on to 'die and fall and nourish the rich earth / From which they lately had their birth' (10–11). The stanza makes use of a Tennysonian rhyme and motif found in 'All Things Will Die' (*TP* 2: 250): 'The old earth / Had a birth', and 'the old earth must die' (ll. 37–8, 41). In alluding to

Tennyson, Rossetti's 'Sweet Death' enacts its own message; from poetry of the past, new poetry has its birth. The poet imbues the natural cycle with Christian meaning, and literary significance, in order to accommodate the conflicting conclusions of Tennyson's companion poems, 'All Things Will Die' and 'Nothing Will Die' (1: 47). His first poem ends with, 'For all things must die', while the second with, 'Nothing will die; / All things will change' (ll. 49, 37–8).

Rossetti addresses the difficulties of accommodating death and change by interrelating the concepts of prayer and the cycle of nature to create a metaphor about Man's relationship to God. Line 16 of the poem, 'The grass hath lasting worth', is taken from Isaiah 40:6 which reads, 'All flesh is grass, and all the goodliness thereof is as the flower of the field', and 40:7: 'The grass withereth, the flower fadeth: because the spirit of the Lord bloweth upon it: surely the people is grass'. Relating to Isaiah's metaphor of the flower as an expression of the 'goodliness' of the flesh, the poet sees the rising perfume of flowers as an expression of prayer. The actions of praise and prayer in line three correspond to the blossoms falling and their perfume rising in lines 6–7. The image also has further metaphysical dimensions in terms of the decay of the body and the resurrection of the spirit.

The 'lasting worth' of the flesh is proved only in death, as the spirit is then freed to rise up to heaven, while the body decays again into earth which will foster new life. Rossetti's interpretation of Isaiah is also filtered through the New Testament, 1 Peter 1:24 where 'the glory of man' replaces man's 'goodliness' as the flower of the grass.[24] Human goodness and glory will outlast the flesh, thus the best parts of humanity will become immortal. This idea is reinforced by the language of flowers, where grass signifies both submission and utility. The poem's conception of man's lasting worth relates back to 'Song', where the speaker chooses the melancholy of withered leaves over the glory of the bay, not simply out of modesty (symbolized by the rejected violets) but out of a belief that true glory will survive death.

Rossetti's second stanza reverses the usual order of ideas on death and life: 'Sweet life, but sweeter death that passeth by / As though it had not been: ... / All colours turn to green' (12–14). The fact that it is not the expected life that passes, but death, reflects the Christian view of death as not an end in itself but as a prelude to life everlasting. Rossetti carries Isaiah 40:7 further by not only relating man to grass, but by recontextualizing both man and grass in the larger cycle of Nature. Even things whose 'bright hues vanish' and 'odours fly' in death have 'lasting worth' because they will eventually produce new life. Rossetti reasons that, as life passes, so too does death, and both form an integral part of a cycle whose eventual goal, it is revealed in the last stanza, is afterlife:

> And youth and beauty die.
>   So be it, O my God, Thou God of truth:
>   Better than beauty and than youth
> Are Saints and Angels, a glad company;
>   And Thou, O Lord, our Rest and Ease,
>   Art better far than these.
> Why should we shrink from our full harvest? why
>   Prefer to glean with Ruth?

> (17–22)

This stanza is bursting with allusions to Keats's 'Ode on a Grecian Urn', 'To Autumn' and 'Ode to a Nightingale'. Rossetti begins by critiquing Keats's creed, 'Beauty is truth, truth beauty' ('Ode on a Grecian Urn', *KCP* 49, 282), by dismantling the phrase and associating 'truth' with 'God' (18). The original Keatsian emphasis is not destroyed in the process, but reconfigured in the new, theological context: Rossetti allows it to linger through the informal rhyme of 'youth and beauty' in line 17 and 'truth' a line later. By the time she asks the stanza's penultimate question, it is 'To Autumn' that seems to have come to mind. The suspicion is reinforced by the final line's reference to 'glean', a more explicit allusion to Keats's 'To Autumn': 'And sometimes like a gleaner thou dost keep / Steady thy laden head across a brook' (ll. 19–20, 360).

The final plaintive question ends the poem on an ambiguous note. The use of the gleaning of Ruth has both literary and biblical implications. Read as a response to Keats's Ruth in 'Ode to a Nightingale', Rossetti's Ruth is a criticism of Romantic communion with nature. The song of Keats's nightingale '… found a path / Through the sad heart of Ruth, when, sick for home, / She stood in tears amid the alien corn' (ll. 65–7, 279). His Ruth feels unhappy and displaced, and it is this melancholy to which Rossetti responds in the final line of 'Sweet Death'. Ruth, divested of divine meaning by Keats, is re-located in her original, biblical context: her homesickness becomes a metaphor for divine longing as the 'Rest and Ease' of heaven's "full harvest" are preferable to the momentary glimpses of happiness available on earth (21, 23).

The use of the story of Ruth as a warning against earthly pleasures is inconsistent with biblical tradition, as the gleaning of Ruth led to her marriage with Boaz, and eventually gave rise to the house of David, and thus the earthly lineage of Christ.[25] The poem's last question is thus a difficult one. It functions paradoxically as both a criticism of earthly concerns and a celebration of life on earth. As if in imitation of the Biblical texts she quotes, Christina's exegesis of Isaiah, Peter, and Ruth in 'Sweet Death', in addition to her allusion to Keats, is both intertextual and inconclusive. In this sense, the poem's final line does not function rhetorically, but is truly an open question. Even as Rossetti challenges parts of her Keatsian inheritance, her final questions establish what she has gleaned from it. By refusing to provide answers, Rossetti leaves us at the poem's end in the familiar Keatsian territory of 'doubts, mysteries, uncertainties'.[26]

Keatsian sweet death is the subject of Rossetti's sonnet about the poet himself, 'On Keats' (3: 168). Written on St. Agnes's Eve in 1849, this sonnet was unpublished during Rossetti's lifetime, first appearing in William Michael's *Poetical Works*. It portrays Keats not as a weak boy slain before his prime, but as 'a strong man grown weary of a race / Soon over' (3–4). Though it takes death as its theme and a graveyard as its location, this tribute to Keats is notable not for anguish or resignation, but hope, showing the beginnings of Rossetti's movement from a renunciatory to a redemptive aesthetic. Its contemplative and peaceful tone distinguishes it from the prevailing nineteenth-century view of Keats, fostered by the Pre-Raphaelites, which reclaimed the poet as a tragic martyr to his art and a victim of his cruel critics. For example, Dante Gabriel's sonnet 'On Keats'[27] mourns a 'pang-dowered poet' (9) who 'toiled though sands of Lethe; and long pain, / Weary with labour spurned and love found vain' (6–7).

Susan J. Wolfson points out that a similar view of Keats as a victim was also held by the period's female readers: 'Keats continued throughout the [nineteenth] century to be marketed to female audiences,' not only because 'qualities in his poetry' were 'deemed to have particular appeal to women,'[28] but also because of the way in which 'Keats was culturally installed as a sensitive and vulnerable boy, a creature of too-feminine delicacy.'[29] Wolfson writes further of 'Keats's adoration by female readers, for whom the 'Adonais' myth was intrinsic to Keats's biography.'[30] Obviously influenced by Shelley's version of Keats's literary martyrdom at the hands of the critics, Elizabeth Barrett Browning, for example, expressed a typical female Victorian viewpoint when she wrote of 'Poor Keats! ... slain outright and ingloriously by the Quarterly Reviewer's tomahawk'. Rossetti, an admirer of both Barrett Browning and Shelley, addresses questions of Keats's effeminacy and victimhood in her sonnet.

> A garden in a garden: a green spot
>> Where all is green: most fitting slumber-place
>> For the strong man grown weary of a race
> Soon over. Unto him a goodly lot
> Hath fallen in fertile ground; there thorns are not,
>> But his own daisies: silence, full of grace,
>> Surely hath shed a quiet on his face:
> His earth is but sweet leaves that fall and rot.
> What was his record of himself, ere he
>> Went from us? *Here lies one whose name was writ*
>> *In water:* while the chilly shadows flit
>>> Of sweet Saint Agnes' Eve; while basil springs,
>>> His name, in every humble heart that sings,
> Shall be a fountain of love, verily.

(3: 168)

Milnes's influence can be seen in Rossetti's portrayal of Keats as a 'strong man': until his biography was published, images of the 'effeminate' Keats, such as those in Shelley's 'Adonais', dominated. Rossetti's floral imagery in 'On Keats' echoes that of Shelley's poem, yet her flowers preach a different lesson. In his preface, Shelley characterizes Keats's genius as a 'young flower ... blighted in the bud'.[32] Rossetti's floral arrangement, by contrast, excludes Shelley's flowers that 'mock the corse beneath' with which 'He had adorned and hid the coming bulk of death' ('Adonais', 17–18). For Rossetti, Keats's graveside daisies exist in a natural, cyclic relation to his mortality, and are both expressive of, and nourished by, the poet's death ('On Keats', ll. 4–8).

Both Shelley and Rossetti testify to the triumph of Keats's poetry over his death through their allusions to his verse; Keats's words are literally speaking from beyond the grave. Shelley writes that 'The soul of Adonais, like a star, / Beacons from the abode where the Eternal are' (494–5), while Rossetti predicts that 'His name, in every humble heart that sings, / Shall be a fountain of love, verily'. Where Rossetti differs from Shelley is in her attitude toward Keats's death. Shelley's portrayal of Keats as tragic victim ('The bloom, whose petals, nipt before they blew / Died on the promise of the fruit, is waste') was motivated by immediate personal and political grievances ('Adonais', 52–3); Rossetti, benefiting from historical and emotional distance, interprets Keats's early end as a necessary and natural stage of spiritual and literary immortality. Central to this view was Rossetti's own developing Christian sense of death as part of a process of renewal, one which she relates to the cyclic nature of poetry itself. Rossetti recycles Keatsian imagery ('daisies', 'Saint Agnes' Eve', 'basil') within her own poem about his death. The 'water' in Keats's epitaph is put to work in the 'garden' of Rossetti's poem, nourishing her own version of Keats, not as the delicate and doomed poet of the Pre-Raphaelite vision, but as 'fertile', 'strong', and 'full of grace'. The graveyard described as his 'fitting slumber-place' introduces the possibility of an awakening, conflating the idea of Romantic trance with the Christian hope of resurrection.

Rossetti incorporates Keats's epitaph to simultaneously suggest the earthly transience of the man and the immortality of his work. Her literary treatment of Keats's gravesite as 'a garden in a garden' provides another image of death and renewal. Although this grave among graves is a place of death and decay, it is also 'a green spot / Where all is green', because, like the 'sweet leaves that fall and rot', mankind comes from, and returns to earth. Keats's release from this earthly cycle is suggested by the biblical allusion in lines 4 and 5: 'Unto him a goodly lot / Hath fallen in fertile ground; there thorns are not'. This refers to Christ's parable of the sower, which appears in different versions in Matthew 13, Mark 4, and Luke 8. It describes an episode wherein a sower planted seeds, some of which did not grow because they 'fell by the way side', 'upon a rock', 'among thorns', while others 'fell on good ground, and sprang up, and bare fruit an hundredfold' (Luke 8:5, 6, 7, 8). The seeds falling on the infertile and thorny ground represent the rejection of God's word, while those on good ground represent 'they, which in an honest and good heart, having heard the word, keep it, and bring forth fruit with patience' (Luke 8:15).

Rossetti's use of this parable about conversion to Christianity elides certain truths about Keats's work, which was hardly motivated by an interest in promoting the word of God. However, Rossetti reworks the parable of the sower to link Keats's literary immortality with his spiritual salvation. In the 'fertile ground' of Keats's grave lie not the thorns of worldly distractions,[33] but 'his own daisies'. These daisies represent the flowering of Keats's artistic and fertile imagination in his poems. In Rossetti's hands, Keats's life and work become, not a tragic example of youthful potential cut short, but an illustration of the redemptive force of poetry. The sonnet reaffirms his literary immortality by cultivating

Keatsian motifs alongside cyclic metaphors of death and renewal. Lines 4 and 5 further emphasize Keats's literary legacy, and Rossetti's sense of her own poetic inheritance, in their conflation of Matthew, Mark, and Luke with Psalms 16: 5–6: 'The Lord is the portion of mine inheritance and of my cup: thou maintainest my lot. The lines are fallen unto me in pleasant places; yea I have a goodly heritage'.[34]

The direct influence of Keats is most apparent in Rossetti's early poems, such as those which appeared in *The Germ* and in *Goblin Market* (1862). It began to wane, however, as Rossetti became less able to reconcile the consolations that Keats-inspired art offered with those provided by her faith in God. Still, as Sarah Wootton recently pointed out, 'It is an oversimplification to suggest that Keats merely facilitated the purging of Romantic influences.'[35]

Rossetti's last published volume reveals that Keats remained in her thoughts throughout her life. Forty-six years after writing her sonnet 'On Keats', Rossetti revisited his grave in her final devotional prose-work, *The Face of the Deep*:

> In the Book of Life: or not in the Book of Life. Once more, no neutral book, no neutral ground: no names "written in water," as one death-stricken man predicted of himself, presumably with reference to earthly fame.
>
> *(FD 338)*

In contrast to Rossetti's early sonnet, it is God's 'Book of Life,' and not a book of poetry, that is the unquestioned solution to the Keatsian problem of mortality.

What continues to trouble Rossetti about Romantic poets like Keats, and the Pre-Raphaelite response to them, is not their interest in the sensual, the erotic, or their passionate attachment to the natural world, but the suspicion that such an attachment does not extend to the heavens and is therefore idolatrous. This distinction is vital for an understanding of Rossetti's devotional poetry, which has long been oversimplified as renunciatory, and discussed in terms of complete opposition to Romanticism. However, Rossetti's project goes beyond simple refutation and debate in its attempt to redirect Romantic ideas and language into devotional poetry.

What Rossetti's work shares with that of the Romantics is that it is very much a poetry of the self, though not necessarily that of the author. Rossetti's 'I', in fact, is often as generalized and mysterious as the 'secret' events upon which her poems famously turn. Renunciation of the self often was advocated by Rossetti, but the reason she tries to remove herself from her poems is as much literary as it is religious. The self which Rossetti explores is the more generalized human self of the parable, a representative of various aspects of the human condition.

Rossetti rewrites the Romantic quest for the self into the soul's quest for God. Her Christianity is more speculative than conclusive, probably because it depends so much on the idea that true conclusion takes place only in heaven. Such is the theology behind the ambivalence and confusion in Rossetti's work. As Catherine Cantalupo writes, 'In some poems [Rossetti] struggles to the conclusion that God is wholly transcendent, not immanent, and that nature can literally be a hindrance to spiritual progress. Detachment, not communion, is her goal. This quite anti-Romantic stance clearly represents a conservative religious view of nature — a form of asceticism'.[36] Yet, as with Wordsworth, it is the learning process, as much as what is learned, that interests Rossetti. Her nature poetry shows that on earth, in fact, it *is* necessary to commune with nature in order to translate God's messages properly. Detachment is, I think, an imprecise or incomplete definition of Rossetti's goal, simply because much of her poetry seeks to transcend, and in order to transcend, it must engage.

The hopeful imagination

For Rossetti, it is hope which sustains the imagination in its quest to seek out divinity in a fallen world. Hope plays as much a part in Rossetti's aesthetic as does the renunciation for which she is better known. Often the two operate together, as in the three sections which comprise the poem 'Three Stages'.[37] The first part, 'A Pause of Thought' (1: 51), was published in the second issue of *The Germ*. Written a year after 'Repining', this poem's religion is murmured in undertone, with only a biblical quotation to hint at devotional aspirations. It is here that the generalized world-weariness for which Rossetti is famous starts to take shape, with the precocious observation of its first stanza, 'But years must pass before a hope of youth / Is resigned utterly' (3–4). The biblical quotation, 'hope deferred made my heart sick in truth' (2) is taken from Proverbs 13:12, but here its use seems secular, as the undefined object of that hope is 'that which is not, nor can be' (1). Whatever the object, its significance lies in its unattainability, and its earthliness, for the speaker's quest for it is described as a useless chase (19) and 'an empty name' (13). Given Rossetti's religious feeling, it is unlikely that she would describe the quest for God as useless or an empty name. The unnamed referent of the poem allows 'that which is not, nor can be' to stand in for any worldly desire. The poem's refusal to reveal the object of its hope has been characterized as typically Rossettian in its secrecy, but the authorial decision not to define that hope also allows the concept of hope to remain free-floating and generalized. Strains of Romantic melancholy can be heard in Rossetti's recontextualization of ancient biblical language, while a general sense of thwarted Romantic quest pervades the poem. The sense of longing, of watching and waiting, is also congruent with the Lady of Shalott and Mariana. The undefined object of her speaker's hope also recalls the mystery surrounding the source of the soul's guilt in Tennyson's 'The Palace of Art', while it uses the same stanza form as 'The Palace of Art' and 'A Dream of Fair Women'. That this stanza form was also used in Henry Vaughan's 'Psalm 104' suggests a devotional layer of meaning. While Vaughan's poem, a re-writing of a psalm which praises God's rule over the earth and its creatures, bears no direct thematic link, this poet's echo within Rossetti's formal structure adds to the sense of metaphysical quest in the poem. A structural allusion to Vaughan reinforces the poem's interest, not just in the specific object of the speaker's desire, but in the general nature of human longing.

The speaker's waiting is also, in some sense, devotional, as another biblical allusion occurs in the second stanza: 'And though the object seemed to flee away / That I so longed for, ever, day by day / I watched and waited still' (6–8). This comes from Matthew 25: 1–13 and Luke 12: 35–40, a parable of wise virgins watching and waiting for Christ. Again, Rossetti has secularized a biblical concept by making 'the object' earthly rather than heavenly, which we know from the third stanza, when the speaker contemplates resigning her hope in order to 'be at peace' (11). If the hope were God or heaven, resigning belief in either would be a strategy unlikely to achieve a Rossettian speaker's peace.

In the first four stanzas the speaker addresses us in the first person, but the identity of the woman in the last stanza is ambiguous:

> Alas, thou foolish one! alike unfit
> For healthy joy and salutary pain:
> Thou knowest the chase useless, and again
> Turnest to follow it.

> (17–20)

This voice could be one of bitter self-recrimination, as the speaker turns away from the reader and withdraws into herself. However, the final stanza's tone lacks the self-pity which characterizes the preceding stanzas, and also notably lacks the quotation marks which the poet has so far used to indicate that the speaker is talking to herself. This suggests the possibility that 'thou foolish one' might directly address the reader, implicating him / her in the speaker's quest for hope deferred (17). This last stanza could also be introducing a new voice which addresses the speaker, and is possibly a divine voice. The phrase 'hope deferred maketh the heart sick' became one of Rossetti's characteristic refrains, and continued through to her last works. In 'A Pause of Thought', the proverb significantly is not quoted in full: 'Hope deferred maketh the heart sick: but when the desire cometh it is a tree of life' (Proverbs 13:12). 'Hope deferred' in Rossetti's poems almost always refers to an earthly aspiration, with the hope of heaven as a second, quieter referent. For Rossetti, the 'tree of life' can only be found in heaven, and so life on earth is one long instance of hope being deferred, thus making earthly hopes futile, a useless chase. However, by quoting this proverb in part, Rossetti alludes to it in full, enacting the proverb's power simultaneously to offer and withhold hope. The Psalms to which the poem alludes are 39:7 and 130:5, which also deal with the conflict between having to wait and needing to hope.[38] As the ambiguous title suggests, the poet is both pausing to think and pausing thought, in order to allow the poem's heart to speak.

Here, the development of Rossetti's religious philosophy about the value of contrast and contradiction in a fallen world begins to take shape. Rossetti has not yet bridged, nor entirely recognized, the gap between a Romantic attachment to experience and an Anglo-Catholic proclivity for renunciation, and so the poem's last line, like the end of 'Repining', has a tone both rebellious and resigned. As the woman in 'Repining' agrees to be returned to her solitary room in terms which both suggest she has learned a lesson, but has also learned how to use her learning to advantage, so the last stanza of 'A Pause of Thought' suggests both capitulation and defiance.

'A Pause of Thought' later appeared in manuscript as part of a longer poem entitled, 'Three Stages', the writing of which spans seven years, from age 18 to 25 (3: 232). The poem can be read autobiographically, as an exploration of the stages of falling in love, being rejected, and recovering, but can also be read as literary autobiography, as it traces the poet's writing process, which begins on a note of precocious cynicism, progresses to adolescent angst, and ends with mature resolve at least to keep creating. Written a year later, and more heart-sick in tone than its predecessor, the second part of 'Three Stages' bemoans a 'weary wakening from a life-true dream!' and grieves that 'the cherished secrets of my heart, / Now all my hidden hopes are turned to sin' (5, 13–14). The speaker, like the soul of 'The Palace of Art', resolves to renounce the world: 'I must pull down my palace that I built, / Dig up the pleasure gardens of my soul' (9–10). She will transform her palace of art into a lonely home:

> But where my palace stood, with the same stone,
>   I will uprear a shady hermitage;
> And there my spirit shall keep house alone,
>   Accomplishing its age:
>
> (21–4)

However, in the poem's third 'stage', written six years later, the speaker finds herself in an unexpectedly different place, having imagined that her 'life would lapse, a tedious monotone: / I thought to shut myself, and dwell alone' (18–19). Like Keats's 'To Hope', which begins, 'When by my solitary hearth I sit, / And hateful thoughts enwrap my soul in gloom' (*KCP* ll. 1–2, 6), Rossetti's poem opens on a note of despair and isolation, which is then tempered by imagination. Though the speaker promises she 'will not hope again', that she has 'Gone dead alike to pulses of quick pain, / And pleasure's counterpoise' (14, 15–16), her imagination is awakened:

> But first I tired, and then my care grew slack;
>   Till my heart slumbered, may-be wandered too: — [39]
> I felt the sunshine glow again, and knew
>   The swallow on its track;
>
> (21–4)

When Keats's speaker finds that 'no fair dreams before my "mind's eye" flit' ('To Hope', 3), he asks Hope to 'wave thy silver pinions o'er my head' and 'Peep with the moon-beams through the leafy roof' (6, 11). Rossetti's speaker too experiences a time 'in silence and the dark', and also finds solace in an image of light, and in her own imagination. The 'sunshine glow' melts away her resolve to 'not hope again'. Nature, or, more precisely, the way in which her imagination (symbolized by her slumbering and wandering heart) acts upon nature, brings both the speaker and the natural world back to life. Nature, both external and

internal, comes temporarily to the speaker's rescue, as, despite her former resolve to renounce the world, she observes:

> All birds awoke to building in the leaves,
>   All buds awoke to fulness and sweet scent,
> Ah, too, my heart woke unawares, intent
>   On fruitful harvest sheaves.

(25–8)

Her heart is awakened by nature, yet the speaker's experience here is
similar to that of the woman of 'Repining', in that the awakening is
painful as well as instructive. Like the woman in 'Repining', who envies
the birds' mating ritual, the speaker in 'Three Stages' is aware from the
outset, 'I cannot build myself a nest' (31). She is made vulnerable again
to pain and regret in the renewed knowledge that,

> I may pursue, and yet may not attain,
>   Athirst and panting all the days I live:
> Or seem to hold, yet nerve myself to give
>   What once I gave, again.

(37–40)

However, the difference here is that while the woman of 'Repining' is
given nothing to do except, presumably, to return to her lonely spinning,
the speaker in 'Three Stages' determines at least to fight hopelessness, to
'nerve' herself 'to give'. Again, there is the theme of heartsickness caused
by hope deferred, but the speaker has made up her mind to pursue her
goal, despite an understanding that she may never attain it. The speaker
no longer avoids 'pleasure's counterpoise' as she tries to be fit for the
healthy joy and salutary pain of the poem's first part. As much as this
poem probably documents a heartbreak, it also, like Keats's 'To Hope',
documents a creative and imaginative process of writing *through* disappointment. Though a poem about love and loss, it must be remembered
that, objectively, this is a *poem*, and that the act of writing here is
redemptive, and tentatively life affirming.

Rossetti, in the last part of her seven-year trilogy, writes of both the
bitter and the sweet of the renewal of desire. While she doesn't quite
find hope's silver pinions waving o'er her head, what the speaker does
find is a kind of solace as her imagination dreams and wanders. This

last part of this poem qualifies the advice of the first, as the speaker decides that though the chase may be useless and painful, there is a redemptive element in the choice to turn again to follow it. The poem's penultimate line gets to the heart of critical overemphasis on Rossetti as a renunciatory poet, which, by confusing poet and speaker, often overlooks that as much as Rossetti's poetry seems to hold back, equally it nerves itself to give.

3
'Great Love and Long Study': Dante, Petrarch, and *Monna Innominata*

Monna Innominata is a sonnet sequence consisting of 14 sonnets, each one preceded by a double epigraph from Dante and Petrarch. Its daunting length has meant that individual sonnets have often garnered more critical attention than the sequence as a whole.[1] Rossetti herself would have resisted this practice. Refusing an American editor permission to excerpt *Monna Innominata*, she explained: 'Such compound work has a connection (very often) which is of interest to the author and which an editor gains nothing by discarding'.[2] In the interest of reading in the spirit of Rossetti, this chapter addresses the sonnet sequence in its entirety. Although I do not, for reasons of space, include the whole text of *Monna Innominata*, it can be found on pages 86–93 in Volume 2 of the Crump edition.

'Romantic' and 'Victorian' Dante

After the struggles of the early poetry to reconcile Romantic and Tractarian philosophy, Rossetti's mature work looks further into the past for guidance. The untranslated epigraphs from Dante and Petrarch in *Monna Innominata* reveal that while the Anglo-Italian Rossetti may have been home-schooled, she had not come by Italian poetry second hand. That she could read these poets' works both in translation and in their original form made her conscious of translation as an interpretative and creative tool. The sonnet sequence itself reacts to the ways in which poets translate each other, their muses and God. *Monna Innominata* is also influenced by the Romantic and Victorian reception of Dante, so it is worth examining Dante in this context before moving on, in this chapter's second section, to Rossetti's own response.

From both Romantic predecessors and Victorian contemporaries, Rossetti inherited a legacy of Dante interpretation which sat uncomfortably with her devotionalist aesthetic. While Romantic critics had embraced the political, philosophical, and dramatic implications of Dante's works, they were much less interested in his devotional imagination. A Romantic distrust of poetry with what Keats called 'a palpable design' informs the lack of attention to Dante's Christianity. His religious faith was considered more a relic of his historical period than an integral part of his poetics, and his allegorical design was often subordinated to the human drama of the poem.[3]

The Romantic re-engagement with Dante served to rehabilitate him as an important poet, a revival confirmed and extended throughout the nineteenth century. Michael Caesar notes that 'The nineteenth century produced more than ten times as many new editions of the *Divine Comedy* as the eighteenth ... the most rapid and constant expansion occurred between the 1820s and the 1860s, in a fifty-year period which saw an average of nearly 4 new editions every year'.[4] Early Victorians continued to read Dante as a Romantic precursor, and to emphasize the qualities appropriate to such a figure. Thomas Carlyle, for example, gives Dante's genius a Keatsian twist in his lecture, 'Dante as Poet-Hero':

> Perhaps one would say, *intensity*, with the much that depends on it, is the prevailing character of Dante's genius. Dante does not come before us as a large catholic mind; rather as a narrow, and even sectarian mind: it is partly the fruit of his age and position, but partly too of his own nature. His greatness has, in all senses, concentrated itself into fiery emphasis and depth. He is world-great not because he is world-wide, but because he is world-deep.[5]

'The excellence of every Art is its intensity', Keats had written, 'capable of making all disagreeables evaporate'.[6] He was thinking of *King Lear*, the most Dantesque of Shakespeare's plays; for Carlyle, however, the 'disagreeables' in Dante are less to do with violence and horror than with his 'narrow, and even sectarian mind'. Like the Romantics, Carlyle sees Dante's religious feeling as a product of 'his age and position', though he concedes it is 'partly too of his own nature'. He also reaffirms Coleridge's observation that Dante's work shows 'profoundness rather than sublimity; for Dante does not so much elevate your thoughts as send them down deeper'.[7] For Carlyle as for Coleridge, Dante's lack of scope is recuperated by a kind of pre-Romantic intensity responsible for the 'fiery emphasis and depth' of his poetry.

While the Romantics generally had more to say about the passion of Paolo and Francesca or the tragic suffering of Ugolino, Victorians were most fascinated by Dante's relationship to his own muse. Mid-Victorian readings of Beatrice, in particular in the *Vita Nuova*, were influenced by the idea of woman assuming nature's role as the mediator between man and art, or man and God. Steve Ellis associates Gabriele Rossetti's publications on the cult of the *Vita Nuova* with the start of this trend: 'the mid-century insistence on a very human Beatrice was provoked by Gabriele Rossetti's controversial final work on Dante, *La Beatrice di Dante*, of 1842'.[8] Gabriele's notorious assertion that Beatrice was no real love, but a poetic device through which Dante objected to the tyranny of church and state, was famously rubbished by the critics. Certainly Gabriele's youngest son, Dante Gabriel, made a career out of challenging his father's line of thought. The 'intensity' with which Carlyle credits Dante's work informs Dante Gabriel's vision of the poet to the extent that he finds Dante's work and life utterly inseparable. Ellis notes that Dante Gabriel's investment in the earthly Beatrice stemmed from his almost exclusive devotion to the *Vita Nuova*, which he translated in 1862, over the *Commedia*.

Dante Gabriel also took his cue from the Romantic interest in the love story of Paolo and Francesca; amatory medievalism was always more compelling to him than the ascetic Christianity which often accompanied it. Romantic readings of the tale had stressed Dante's sympathy with the adulterous pair, using their presence in hell more as a dramatic backdrop to their doomed love story than as a signal of divine displeasure. Romantic poets found both erotic and artistic pleasure in the episode, re-imagining the cautionary tale of Paolo and Francesca as a fable reinforcing the strong bonds of earthly love. Keats brings not only sympathy but also eroticism to the story of Paolo and Francesca; in a letter of 1819 he writes that the fifth canto 'pleases me more and more', and relates the dream he had of being 'in that region of Hell':

> The dream was one of the most delightful enjoyments I ever had in my life — I floated about the whirling atmosphere as it is described with a beautiful figure to whose lips mine were joined at it seem'd for an age ... [9]

The same letter includes a sonnet inspired by Keats's dream. The poem's eroticism heightens the sympathy for the lovers' predicament:

> Of Rain and hailstones lovers need not tell
> Their sorrows — Pale were the sweet lips I saw

> Pale were the lips I kiss'd and fair the fo[r]m
> I floated with about that melancholy storm —
>
> (11–14)

Like Keats, Dante Gabriel differs from his source when describing the passions of the *Commedia*, but not because he is seeking imaginative truths or critiquing Christianity's system of punishment and reward. He is more interested in expounding the relationship of Dante to his muse, a focus which becomes myopic as Dante's divine love for God falls away completely in the face of his erotic love for Beatrice. In Dante Gabriel's poem, 'Dante At Verona', this view is made explicit in a stanza regarding Beatrice:

> Each hour, as then the Vision pass'd,
>   He heard the utter harmony
>   Of the nine trembling spheres, till she
> Bowed her eyes towards him in the last,
>   So that all ended with her eyes,
>   Hell, Purgatory, Paradise.[10]

Though Dante Gabriel has taken this moment from canto 30 of *Purgatorio*, no sense of Beatrice's rebuke to Dante remains, and 'Hell, Purgatory, Paradise' are contained in her gaze, utterly secularized. Throughout his poem, Dante Gabriel uses Beatrice's words as a refrain: 'Look on me well: I am, I am Beatrice' (*Purgatorio* 30: 73), but he divests her words of anger. She does not speak 'as one ... whose purpose is / To keep the hottest word awhile unsaid' (30: 71–2), but in fact, is one whose 'voice brought peace' ('Dante At Verona', 455). If Beatrice is allegorical at all for Dante Gabriel, hers is an allegory of the power of earthly desire. His interpretation, however, does not simply reflect a younger son's rebellion against his father, nor is it just an outgrowth of Pre-Raphaelite 'fleshly' concerns. Although, or perhaps because Dante Gabriel was a religious skeptic, his approach to the legendary relationship of Dante and Beatrice reveals a classic kind of Victorian doubt, as Ellis points out: 'his sense of the woman as a repository of ultimate values in not an act of defiant idolatry but comes rather from his sheer religious uncertainty: he clung to what he knew' (134).

Christina Rossetti and Beatrice

Christina Rossetti rejects the figure of Beatrice as 'a repository of ultimate values', not only because of the whiff of idolatry, but also because of worries about the corrupted poetic imagination and its effects on both artist and muse. About the very same scene, *Purgatorio*, 30, she writes as if to refute Dante Gabriel's sonnet:

> Hear how, even amid the peace and bliss of the Terrestrial Paradise, Beatrice, with veiled countenance and stinging words, addresses [Dante], *"Guardami ben; ben son, ben son Beatrice"* ("Look on me well; yes, I am Beatrice"), and despite his overwhelming shame, resumes the thread of her discourse by speaking no longer *to* but *at* him ...[11]

In Christina's view, the 'I am' of Beatrice is assertive and angry rather than soothing, this moment of reunion tense and dubious rather than fully redemptive.

Rossetti's essay for the *Century* addresses both the historicity and the legend of Dante. Like her brother Dante Gabriel, Rossetti is interested in the relationship of an artist to his muse, but this interest is troubled by two potential problems which can appear at the crossroads of the literary and the religious: misrepresentation and idolatry. Rossetti is attracted to the way Romantic imagination operates in the story of Dante and Beatrice, but unsettled by Victorian secularization of the narrative. Aware of the burden of critical and family history, she begins her essay by acknowledging that 'it is not least formidable for one of my name, for *me* to enter the Dantesque field'.[12] She tries to reconcile differing critical opinions, not to mention family disagreements, with an argument which relies on the Keatsian idea of 'negative capability':

> Still, acute thinkers abide at variance as to his ultimate meaning; and still able writers record the impressions of wonder, sympathy, awe, admiration, which — however wide and manifold his recondite meanings may be — he leaves even on simple hearts so long as these can respond to what is lovely or is terrible. *"Quanti dolci pensier, quanto desio"* ("How many sweet thoughts, how much desire"), has he not bequeathed to us!
>
> ("Dante: The Poet Illustrated Out of the Poem", 566)

This passage shows the influence of Romantic ideas about reader response, about how meaning may vary, but what is most important is the sense of 'wonder' and 'sympathy' great poetry engenders. Rossetti's point ties neatly to a brief discussion of her family's diverse, and diverging, accomplishments in Dante studies. Despite her obvious omission of Gabriele's academic works on Beatrice, a sense of family pride accompanies her list of their achievements. In reference to her own work, she writes with characteristically ambiguous humility: 'I, who cannot lay claim to their learning, must approach my subject under cover of "*Mi valga ... il grande amore*" ("May my great love avail me") leaving to them the more confident plea, "*Mi valga il lungo studio*" ("May my long study avail me")' (567).[13]

The modesty of this statement is belied by Rossetti's biography and family history, as her readers in 1884 would have been well aware. Her 'knowledge' of Dante (her sense of his significant presence) would have begun at a very early age, with her father's scholarly obsession and her family's sense of its Italian roots. Her own study of the poet's work began in adolescence and continued throughout her life, despite her claim to rely on 'love' alone. In later years her interest was not just poetic, but also academic, as she attended Charles Tomlinson's lecture series on the *Inferno* and *Paradiso* at University College London from 1879–80 (*LB* 509). Although a poet at heart, Rossetti's awareness of what is at issue in Dante studies still shines through her essays on Dante. While Rossetti's poetic instinct is to endorse the power of Dante's imagination, as a religious thinker reacting to perceptions of Dante in her day, she needs somehow to sanctify that imaginative impulse:

> For, taught by bitter experience in what scales to weigh this world and the things of this world, [Dante] bequeathed to future generations the undying voice of his wisdom, — a wisdom distilled in eloquence, modulated to music, sublimed by imagination, or rather subliming that imagination which is its congruous vehicle and companion.
>
> (570)

Here Rossetti makes a case for the inseparability of Christian wisdom from the sublime imagination. By acknowledging both Dante's 'experience' and 'wisdom', Rossetti casts the poet as the medieval equivalent of Solomon, relocating the poet in a specifically religious context. However, she partially preserves Romantic readings of Dante by alluding to, and taking issue with, Keats's theory of the Imagination: 'What the imagination seizes as Beauty must be truth — whether it existed before or not — for I have the same Idea of all our Passions as of Love they are all in their sublime, creative of essential Beauty.'[14] By rewriting the sublime imagination as wisdom's 'congruous vehicle and companion', Rossetti carries Keats's secular theory in a new direction: Imagination is no longer the force which creates essential beauty, but the vehicle which expresses it. Rossetti aligns Keatsian ideas of the sublimity of the poetic imagination with the Christian tradition of wisdom literature in order to frustrate Romantic and Victorian tendencies to separate Dante's religious feeling from his art.

For Rossetti, the imagination is subject to the will and wisdom of God, and does not originate from the will of the dreamer, as it does in Keats's discussion of 'Adam's dream'.[15] Imagination ought to be 'sublimed' by wisdom, not the other way around. The impact of the transitive 'sublimed' renders the imagination the more passive in this combination: the imagination is acted upon by wisdom, the imagination is a vehicle powered by wisdom. In Rossetti's conception, the imagination is not creative, but expressive.

At the crossroads of faith and imagination lies Dante's love for Beatrice, which is perhaps why the relationship intrigues Rossetti. Like her father, Christina Rossetti read Dante's love for Beatrice as a 'hidden paraphrase', but she diverges from his thesis in terms of exactly what it is that is being hidden. For Gabriele, Dante's love hides the poet's political conviction; while for his daughter, the human longing of Dante for Beatrice is also an allegory of the divine longing of the soul for God.

Rossetti does not explicitly resolve the question of Beatrice's specific significance, whether religious, political, or erotic; her view emerges not as argument, but inference:

> Some students speak of hidden lore underlying the letter of our poet's writings: in Beatrice they think to discern an impersonation rather than a woman, in the Divine Comedy a meaning political rather than dogmatic ... So obscure a field of investigation is not for me or for my readers; at least, not for them through any help of mine: to me it is and must remain dim and unexplored, even as that *"selva oscura"* (dark wood) with which the Cantica of the Hell opens.
>
> (572)

Though 'so obscure a field of investigation' had ruined the career of Rossetti's father, his polite and private daughter does not go so far as to disagree openly with his theory that Beatrice is 'an impersonation rather than a woman' or that the *Divine Comedy* holds 'a meaning political rather than dogmatic'. Yet her tone is dismissive, however neutral her words; their author's true opinion is hinted at when she states her intention not to expound such theories to her readers, in language simultaneously humble and assertive: 'not for them through any help of mine'.

For Rossetti, the key to Dante's imagination lies not just with Beatrice, but with the tradition of translation itself. While she mourns what is lost in translation, she also is aware of other meanings which can be teased out during the project. Her theories about the difficulties of translation are formed at the intersection of her personal, devotional, and poetic beliefs. Tractarian ideology, for example, pervades a passage concerning the act of literary translation in her article, 'Dante, An English Classic':

> To reproduce Dante in all fulness and subtlety of beauty would demand Dante's self, and must be abandoned as hopeless: indeed, a question may be raised whether, as no two things can be absolutely the same as each other, and thus apparently one must exceed, one fall short, he is not the consummate translator who sits nearest, yet below not above, his original; invested with all communicable glory, not shining with independent lustre; though, as most rules admit of some exception, an occasional added grace may be condoned to the ideal translator as some balance against frequent inevitable shortcomings.[16]

Here Rossetti connects the Tractarian doctrines of reserve and analogy to literary production. Just as the world is only a shadow of heaven, so a translation is a shadow of its original. Because no two things 'can be absolutely the same as each other', the representation of the original object must 'fall short'. She is aware that a translation exists at one remove, and thus can never reproduce exactly the 'subtlety of beauty' of the original. The best a translator can hope for is for his / her work to sit 'nearest, yet below not above' the original, and hope for reflected glory. The advice against 'shining with independent lustre' merges Keble's maxim, 'Don't be original', with the Tractarian investment in the idea that one who occupies 'the lowest place' on earth will enjoy the higher position in heaven.[17] Despite the Tractarian philosophy used to defend its argument, Rossetti's advocation of writerly humility here betrays a literary, not a religious, anxiety. Having brought her argument onto secular ground, she is free to allow for the possibility of the 'added grace' (in both the artistic and the religious sense) of new interpretation. The passage shows Rossetti engaging self-consciously with the idea of poetic legacy, providing a retrospective literary gloss on these lines of resignation in her poem, 'The Lowest Room' (1856):

> Not to be first: how hard to learn
>   That lifelong lesson of the past;
> Line graven on line and stroke on stroke;
>   But, thank God, learned at last.

> ("The Lowest Room" 265–8, 1: 200)

Monna Innominata: The preface

Rossetti's awareness that she is not the "first" flavors the famous preface to her sonnet sequence *Monna Innominata* (2: 86–93). It reworks the relationship of poet to muse, and of sonnet tradition to the poet, since the female subject is imagined as a poet in her own right. The poem's measured rhythms, attributed yet untranslated quotations from Dante and Petrarch, and studied form which is in itself a commentary on the sonnet tradition, work together to create a contemplative love letter possibly to a real person, but more importantly to Rossetti's poetic heritage, to God, and to the idea of love itself. Self-consciously constructing a poetic trajectory from Dante and Petrarch and the troubadour tradition to Elizabeth Barrett Browning, the preface is the closest Rossetti ever comes to a statement of authorial intent with regard to a specific work. She begins it with the name Beatrice, a word with so many resonances for Victorian readers and writers that its use alone throws down a poetic gauntlet:

> Beatrice, immortalized by "altissimo poeta ... cotanto amante"; Laura, celebrated by a great tho' an inferior bard, — have alike paid the exceptional penalty of exceptional honour, and have come down to us resplendent with charms, but (at least, to my apprehension) scant of attractiveness.
>
> (2: 86)

The tone of the opening paragraph is unusually strong for Rossetti. Although she uses a characteristic parenthesis to temper her criticism, this humble aside fails to detract from the confidence of the words surrounding it. Beatrice and Laura have been penalized as well as honored by their literary immortalization. The penalty they have paid, it seems, is that they have 'charms' rather than 'attractiveness'. 'Charms' has associations of conventional, physical beauty; 'attractiveness' comes from within. Rossetti suggests the shallowness of one and the profundity of the other. Jan Marsh points out how Franz Hueffer's *The Troubadours* (1878), which Rossetti knew, more explicitly states what she implies.[18] Hueffer writes that the troubadours tell us of women's 'incomparable charms' 'loving-kindness' or 'cruelty,' yet 'in few cases ... are we enabled to realise from generalities of this kind an individual human being with individual passions or caprices ...'.[19]

Though Rossetti shies away from Hueffer's notion of individuality with the euphemistic 'attractiveness', something of Hueffer's recognition of female agency is retained in her critical tone. Rossetti's preface claims that 'one can imagine many a lady as sharing her lover's poetic aptitude'. Although 'one' is gender-neutral, and refers to all readers, the rest of the passage certainly does not encourage us to read it this way. When its author, a famous female poet, writes 'one can imagine', she is asserting that *she herself* can imagine, and has imagined. Rossetti links the capacity to imagine both to contemporary and past female poets, *many* female poets. In Keats's famous discussion of the imagination, it is compared to *Adam's* dream — Eve is a product of the imagination, but not its producer. Imagination was not something traditionally associated with women artists, as can be seen even in Hueffer's mainly positive argument for their rehabilitation. But Rossetti makes clear her view than an entire history of women's creativity has been suppressed. Her defense of female imagination and poetic ability, even-toned though it is, fairly leaps off the page.

Elizabeth Barrett Browning famously lamented the absence of literary 'grandmothers'; for Rossetti, Barrett Browning herself fulfilled this role, yet the preface which invokes her great precursor also yearns to 'imagine' a more distant ancestry, the 'many a lady' who 'shar[es] her lover's poetic aptitude' — though not his bed.

Romantic echoes are heard in the argument that Barrett Browning's love poetry may have benefited from her unhappiness:

> had the Great Poetess … only been unhappy instead of happy, her circumstances would have invited her to bequeath to us, in lieu of the "Portuguese Sonnets," an inimitable "donna innominata" drawn not from fancy but from feeling, and worthy to occupy a niche beside Beatrice and Laura.

Rossetti's thoughts on Barrett Browning recall Byron's lines from *Don Juan*: 'Think you, if Laura had been Petrarch's wife, / He would have written sonnets all his life?'[20] Though it lacks Byron's facetiousness, Rossetti's argument makes a similar connection between the act of longing and the creative impulse.

Just as important as what Rossetti says about her contemporary and her competition is what her preface begins to say about female creativity, and the emotional legacy of women's love. What Rossetti suggests in both preface and poem will eventually become cornerstones for feminist debate, not only about women as the subject of art, but women as producers of art. However, it is important to remember that Rossetti's stance is not just politically or socially motivated, but has religious dimensions. Her sonnet sequence goes on to argue that the emotional and social segregation of men from women is an earthly indicator of their post-lapsarian status.

Monna Innominata: The poem

Although at first one could suspect that Rossetti's gothic imagination might be drawn to the *Inferno*, it is entirely fitting that she chooses *Purgatorio* as the primary source for her Dantean epigraphs in *Monna Innominata*. Rossetti often writes about the fallen, but seldom about the damned. Her goblins, ghosts, and otherworldly monsters are figures between life and death, trapped on earth. Their function in the poems is usually to force the speaker or the hero / ine of the poem into making a moral choice. They are shape-shifters and tempters of human nature, there to test but not to condemn. Unlike Dante's *Inferno*, the nightmare of hell is never fully realized in Rossetti's work. The concept of Purgatory, however, fits the politics and poetics of *Monna Innominata*, a love poem, like so many of Rossetti's, that deals in the bittersweet pain of separation and hope of reunion.

Hope (deferred) is a strong theme of Dante's *Purgatorio*, one which Rossetti stresses with her choice of quotations in the epigraphs to each sonnet of *Monna Innominata*. Of the fourteen Dante epigraphs, nine come from the *Purgatorio*, one from the *Inferno*, and four from the *Paradiso*. Each sonnet also has an epigraph from the *Canzoniere* of the 'alike, tho' inferior bard', Petrarch, whose secondary position in the epigraphs is a structural illustration of his inferiority. The Petrarchan poems Rossetti uses also engage with the theme of hope, though his hope seems more for the love of Laura than the love of God, which is perhaps why Rossetti gives him 'inferior' status. The sonnets themselves reverse poetic convention in both Dante and Petrarch because they are spoken by a female artist about her male lover and muse: here Rossetti follows the example of *Sonnets from the Portuguese*, even though she is taking Barrett Browning's female artist / speaker in a different direction. Female interpretation remains a subtext of the epigraphs: just as her female troubadour sings of herself in the sonnets, Rossetti offers a personal and professional homage to, interpretation of, and claim to, a legacy of great poetry.

Rossetti's first sonnet immediately introduces the idea of hope deferred both thematically and formally. Its Dantean epigraph is taken from *Purgatorio* 8: 3, 'Since morn have said Adieu to darling friends' ['*Lo dì che han detto a' dolci amici addio*'].[21] That the epigraph itself is only a fragment emphasizes the speaker's Platonic sense of emotional incompleteness and her anticipation of a reunion. The quotation prefaces an episode in *Purgatorio* when one of its spirits 'joined and lifted both its palms in prayer', leading the others in a hymn (10). Like *Purgatorio* 8, Rossetti's sonnet 1 begins with a moment of prayer: With the combination of a request, ('Come back to me', 1), praise ('For one man is my world of all the men / This wide world holds', 7–8), and lament ('So far between my pleasures are and few', 4), this sonnet fulfills a prayer's requirements as well as a love poem's. Like a prayer too, it both acknowledges separation and anticipates togetherness. The whole sonnet struggles with 'hope deferred', most explicitly in line 11: 'My hope hangs waning, waxing, like a moon'.

Rossetti takes pains to assert her speaker's gender in order to differentiate hers from an active, Dantean quest. Her speaker is not a 'new-made pilgrim on his way' (*Purgatorio* 8: 4), but a woman defined by the acts of watching and waiting. The fact that 'long it is before' her lover returns could signify either reluctance or preoccupation on his part, but his motivation is less important than the speaker's expression of frustration (3). While he is gone, she explains, 'So far between my pleasures are and few. / While, when you come not, what I do I do / Thinking, "Now when he comes," my sweetest, "when"' (4–6). Unlike, for example, Tennyson's 'Mariana', this speaker is not emotionally paralyzed, but stimulated by her lover's absence. She finds some enjoyment both in 'Thinking' about his return and in 'Thinking' during his absence. Here, the condition of waiting is embraced as imaginatively active and fertile, not static and morbid. She is a speaker who not only waits, but also watches. This secular kind of alertness has biblical resonance also, as watching and waiting are the duties of the wise virgin brides of Christ in Matthew 25, and by extension, all Christians who await his return. This poem explores absence and reunion from a specifically female perspective which involves, not adventuring, but vigilance.

Love and separation are also themes of Rossetti's second epigraph, which uses the twelfth line from the final tercet in Petrarch's *Canzoniere* sonnet: '*Amor, con quanto sforzo oggi mi vinci!*'[22]:

> Love, with what force thou dost me now o'erthrow;
> For, were not hope with passion multiplied,
> I should fall dead, when life is joy supreme.
>
> (ll. 12–14, sonnet 64, 'Now and Then')

The shifting forces of Petrarch's 'passion' and 'hope' also affect Rossetti's speaker, whose 'hope hangs waning, waxing, like a moon'.

Like Petrarch, Rossetti's speaker has a muse whose absence she finds both emotionally crippling and imaginatively stimulating. In alluding to Petrarch, Rossetti both pays homage to the legacy of the sonnet and locates herself, and her female speaker, within the sonnet tradition. The speaker's poetic aptitude is hinted at in the sonnet's conclusion which links love to both the act of writing itself and its reception: 'where are now the songs I sang / When life was sweet because you called them sweet?' (13–14). This epigraph is a reminder of Rossetti's preface which imagines a female troubadour 'sharing her lover's poetic aptitude'.

The Dantean epigraph of sonnet 2 inspires a meditation on writing as an act of nostalgia. Dante's line is the first of *Purgatorio* 8, which describes how nightfall causes a kind of home-sickness:

> It was that hour, which thaws the heart and sends
>   The voyagers' affection home, when they
> Since morn have said Adieu to darling friends.
>
>   (1–3)

Rossetti has used this canto already as a source for her first sonnet's epigraph. Her first sonnet uses the third line of *Purgatorio* while her second sonnet uses its first line. Like Dante's lines quoted out of order, Rossetti's speaker's feelings of love function retrospectively:

> I wish I could remember that first day,
>   First hour, first moment of your meeting me,
>   If bright or dim the season, it might be
> Summer or Winter for aught I can say;
> So unrecorded did it slip away,
>   So blind was I to see and to foresee,
>   So dull to mark the budding of my tree
> That would not blossom yet for many a May.
> If only I could recollect it, such
>   A day of days! I let it come and go
>   As traceless as a thaw of bygone snow;
> It seemed to mean so little, meant so much;
> If only now I could recall that touch,
>   First touch of hand in hand — Did one but know!

As memory feeds anticipation in her first sonnet, forgetfulness aids imagination in the second. The lovers' first meeting is all the more affecting because of the speaker's loss of the moment that 'seemed to mean so little, meant so much'. Rossetti's speaker cannot use her memory of first meeting her lover to inspire her verse, and so she uses the fact of her own forgetfulness to create her tribute.

The Petrarchan epigraph to the second sonnet in Rossetti's sequence, 'I've called to mind how I beheld you first [*Ricorro al tempo ch'io vi vidi prima*], also relates memory to creativity (Cayley trans., 'Delayed Praises', 3). It is a sonnet about Petrarch's inability to express in words his love for Laura. He concludes, 'Verse have I more than once begun to write; / But intellect alike, and hand, and pen / In the first onslaught were discomfited' (12–14). Although Petrarch finds his literary skills unequal to the task of describing the significance of his first glimpse of Laura, he regains authorial control by using this inadequacy as his inspiration.

The excitement Rossetti's speaker did not feel at the time is felt all the more forcefully in retrospect as her imagination allows her to bypass time in her attempt to recreate a memory. The 'thaw of bygone snow' represents a kind of nostalgia. The 'thaw' is significant also because it recalls the Petrarchan sonnet's description of writer's block: 'My brain, considering nicely what it durst, / Was by this study frozen to the core' (7–8). In the context of Rossetti's poem, the 'traceless' thaw of the snow is a metaphor for the speaker's forgetfulness. At the same time, it is a figure for poetic inspiration. The simple image of a snow-thaw represents a poetic breakthrough, a creative ability to thaw the 'brain' that is 'frozen to the core' by the challenge of writing. Here, Rossetti's speaker, instead of being paralyzed by the failure of memory, writes around the problem by describing instead what it is like to forget. The metaphorical power of thawing is first suggested in this sonnet's Dantean epigraph, 'It was that hour, which thaws the heart [*Era già l'ora che volge il desio*] (*Purgatorio* 8:1). In following this with the Petrarchan epigraph, 'I've called to mind how I beheld you first', Rossetti uses Dante to thaw Petrarch's sonnet's 'frozen' poetic imagination.

Despite her faulty memory, the attempt of Rossetti's speaker to pen her affection is not, like Petrarch's, 'discomfited' at 'the first onslaught'. Her eyes, though formerly 'blind ... to see and to foresee' events as they happened, now have the power of hindsight. The power of this retrospective vision represents more than nostalgia — it is a poetic manifestation of Tractarian typological principles. Just as the Old Testament can be read as retrospectively forecasting New Testament events, so too can emotional history be re-examined in the light of current emotion.[23] Like the Bible, the *Divina Commedia* and the *Canzoniere* are texts whose journeys are as much emotional as they are chronological. In continually quoting the lines and cantos of *Purgatorio* and the *Canzoniere* out of order, Rossetti's entire sequence enacts the challenge to chronological significance that her second sonnet constructs.

Rossetti's shifting chronology continues in her third sonnet's selection from *Purgatorio*, 2: 79, 'Ah shadows, that are but for sight inane! [*O ombre vane, fuor che ne l'aspetto!*]' Here, Dante, in attempting to embrace a spirit, finds him insubstantial. The previous Dantean epigraph takes place at nightfall, while this one happens at sunrise. In *Purgatorio*, the sun rises in canto 2 and sets in canto 8, but in Rossetti's sonnet sequence, Dante's sun sets before it rises. This temporal switch highlights the transience and insignificance of earthly events, emphasized with Rossetti's sonnet's last line, one of her favorite quotations from Ecclesiastes: 'there be nothing new beneath the sun' (Ecclesiastes 1:9). In Rossetti's third sonnet, Dante's 'shadows' are the speaker's dreams, whose insubstantiality is revealed at the moment of waking:

> I dream of you to wake: would that I might
>   Dream of you and not wake but slumber on;
>   Nor find with dreams the dear companion gone,
> As Summer ended Summer birds takes flight.
> In happy dreams I hold you full in sight,
>   I blush again who waking look so wan;
>   Brighter than sunniest day that ever shone,
> In happy dreams your smile makes day of night.
> Thus only in a dream we are at one,
>   Thus only in a dream we give and take
>   The faith that maketh rich who take or give;
>   If thus to sleep is sweeter than to wake,
>   To die were surely sweeter than to live,
> Tho' there be nothing new beneath the sun.

The sonnet exhibits a desire for escape from the demands of the material world that borders on a death wish: 'would that I might / Dream of you and not wake but slumber on' (1–2). Drawing on Shakespeare's *Hamlet* and Keats's odes to a Nightingale and on a Grecian Urn, the attraction to visionary oblivion running for thirteen lines is expressed through a series of logical and familiar tropes: the central images of life / wakefulness and death / sleep invert Hamlet's own comforting metaphors in his 'To be or not to be' soliloquy.

Rossetti carefully manipulates these two states in the octave to promote the speaker's desire for sleep, enacting in the process the gradual progress from unconsciousness to consciousness through a series of apparently opposed images: the imaginative height — or depth — of the dream-state inspires a 'blush' whereas she is 'wan' upon waking, while her companion's 'smile makes day of night'.

Yet the happy dream itself unravels, despite the sonnet's best efforts to hold it together. The sorrow of waking is promoted as a constant presence; yet, the idealized experience of dreaming is not guaranteed to be a happy one. The speaker's repeated reference to 'happy dreams' (5, 8) suggests their opposite, *unhappy* dreams, as even oblivion seems no guarantee of fulfillment. The poem's apparent confidence in the desire for oblivion is challenged by an underlying skepticism, almost as soon as it is voiced. The opening words 'I dream of you to wake', suggest a paradoxical tension from the very start: is the speaker concerned with this unnamed 'you' or with her own happiness? In the octave, the speaker is straining after the happiness of these dreams, even as it dissipates.

This sense of disturbance persists in the sestet, despite the assertive and unequivocal language of its first three lines. The conclusive logic of the statements, 'Thus only in a dream we are at one, / Thus only in a dream we give and take', is challenged by the conditional syntax of lines 11–12, '*If* thus to sleep is sweeter than to wake, / To die *were surely* sweeter than to live'. In this case, 'To sleep is sweeter than to wake' only '*If*' the dream is of being 'at one'. The sleep's 'sweetness' is dependent upon the occurrence of the 'happy dream' (as opposed to the possibility of a nightmare). Like Keats, this speaker's suicidal yearnings are conditional, as she is only '*half* in love with *easeful* death', while like Hamlet, her ambivalent consideration of the escapist possibilities of dying, sleeping, and dreaming betrays as much uncertainty about the insubstantial as it does about the concrete.

The quotation from Ecclesiastes in the final line recognizes that the speaker's uncertainty is a fundamental aspect of the human condition. Ecclesiastes posits that human life itself is a vain illusion, and concludes that obedience to God is mankind's only purpose. Rossetti's use of Ecclesiastes synthesizes the literary and the devotional. By alluding to Dante, Petrarch, Keats, and Shakespeare's meditations on waking and dreaming, and life and death, Rossetti positions the work of her female speaker in the same literary tradition. She traces this tradition's roots back to Ecclesiastes; there is 'nothing new beneath the sun', in human thought or its expression. Furthermore, these thoughts are not exclusive to its male artists. The speaker's thoughts, as well as Rossetti's, are both haunted and shaped by the shadowy presence of her great literary predecessors.

The sonnet's Petrarchan quotation, 'Now by a phantom guide it is con-trolled' ['*Immaginata guida la conduce*'] also plays on a kind of haunting (9). In Petrarch's sonnet 236, Laura's death means that a 'phantom guide' now controls his life because his 'true guide' is 'gone to heaven' (10). Though Petrarch still feels Laura in his heart, he cannot see her with his 'eyes, for their desired light / Is hid from them by sorrow's blinding fold' (12–13). While Dante can see the spirits, but cannot feel them, Petrarch can feel Laura ('on [his] heart shining') but cannot see her (11). Though each is distanced from the spirits in a different way, Rossetti uses both poets to make a similar point about the pain of separation which ges-tures to the impossibility of lasting union on earth.

The fleeting pleasures of the earth are also alluded to in Rossetti's Dante selection for her fourth sonnet, this time from *Paradiso* 1: 34: 'Great fire may after little spark succeed' ['*Poca favilla gran fiamma seconda*']. Aware of the transience of his life, Dante hopes to achieve a kind of immortality through his work. He asks Apollo to 'Rend me such a vessel of thy might / As to the longed-for laurel may suffice', hoping that the 'little spark' of his verse might ignite 'a great flame' of inspira-tion in future poets 'with better voice than mine' (14–15, 35).[24] Beatrice later explains to Dante that each soul rises naturally like a flame to heaven, but that remaining loyalties to earthly pleasure can cause the soul to swerve off course (131–5). Dante's quotation acts as Rossetti's 'little spark' to inspire her own quest for poetic achievement. Dante's 'longed-for laurel' provides a link to Petrarch, both because of his quest for *gloria* and the word's close resemblance to the name of his beloved. As well as locating herself in their poetic tradition by invoking her lit-erary forefathers, Rossetti also refashions them in her fourth sonnet by using a Dantean vision of unity to resolve traditional Petrarchan anxi-eties about love:

> I loved you first: but afterwards your love
>   Outsoaring mine, sang such a loftier song
> As drowned the friendly cooings of my dove.

(1–3)

The sonnet's Petrarchan quotation, 'Take flight all thoughts and things that it contains, / And therein Love alone with you remains' ['*Ogni altra cosa, ogni pensier va fore, / E sol ivi con voi rimansi amore*'] read along with Dante's 'little spark', maintains the sense of upward movement which defines Dante and Beatrice's ascension to the sphere of fire in *Paradiso* 1 (canzone 9, 44–5). Rossetti's fourth sonnet, like Dante's spark and Petrarch's flight, also rises, not only with the description of a love 'out-soaring' her speaker's, but also within the context of her sequence (2). The anxious tone of the first three sonnets, defined by plaintive request, lament, and escapist desire, hints at conflict. The fourth sonnet is the first to abandon complaint and embrace the joy of love. It represents the 'great fire' of love which follows the 'little spark' of love's beginnings. Although the octave begins by comparing and contrasting each person's love, its final line takes Petrarch's advice to send into 'flight all thoughts and things that it contains' as the speaker concludes, 'Nay, weights and measures do us both a wrong' (8). Human thought, like weights and measures, can quantify, and therefore limit love. Line 10, 'With separate "I" and "thou" free love has done', liberates the concept of love from the language of economy, transforming literal value into spiritual value. The octave's question, 'Which *owes* the other most' is answered in the sestet: '*Rich* love knows nought of "thine that is not mine"' (4, 12, emphasis mine). The final tercet resolves not to attempt to contain love through quantification or qualification: 'Both have the strength and both the length thereof / Both of us, of the love which makes us one' (13–14).

The final line also echoes Zechariah 2:2, 'Then said I, Whither goest thou? And he said unto me, To measure Jerusalem, to see what is the breadth thereof, and what is the length thereof'. In this chapter, Zechariah meets an angel who has come 'with a measuring line in his hand' to measure Jerusalem in preparation for God's planned return to the city (2:1). Rossetti's use of Zechariah here suggests that 'weights and measures' are best left to angels, and not to fallible humankind. It is an ominous forecast of the turmoil to come later in the sequence. Although 'weights and measures do us both a wrong' (8), the speaker has measured the 'strength' and 'length' of their relationship, and, as will be shown later, may have miscalculated.

The Dante epigraph of sonnet 5 reminds us of love's flame, but this time hints at its dangers: 'Love, who from loving none beloved reprieves' ['*Amor che a nulla amato amar perdona*'] (*Inferno*, 5: 103). The next line is, 'So kindled me to work his will again' (104). Spoken by Francesca, who is damned by the sin of incontinence to spend eternity in hell, the lines refer to her inability to control her love for Paolo, brother of her husband.

> O my heart's heart, and you who are to me
> More than myself myself, God be with you,
> Keep you in strong obedience leal and true

To Him whose noble service setteth free,
Give you all good we see or can foresee,
  Make your joys many and your sorrows few,
  Bless you in what you bear and what you do,
Yea, perfect you as He would have you be.
So much for you; but what for me, dear friend?
  To love you without stint and all I can
Today, tomorrow, world without an end;
    To love you much and yet to love you more,
  As Jordan at his flood sweeps either shore;
Since woman is the helpmeet made for man.

In canto 5 of *Inferno*, Francesca explains to Dante that love mastered her, obliged her to obey its human law, but in Rossetti's sonnet, the quotation applies also to the relationship between God and man. This sonnet invokes God, asks for his blessing, and outlines the duties of lovers to each other, formally resembling a prayer. God's love for man obliges man to love, and to serve that love in return. Rossetti's speaker expresses the wish that her lover remain 'leal and true / To Him whose noble service setteth free' (3–4). Her own promise 'to love you without stint and all I can', implies that this same freedom extends to her (10).

The octave promises that man's obedience to God will be rewarded with blessings while the sestet turns the reader's attention toward the woman's place in this union. The ninth line 'So much for you; but what for me, dear friend?' has a double meaning. Idiomatically, it functions as an indicator of a shift in subject from the man to the speaker (So much for you …) but taken literally, it is also a wry account of the vast gains to be had from the man's relationship to God (So *much* for you). The rest of the line, 'but what for me, dear friend?' becomes more plaintive in this reading, as the speaker contrasts the 'much' promised by God to her lover with 'what' she might expect. She can express obedience to God by loving and aiding man, which is woman's appointed role. As her lover is subordinate, yet free in his service to God, she will be subordinate, yet free, in her love for him. Her role as 'the helpmeet made for man' alludes to the creation of Eve in Genesis 2:18, 'And the Lord God said, It is not good that the man should be alone; I will make him an help meet for him'.

Female subservience in this sonnet does not necessarily equal spiritual inferiority. The desire to redress the problems caused by Eve's disobedience speaks of both humility and spiritual ambition. The speaker takes an active role in her own salvation by invoking God's blessing in the octave and asserting her own spiritual power in the sestet. The 'So much' that God gives to and expects from the speaker's lover is echoed in her promise 'To love you much' (12). Christ is the speaker's model here, as he provides the opportunity for the salvation of Eve's female descendents. Furthermore, he is most closely associated with the redemptive capability of love. Christ is further alluded to in line 11, where the speaker states her intention to emulate Christ by loving 'Today, tomorrow, world without an end'. Her words echo Ephesians 3:21, 'Unto him be glory in the church by Christ Jesus throughout all ages, world without end'. Rossetti's speaker wants her love to be unifying and mutually redemptive, saving both giver and receiver, just as the river Jordan, which borders the Promised Land 'sweeps either shore' (13).

The uncontrollable nature of Francesca's love in the Dantean epigraph is maintained in the sonnet's Petrarchan quotation: 'Love ... / *required* me into such sweet hopes to fall' ['*Amor m'addusse in sì gioiosa spene*'] (sonnet 43, 'Disappointed', 10–11, emphasis mine). Rossetti's sonnet relates the substance of this poem to the story of Francesca, as both become warnings about the sin of incontinence. Petrarch reveals his hopes of true love on earth to be false and fleeting, as 'previous to the last leave-taking hour, / There lives no man, that happy we should call' (13–14).

Rossetti's sonnet 5 itself provides few clues as to the quandary gradually forming, but read in the context of the entire sequence and its epigraphs, sonnet 5 presages trouble. The 'free love' of sonnet 4 is disrupted by an imbalance both in feeling and in duty. Rather than praising the equal 'strength' and 'length' of their love in sonnet 4, here the speaker assumes almost total responsibility for the relationship. The sestet outlines her obligations to her lover, but not his duties to her. This unbalanced division of labor is reflected by the sonnet's formal division; the lover gets the major part (the octave), and she the minor (the sestet). At the same time, the speaker, as a female troubadour composing the sonnet, controls this very fact. This friction between surrender and control produces this sonnet's 'little spark'.

The speaker's pledge to love a man alludes to her duty to God, without giving any explicit assurance that love of God is her primary obligation. There is a fine line between loving another person and worshipping him at the expense of the primary relationship with the divine creator. The speaker's vow to love 'Today, tomorrow, world without an end', though given in biblical language, is made more secular in the context of this sestet. It hints at idolatry, the kind which led Francesca, whose words serve as the poem's Dantean epigraph, to hell.

The speaker, aware of idolatrous resonance, hastily relates her love of God and man in sonnet 6:

> Trust me, I have not earned your dear rebuke,
>   I love, as you would have me, God the most;
>   Would lose not Him, but you, must one be lost,
> Nor with Lot's wife cast back a faithless look
> Unready to forego what I forsook;
>   This say I, having counted up the cost,

(1–6)

The 'me' of the first line has a double referent — as the speaker seeks the trust of her lover, so Rossetti seeks the trust of her audience. Although the specific cause of the 'rebuke' remains unclear, the rest of the sonnet tells us that it involves the speaker's love for both God and her lover. In order to overcome the contradictions between a tribute to human love and a tribute to God, Rossetti expands the boundaries of sonnet convention to incorporate the love between God and woman. This effort reflects the preface's determination to create a female figure not just 'resplendent with charms' but possessing genuine 'attractive-ness' and depth of character. This happens in the sixth sonnet's sestet which writes the love of woman for God and woman for man as utterly interdependent.

> Yet while I love my God the most, I deem
>   That I can never love you overmuch;
>   I love Him more, so let me love you too;
> Yea, as I apprehend it, love is such
> I cannot love you if I love not Him,
>   I cannot love Him if I love not you.

(9–14)

The sonnet's Dante quotation concerns, not just the strength, but the value of love. In canto 21, when Statius praises Virgil and tries to embrace him, he is reminded by Virgil that both are spirits, and thus cannot physically touch. It is the force of his love that caused Statius temporarily to forget that both are insubstantial spirits, as he explains to Virgil: '"Now," said he, rising, "mayest thou rightly set / A value on the love with which I flame"' ['*Or puoi la quantitate / Comprender de l'amor che a te mi scalda*'] (*Purgatorio*, 21: 133–4). Rossetti's sonnet follows from

Statius' declaration that love carries a value which can be quantified, but asserts, like Virgil, that this value must ultimately be judged according to God's will, not man's. Without God, who is both the origin of love and love itself, human love is an illusion, its pursuit like trying to embrace a shadow.

In sonnet 6, the rejected 'weights and measures' of sonnet 4 ('Nay, weights and measures do us both a wrong'), are reinstated. When God's will is not taken into account in the weighing and measuring of human love, its 'cost', as the case of Lot's wife proves, is too dear. While on earth, it is necessary to keep the love of humanity proportional to love of God: 'I love Him more, so let me love you too' (11). This attention to proportion also addresses the speaker's sense of imbalance in sonnet 5: 'So much for you; but what for me, dear friend?'(9).

Rossetti's final tercet re-asserts the speaker's perspective with its authoritative, biblical 'Yea' and confident tone ('as *I* apprehend it'). It articulates a philosophy of love which derives both strength and value from love's interdependence. The meaning of the first tercet, 'I love Him more, so let me love you too' is refined by the second tercet's final line, 'I cannot love Him if I love not you'. Here, the love the speaker feels for her lover is not opposed to the love she feels for God because it is equivalent in nature, if not in degree. The knotted structure of Rossetti's final tercet, with its interlacing of love for man and love for God, lends a religious dimension to her Petrarch quotation, 'Me shall not Love release, / From such a knot, by pain or by decease' ['*Non vo'che da tal nodo amor mi scioglia*'] (Ballata 6, 16–17). Petrarch's sentiment was solely for the dead Laura, but in Rossetti's hands, the 'knot' of love embraces God as well as muse.

The sense of interdependence is further elaborated in Rossetti's sonnet 7, where equality and togetherness contribute to an idealized vision of love's strength:

> "Love me, for I love you" — and answer me,
>   "Love me, for I love you" — so shall we stand
> As happy equals in the flowering land
>
> (1–3)

Here, the speaker proposes that man and woman can be made 'happy equals' through the reciprocity of their love. This is a rhetorical reciprocity too, with the exchange of identical vows of love in lines 1 and 2. With equality comes unity, because 'the flowering land / Of love ...

knows not a dividing sea' (3–4). The tone of the octave is confident and strong as the speaker imagines an edenic love uncomplicated by separation and difference. However, trouble is forecast in a shift in the sequence's rhyme scheme, from abba abba in sonnets 1–6 to abba abab in sonnet 7. The last two lines of the octave, 'And who hath found love's citadel unmanned? / And who hath held in bonds love's liberty?', are questions which should be defiantly rhetorical, but which might easily modulate into real anxiety, an anxiety also reflected structurally in a different rhyme-scheme (7–8).

The sonnet's first epigraph is from *Purgatorio* 28: 143, a canto which warns us that this paradise is not yet achieved. Matilda explains to Dante the workings of the Earthly Paradise, whose self-perpetuating and restorative waters see to it that 'Here spring was always, and each plant' ['*Qui primavera sempre ed ogni frutto*']. The two waters which pour from a fountain in the Earthly Paradise have different powers — one erases the memory of sin and one restores the memory of good deeds. This Dantean image of perpetual fruition and supernatural transformation emphasizes the reciprocal energy of love in the first two lines of sonnet 7.

Reciprocity is also the subject of the Petrarchan epigraph, 'Love with me walks and talks, and with him I' ['*Ragionando con meco ed io con lui*'] ('A Lover's Walk', 14). Though Petrarch's anxiety about his separation from Laura discourages human company, love does not desert him. Like Petrarch, Rossetti personifies love in her sonnet in order to demonstrate its tenacity, as it 'builds the house on rock and not on sand' and 'laughs while the winds rave desperately' (5, 6). This line also borrows its authority from Christ's words in Matthew 7:26, 'And every one that heareth these sayings of mine, and doeth them not, shall be likened unto a foolish man, which built his house upon the sand'. It also recalls the personification of love / charity in 1 Corinthians 13.

Yet the anxiety which pervades Petrarch's sonnet is also reflected in Rossetti's sestet where the speaker confesses 'My heart's a coward tho' my words are brave' (9). The speaker realizes that her idealized vision of togetherness is far from the truth of the situation, and challenges her lover to solve the 'problem' of prolonged separation, both in life and in his own poetry: 'We meet so seldom, yet we surely part / So often: there's a problem for your art!' (10–11). The word 'art' has a double meaning, playing on both poetic creativity and the idea of artifice. The accusatory exclamation point challenges both her lover's 'poetic aptitude' and his ability to justify his absence. The speaker uses her own 'art' to answer this challenge in the final tercet. She takes 'comfort in his Book' with two inverted lines from *The Song of Solomon*, 8: 6, 'Tho' jealousy be cruel as the grave / And death be strong, yet love is strong as death' (12, 13–14). More important than this inversion, though, is the fact that Rossetti has dismantled the parallelism between jealousy and love in the original and transformed it into an opposition. The test of parting in life is seen as a preparation for the lover's inevitable parting — death. The speaker takes comfort from the idea that love is as strong even as death, the most extreme kind of separation. Just as the love in Petrarch's sonnet 'walks and talks' with him while he despairs, the love in the Bible comforts Rossetti's speaker.

Rossetti's allusion to *The Song of Solomon* also brings the reader's attention to the tradition of love poetry. The literary immortality of *The Song of Solomon* illustrates the enduring truth of its proposition that love is as strong as death. The sonnet's epigraphs strengthen this resonance. Rossetti's biblical allusion is particularly significant because it references a poem well-known for having a female speaker, a woman 'resplendent with charms' but also a woman willing to testify to her own attractiveness: 'I am black, but comely' (*The Song of Solomon* 1: 5). Like Rossetti's speaker, this woman longs for her lover and demands his return: 'I will rise now, and go about the city in the streets, and in the broad ways I will seek him whom my soul loveth' (*The Song of Solomon* 3: 2). The inclusion of a female speaker in the tradition of love poetry is defended on literary and religious grounds.

Sonnet 8 of *Monna Innominata* contains the poem's only named woman. Again there is a biblical allusion, this time from Esther, whose story illustrates the desire of the sonnet sequence's speaker to be the equal of her lover:

> "I, if I perish, perish" — Esther spake:
> And bride of life or death she made her fair
> In all the lustre of her perfumed hair
> And smiles that kindle longing but to slake.
> She put on pomp of loveliness, to take
> Her husband thro' his eyes at unaware;
> She spread abroad her beauty for a snare,
> Harmless as doves and subtle as a snake.
> She trapped him with one mesh of silken hair,
> She vanquished him by wisdom of her wit,
>   And built her people's house that it should stand: —
>   If I might take my life so in my hand,
> And for my love to Love put up my prayer,
> And for love's sake by Love be granted it!

Here Rossetti gives us an example of a woman who lays claim to both charm and attractiveness. The predatory Esther of the octave is figured as a *femme fatale* who uses her charms when she '[spreads] abroad her beauty for a snare'. [25] Yet both 'spread abroad' and 'snare' also have Old Testament associations which suggest a tradition not only of female sexuality, but of female intelligence and influence. Saul's daughter Michal, for example, is promised to David as a reward for fighting the Philistines, during which battle Saul secretly hopes David will be killed. Saul wants Michal 'to be a snare to [David]' so that 'the hand of the Philistines may be against him' (1 Samuel 18:21). David lives, however, to claim Michal, and finally, it is Saul who is snared. Upon learning of her father's plan to send messengers to arrest David, Michal plants a dummy in her husband's place in bed. This action fools Saul's hired assassins and David flees to safety (1 Samuel 19:11–17).

In alluding to Michal's story, Rossetti identifies a tradition of female subversiveness which is defined as much by intelligence as sexuality. Although Saul wanted Michal to be a sexual 'snare' for David, instead she snares Saul by outwitting him. Esther's beauty is characterized as a sexual snare in the same way, but, for Rossetti, it is 'her wit' which persuades her husband not to slaughter her people.

Rossetti's use of the phrase 'spread abroad' in her re-telling of Esther is typological because it resonates with Old and New Testament meaning. In the Old Testament, the biblical phrase 'spread abroad' generally describes the Jewish diaspora. For example, during Jacob's dream, God says to him, 'And thy seed shall be as the dust of the earth, and thou shalt spread abroad to the west, and to the east, and to the north, and to the south: and in thee and in thy seed shall all the families of the earth be blessed' (Genesis 28:14).[26] In the New Testament, it becomes a way of describing the reach of Christ's influence. After Christ restores sight to blind men sight in Matthew, they 'spread abroad his fame in all that country' (9:31), while in Mark, Christ performs an exorcism, 'And immediately his fame spread abroad throughout all the region round about Galilee' (1: 28). In Thessalonians, it is not only the news of Christ's miracles but of the Christian faith which is spread abroad: 'For from you sounded out the word of the Lord not only in Macedonia and Achaia, but also in every place your faith to God-ward is spread abroad' (1 Thessalonians 1: 8). Just as Christ spreads abroad his influence to redeem mankind, Esther spreads abroad her beauty to save the Jewish people,.

This parallel is further suggested in the octave's last line, 'Harmless as doves and subtle as a snake'. The biblical quotation, from Matthew,[27] is a part of Christ's advice to his disciples as they prepare to convert 'the lost sheep of the house of Israel' (Matthew 10: 6). Its use is startling because the Old Testament story of Esther, which concerns saving the Jews from slaughter, is clearly at odds with the New Testament tale of the necessity of their conversion to Christianity. Rossetti, however, constructs a typological interpretation of the Old Testament, wherein Esther's saving Jewish lives is read as a precursor to Jesus' saving Jewish souls through conversion to Christianity. What is significant here is that Esther, and not a male figure, such as the more common choices of Solomon and David, is treated as a precursor to Christ. That she is a virtuous temptress also makes her a redemptive type of Eve. In pointing out the role of wisdom in Esther's plan to save her people, Rossetti gives depth to the notably Pre-Raphaelite characterization of Esther in the octave. By drawing her in relation to the Old Testament wise king, Rossetti elevates Esther within her poem to the level of power which Esther herself seeks in her own tale.

Rossetti's Dantean epigraph for this sonnet returns to canto 8 of *Purgatorio* when a spirit leads the other spirits in a hymn: 'And breathe to God, "Nought recketh me, but thou"' ['*Como dicesse a Dio: D'altro non calme*'] (*Purgatory*, 8: 12). The spirit's acknowledgement of God's power mirrors Esther's self-subjugation to her king, when she falls prostrate before him to beg for her people.[28] By capitalizing the word 'love' and suggesting it has the power to grant a prayer, Rossetti makes Love a metaphor of God in the final tercet: 'for my love to Love put up my prayer, / And for love's sake by Love be granted it!' The speaker invokes both Esther and the female spirit in *Purgatorio* in her own kind of 'hymn' to persuade her love and her God of her sincerity.

The Petrarchan epigraph employs the same mixture of humility and self-assurance as Rossetti's final tercet. The line, 'I hope to miss not pardon — pity I mean' ['*Spero trovar a pietà non che perdono*'] (8) comes from 'To Readers and the Experienced', a confessional sonnet, where Petrarch, looking back on his 'scattered rhymes', finds them flawed in their aspirations toward earthly love (1). He asks for sympathy for his former perspective from 'Love's true tryers' (those experienced in love), and concludes 'That what here pleaseth is a passing dream' (7, 14). The 'vain anguish' (6) and 'vain hope' (7) of love during humanity's temporary life on earth cannot lead to fulfilment. Rossetti has chosen this quotation to show that Petrarch has reached the same conclusion as the female spirit in *Purgatorio* — nothing is as important as God. The request for 'pardon' and 'pity' also continues the theme of prayer, working with the selections from Esther and *Purgatorio* to seek forgiveness, understanding, and redemption.

Redemption is the dominant theme of sonnet 9, the *volta* in this sonnet sequence, where the speaker, because of unspecified circumstances,
relinquishes her hope of earthly love:

> Thinking of you, and all that was, and all
>   That might have been and now can never be,
>   I feel your honoured excellence, and see
> Myself unworthy of the happier call:

(1–4)

The sonnet's epigraph from *Purgatorio* 3:8, 'Ah! white and honourable!'
['*O dignitosa coscienza e netta!*'] refers to Virgil's conscience and 'how it
made / a bitter morsel of the small offence' of dying unbaptized (8–9).
Here the speaker's feeling for her lover's 'honoured excellence' echoes
Dante's admiration of Virgil's character. The working relationship of
Dante and Virgil is also paralleled by the suggestion of creative exchange
between troubadour and muse within the sonnet sequence. 'White and
honourable' refers also to the love in sonnet 9, which is a force strong
enough to give the speaker faith and hope, despite her apparent defeat:

> And yet not hopeless quite nor faithless quite,
> Because not loveless; love may toil all night,
>   But take at morning; wrestle till the break
>   Of day, but then wield power with God and man: —

(9–12)

The speaker is inspired by the love's endurance, characterized here
with an allusion to Jacob, who wrestled with God all night and prevailed.[29] As Dante follows Virgil in order to be led to heaven, the speaker follows love's lead, willing to 'be spent' like Jacob, in her struggle
toward grace (14).

The Petrarchan epigraph, 'The soul, that warmest breath of virtue
drew' ['*Spirto più acceso di virtuti ardenti*'] is from sonnet 242, which
describes Petrarch's feelings at the death of Laura (4). Here the quotation
is used to underline the speaker's grief at the loss of 'all / That might
have been'. As much as the sestet promises to struggle against despair,
the sonnet's tone overall is despondent and melancholy. Even the elements of self-parody in the speaker's list of her faults '(ah, woe is me!)',
only deepen the sense of her loss of heart (7). In this, it imitates
Petrarch's sonnet wherein Laura's return in spirit form only intensifies

the idea of her loss. The Petrarchan line Rossetti has chosen for sonnet 9 is preceded by 'Thou'st loosened from the fairest, finest ties' (3). Though the ties that bound Laura's body to her soul are 'loosened', the knot tying her to Petrarch is still strong enough that her spirit visits him. The endurance of the love that binds the speaker to her lover and to her faith is emphasized by this chosen epigraph's intratextual reference to the epigraph for sonnet 6 of *Monna Innominata*, 'Me shall not Love release, / From such a knot, by pain or by decease'.

Love's endurance is stressed more explicitly in sonnet 10, which uses quotations from Dante and Petrarch to emphasize the temporary nature of life on earth, and the better life offered in heaven:

> Time flies, hope flags, life plies a wearied wing;
>   Death following hard on life gains ground apace;
>   Faith runs with each and rears an eager face,
> Outruns the rest, makes light of everything,
> Spurns earth, and still finds breath to pray and sing;
>   While love ahead of all uplifts his praise,
>   Still asks for grace and still gives thanks for grace,
> Content with all day brings and night will bring.
> Life wanes; and when love folds his wings above
>   Tired hope, and less we feel his conscious pulse,
>   Let us go fall asleep, dear friend, in peace:
>   A little while, and age and sorrow cease;
>   A little while, and life reborn annuls
> Loss and decay and death, and all is love.

The Dante quotation this time is selected from *Paradiso* 1: 40: 'With better light, with better stars allied' ['*Con miglior corso e con migliore stella*']. As in sonnet 4, Rossetti's allusion to *Paradiso* lifts this tenth sonnet from the earthbound sadness of the ninth. The momentum of the octave is upward, even in its metaphors for the passing of time: 'Time *flies*', 'life plies a wearied *wing*', 'Faith runs ... and *rears* an eager face / Outruns the rest, makes *light* of everything / Spurns earth', 'love ahead of all *uplifts*' (emphasis mine). The faith which 'spurns earth' alludes to canto 1 of *Paradiso* where Dante learns that spirits who retain loyalty to the earth are pulled down and away from heaven. In this canto, Dante is magically transported to the Circle of Fire in Paradise by following Beatrice's gaze toward the sun, then looking into her eyes. Spiritual progress is effected *through* the eyes of the beloved in a literal illustration of salvation through love. Yet it cannot be solely an earthly, idolatrous love, it must have a spiritual dimension which extends to love of God in order for 'transhumanizing' to be successful (*Paradise*. 1: 70). Otherwise, as Beatrice warns Dante, 'we see the flame shoot from heaven, / When'er the first impulsions it lent / Divert it by false pleasures earthwards driven' (1: 133–5).

The tenth sonnet's Dantean quotation also redirects our attention to the epigraph of Rossetti's sonnet 4, the first sonnet to elevate the ambitions of the sequence. Sonnet 4 uses an earlier quotation from *Paradiso* 1: 'Great fire may after little spark succeed' as a metaphor for both spiritual ascension and poetic inspiration. Sonnet 10 reinterprets sonnet 4 in light of the failure of the love relationship. Both sonnets resolve with an image of unity: 'Both of us, of the love which makes us one', and 'Loss and decay and death, and all is love'. Where sonnet 4 in energetic and optimistic, sonnet 10 is weary, though still hopeful. Experience has caused this shift in tone. The momentum of sonnet 4 is so insistently and prematurely *upward* that its speaker fails to take into account the literal and metaphorical *gravity* of earthbound love: 'loss and decay and death'.

The tenth sonnet's quotation from Petrarch's sonnet 231, 'Life flyeth, and will not a moment stay' ['*La vita fugge e non s'arresta un' ora*'], sustains the upward momentum of the octave yet also guides the change of pace in the sestet (1). Petrarch's sonnet is about the certainty of aging and death. He relates his life to a weary sea vessel: 'my mast and sails / Are rent; my pilot with fatigue opprest, / And quenched are the fair lights I used to view' (12–14). This world-weary image controls the pace of Rossetti's sestet, where 'Life wanes' 'love folds his wings'. There is 'Tired hope' whose 'pulse' is slowing, and the suggestion, 'Let us go fall asleep'. As in Petrarch's sonnet, this world-weariness is not quite a death wish, but is expressive of emotional exhaustion. Yet the final tercet hopes for 'life reborn' which 'annuls / Loss and decay and death, and all is love'. The sonnet leaves our thoughts in Paradise, where all is love, fulfilling the promise of its Dantean and Petrarchan epigraphs.

In sonnet 11, a Petrarchan anxiety about separation battles with a Dantean faith in reunion beyond the grave.

> Many in aftertimes will say of you
>   "He loved her" — while of me what will they say?
>   Not that I loved you more than just in play,
> For fashion's sake as idle women do.
> Even let them prate; who know not what we knew
>
>   (1–5)

The octave is inspired by the epigraph from *Purgatorio* 5: 13, 'Let people talk, and thou behind me go' ['*Vien dietro a me e lascia dir le genti*']. These words are spoken by Virgil in response to Dante's discomfort at the spirits' whisperings when they observe that Dante casts a shadow. 'For aye the man, who lets thought over thought / Go flowering, pushes from his drift away', Virgil warns, advising Dante not to be distracted from his goal (16–17).[30]

Although Rossetti partially decontextualizes the quotation by transforming it into advice against listening to gossip, it retains much of Dante's context, as the allusion also references the lovers' shared poetic profession. The speaker assumes the role of Virgil, urging her poet-partner to follow her lead in discounting the judgment of those 'who know not what we knew'. She reminds her lover that she is no ordinary 'idle' woman, but an equal and an artist who loved him 'more than just in play'. The phrase 'More than just *in play*' connotes not only that she loved him deeply, but also suggests that she loved him *in work*, in her songs of love to him (emphasis mine). Like Virgil admonishing Dante for being distracted from his quest by the spirits' whispering, the speaker reminds her lover that, regardless of what 'Many in aftertimes will say', about her love for him, after death her lover must 'make it plain / My love of you was life and not a breath' (13–14).

The sonnet's Petrarchan quotation from sonnet 244 'Counting the chances that our life befall' ['*Contando i casi della vita nostra*'], reinforces the speaker's role of advisor in the relationship. The sonnet compares the connection Petrarch feels with the deceased Laura to the affection of a mother and a loving wife for her children or husband. 'Now mother-like, now love-like', she 'tells [him] all / That on this path I must avoid or choose, / Counting the chances that our life befall' (9–12). Laura's guidance of Petrarch also has spiritual dimensions, because she is 'praying [he] may lift [his] soul with speed' (13).

Rossetti's epigraphs conflate spiritual and maternal guidance to reflect the multiplicity and depth of the speaker's love. Like Virgil and Dante, Rossetti's lovers have a professional and spiritual connection, but like Petrarch and Laura, they also have a sexual and familial connection (husband / wife, mother / child). Her speaker's love is 'life and not a breath' because it is not confined to one category of loving, but embraces a multiplicity of roles, as is further suggested by its word-play on the 'breath of life', which God gives Adam in Genesis. These allusions, from Genesis to *Purgatorio*, draw on stories of both literal and literary creation. *Monna Innominata* itself plays with both kinds of creation, as it is about a poet loving someone and a poet writing about loving someone. The speaker's self-consciousness about the dangers and responsibilities that accompany creation is revealed in line 10, 'My love that you can make not void nor vain'. This implies that the speaker has reason to believe her lover might wish to deny her love. She dismisses what 'Many in aftertimes will say' of their love on earth, but she is adamant that her love be confirmed by her lover 'at the Judgment'. The movement from the 'Many' of the octave to the 'I' and 'you' of the sestet narrows the sonnet's focus from the communal to the private. Acknowledgement of the love between them should be reciprocal, the responsibility shared: 'I charge you' (13). There is also a hint that the speaker's love will survive in the love poem itself: 'Love that forgoes you but to claim anew / Beyond this passage of the gate of death' (11–12).

In sonnet 12, the speaker places her faith in the unifying power of love. The quotation from *Purgatorio* 2: 112, '"Love, that discoursing art within my soul"' ['*Amor, che ne la mente mi ragiona*'] references the Florentine musician Casella, whose song enraptures Dante and the new arrivals in Purgatory. Despite the gravity of his situation, Casella is still capable of communicating love and giving pleasure to his audience. Rossetti's speaker also finds solace in the power of love, and art, in times of suffering:

> If there be any one can take my place
>   And make you happy whom I grieve to grieve,
>   Think not that I can grudge it, but believe
> I do commend you to that nobler grace,
> That readier wit than mine, that sweeter face;
>   Yea, since your riches make me rich, conceive
>   I too am crowned, while bridal crowns I weave,
> And thread the bridal dance with jocund pace.
> For if I did not love you, it might be
>   That I should grudge you some one dear delight;
>   But since the heart is yours that was mine own,
> Your pleasure is my pleasure, right my right,
> Your honourable freedom makes me free,
>   And you companioned I am not alone.

In canto 2 of *Purgatorio*, Casella sings Dante a song to demonstrate that he does not resent the poet's progress toward Paradise, from which he is temporarily barred. Similarly, Rossetti's speaker dedicates a song to her lover's 'freedom' in order to convince him that she does not begrudge him a future relationship. The sestet applies Casella's faith in

the will of God to a human relationship.[31] The final tercet echoes
Purgatorio 2:88–9, when Casella says to Dante, '"As I have loved thee
before ... / In mortal body, so I love thee freed"'. This sonnet takes a
Dantean view of love as a unifying force in which full reciprocation is
not necessarily requisite. Like Dante's love for Beatrice in *Vita Nuova*,
the speaker's affection for her lover does not have to be returned in
order for both her love and her poetry to thrive.

The 'Love' of the Dantean epigraph influences the sonnet's sestet,
while its 'discoursing art' features in the octave. That the speaker is
aware of her own artful discourse is subtly woven into the poem. For
example, the 'art' of the first line is that it is conditional: '*If* there be any
one can take my place' (emphasis mine). The line both releases the lover
and expresses the speaker's skepticism that any other woman could
replace her. The speaker refers to her poetic 'art' when she asserts, 'Yea,
since your riches make me rich, conceive / I too am crowned, while
bridal crowns I weave'. Here, the speaker's crown is probably one of laurel, denoting poetic honor. The sonnet sequence's persistent Petrarchan
epigraphs also maintain this link. 'Conceive' in this context takes
advantage of its multiple meanings, signifying 'consider' and 'create',
and 'procreate'. The speaker wants her lover to conceive (consider) that
she is a poet, and that his 'riches', both his love and his work, inspire
her to conceive (create) poetry. 'Conceive', with its childbearing conno-
tations, also provides a poignant contrast between the poetic creations
of the solitary speaker and the future children of the companioned
bride. At the same time, the possible suggestion of sexual connection
between the man and both women (speaker and bride) contributes to
the unsettling tone of the octave.

The conditional 'If' of the sestet allows the speaker to imagine what
'it might be' *not* to love him, permitting the resentment underlying the
octave's assurances to be expressed. The unequivocal language of the
final four lines, wherein the speaker asserts that 'the heart is yours that
is mine own', and 'Your pleasure my pleasure, right my right', does not
banish the ambivalence of the sonnet's conditional 'if'. While the sonnet's octave seems to release the lover from his obligations to the speaker, the sestet reinforces their irrevocable connection.

This connection is structurally reinforced within the sonnet sequence
itself. Line 11, 'But since the heart is yours that was mine own' restates
lines 1 and 2 in sonnet 5: 'O my heart's heart, and you who are to me /
More than myself, myself'. The speaker's refusal to take back her heart
also confirms the promise of the sonnet 5: 'To love you without stint
and all I can / Today, tomorrow, world without an end' (10–11). In

addition, the Dante epigraph to sonnet 5, 'Love, who from loving none beloved reprieves', has been taken as this sonnet's theme.

The Petrarch quotation for sonnet 12, 'As Love amongst the ladies in your face / Of loveliness appeareth' [*'Amor vien nel bel viso di costei'*] refers us to Cayley's title for Petrarch's poem, 'One In Many' (1–2). The quotation describes how Petrarch's feelings of love increase upon seeing his beloved in the company of women: 'So grow those longings, which your lover sway, / The more as elsewhere I less beauty trace' (3–4). Rossetti inverts this equation so that her speaker, unlike Petrarch's Laura, actually suffers from comparison to another woman: 'I do commend you to that nobler grace / That readier wit than mine, and sweeter face'. The fifth and sixth lines of Petrarch's sonnet, 'Oh then I bless the time and hour and place, / Which my looks lifted to that arduous way', refer us back to sonnet 2 of Rossetti's sequence, where the speaker wishes to 'remember that first day, / First hour, first moment of your meeting me' (1–2). This connection lends the poem extra emotional weight, as it invites us to contrast the happy anticipation of the speaker in the second sonnet with her disappointment in the twelfth. The sestet's rhyme scheme repeats the pattern of sonnet 6 (cde dce), connecting the speaker's effort in sonnet 12 to retain her lover with her struggle between love for God and her lover in sonnet 6. The relationship between the speaker, her lover, and God in sonnet 6 is recast in sonnet 12 with a new triumvirate of speaker, lover, and bride. Here the positions are reversed. Instead of the speaker choosing between God and man, the lover is choosing between the speaker and the bride. Even so, by the end of the sonnet, the speaker regains control, claiming that she and her lover are the same person, and so no matter what his choice, 'you companioned I am not alone'.

The speaker's release of her lover occurs in sonnet 13, which looks to God for love's fulfillment:

> If I could trust mine own self with your fate,
>   Shall I not rather trust it in God's hand?
>   Without Whose Will one lily doth not stand
>
> (1–3)

The octave's biblical allusions to Matthew and Luke remind us of their use in the much younger Rossetti's '"Consider the Lilies of the Field"' (1853), but this poem's 'trust' in God comes from experience as well as faith. The first epigraph, from *Paradiso* 32: 142, 'And set we on the all-first Love our eyes' [*'E drizzeremo glí occhi al Primo Amore'*], bears a direct relation to the sonnet. Both speaker and sonnet set their eyes on Christ, the 'all-first Love' of Dante's *Paradiso*, asking both lover and readers to follow suit. Mirroring Dante's progress, the sonnet sequence now assumes a more paradisiacal outlook than a purgatorial one. The God who 'weighs the wind and water with a weight' (6) refers us back to sonnet 4, 'Nay, weights and measures do us both a wrong' (8). The difficulties of quantifying love also arose in sonnet 6 with the epigraph from *Purgatorio* 21: 133–4, '"Now", said he, rising, "mayest thou rightly set / A value on the love with which I flame."' Unlike the human couple in the sonnet sequence, only God, 'the all-first Love' is capable of weighing and measuring, and ultimately judging, love.[32]

The quotation from Petrarch, 'But for my arms this burden was too sore' ['*Ma trovo peso non da le mie braccia*'] also stresses the human inability to bear the weight of love ('Delayed Praises', 5). The epigraph refers us to sonnet 2 of Rossetti's sequence, which used a quotation from the same Petrarch sonnet. In his sonnet Petrarch bemoans his failure to commemorate in poetry his first meeting with Laura. In sonnet 2, Rossetti's speaker is frustrated at her inability to remember the first sight of her love at all. In sonnet 13, the speaker is frustrated again, this time not because she cannot recall the past, but because she cannot control the future. She speaks ruefully of a God 'Whose knowledge foreknew every plan we planned', and laments the fact that she is 'Helpless to help and impotent to do' (8, 11). These feelings of human helplessness in the face of divine will lend a religious resonance to the creative impotence of Petrarch to express love for his muse. Despite the vow of the Petrarchan epigraph to sonnet 6, 'Me shall not Love release, / From such a knot, by pain or by decease', the speaker here loosens the bonds of love:

> Searching my heart for all that touches you,
>   I find there only love and love's goodwill
> Helpless to help and impotent to do,
>   Of understanding dull, of sight most dim;
>   And therefore I commend you back to Him
> Whose love your love's capacity can fill.
>
> (9–14)

This sense of release is enacted structurally by the rhyme scheme of its sestet, which it shares with sonnet 5 (cdc eed). The shared rhyme scheme calls the earlier sonnet to mind, but also draws attention to the difference between them, notably the spiritual progression of the speaker. It illustrates her maturation, both personal and poetical, as the confidence of youth in earthly union here gives way to the uncertainty brought on by experience. Whereas sonnet 5 declared the speaker's intention to 'love you without stint and all I can / Today, tomorrow, world without an end' (10–11), sonnet 13 finds her 'helpless' and 'impotent'. Confidence is replaced with resignation, as her 'understanding dull' and 'sight most dim' contrasts with her certainty in sonnet 5 that 'woman is the helpmeet made for man'.

The Dante epigraph of the fourteenth and final sonnet, 'In His good pleasure we have each his peace' ['*E la Sua Volontade è nostra pace*'] carries on the conclusion of sonnet 13, that only through pleasing God can true fulfillment be found (*Paradiso*, 3:85). The words are spoken by Piccardia, a spirit who while on earth was forcibly taken from her convent and made to marry. She speaks to Dante in the sphere of the Moon, lower in Paradise to reflect the status of those whose vows were broken or unfulfilled on earth. This sense of broken promise resonates with Rossetti's speaker's regret:

Youth gone, and beauty gone if ever there

> Dwelt beauty in so poor a face as this;
> Youth gone and beauty, what remains of bliss?
> I will not bind fresh roses in my hair,
> To shame a cheek at best but little fair, —
> Leave youth his roses, who can bear a thorn, —
> I will not seek for blossoms anywhere,
> Except such common flowers as blow with corn.
> Youth gone and beauty gone, what doth remain?
> The longing of a heart pent up forlorn,
> A silent heart whose silence loves and longs;
> The silence of a heart which sang its songs
> While youth and beauty made a summer morn,
> Silence of love that cannot sing again.

Unlike Piccardia, the speaker does not seem to find 'peace' in obeying the will of God, but exhibits instead a 'pent-up' anguish, the spirit of which Rossetti borrows from Petrarch's 'The Damsel of the Laurel'. Rossetti chooses line 32 for her epigraph, 'Alone with these my thoughts, with altered hair' ['*Sol con questi pensier, con altre chiome*']. In Petrarch's sestina, he worries that the pursuit of his muse will last a lifetime unsatisfied: 'Sooner will change, I dread, my face and hair, / Than truly will turn on me pitying eyes / Mine idol, which is carved in living laurel' (25–7). Though he may grow old never having won Laura's love, he 'will pursue the shade of that sweet laurel' 'Until the latest day shall close my eyes' (16, 18). Petrarch's wordplay links the poetic 'laurel', to his beloved, 'Laura' throughout the poem.

Although it takes its regretful tone from Petrarch's sestina, Rossetti's sonnet can also be read as a Dantean critique of Petrarch. Rossetti's speaker has arrived at the solitary old age which Petrarch's poem dreads. Not only is her life's journey nearing an end, but her poetic career is coming to a close. Neither laurel nor love proves immortal. While Petrarch's literary legacy and his muse become one as he aspires to 'draw compassion to men's eyes / Not to be born for the next thousand years, / If so long can abide the well-nurtured laurel', Rossetti's speaker has given up such ambitions (34–6). Literally and literarily drained by her unrequited love, she rejects the Petrarchan quest for the beloved ('I will not seek for blossoms anywhere') and for poetic fame ('Silence of love that cannot sing again'). The final tercet's repeated contrast of silence and song itself produces the 'sound' of the speaker's 'silent heart whose silence loves and longs'.

That the sonnet does little to evoke the 'peace' of its Dante epigraph, and refers more obviously to the anxiety of aging in Petrarch's, illustrates the dangers of idolatrous love, both for muses and for poets. The departure of 'youth' and 'beauty', lamented four times, provides an echoic challenge to the Keatsian equation of beauty and truth with knowledge. After youth and beauty fade, the question of 'what doth remain' becomes crucial. Rossetti's final sonnet suggests why she considers Petrarch to be 'a great tho' an inferior bard' to Dante. While Dante's journey to heaven offers the peace of pleasing God, Petrarch's quest for his beloved ends in loneliness and death. Petrarch not only figures Laura and poetic fame as explicitly idolatrous ('Mine idol, which is carved in living laurel'), he closes his poem with an idolatrous reference: 'But gold and sunlit topazes on snow / Are passed by her pale hair, above those eyes / By which my years are brought so fast ashore' (37–9). Rossetti would have recognized this reference to Job 28:19: 'The topaz of Ethiopia shall not equal it [wisdom], neither shall it be valued with pure gold'. Petrarch here substitutes his love for Laura for heavenly wisdom. Rossetti reads this as an admission of idolatry, and as a reason for the futility of his quest. Within the sonnet sequence, it becomes apparent that either the speaker or her lover has given human love precedence over heavenly wisdom, so that 'for love's sake by Love' the wish for love cannot be 'granted' (8:14). Sonnet 14 suggests that the breakdown of the human relationship in *Monna Innominata* has to do with the inability, either on the part of the speaker or her lover, to keep in balance human and divine love.

Monna Innominata mirrors the structure of the Petrarchan sonnet. In the sequence's 'octave', (sonnets 1–8) love is found and plans are made. A risk taken in sonnet 8, when the speaker, like Esther, asks for a wish to be granted. The 'volta' of sonnet 9 makes it clear that the request has been denied, while during the 'sestet' (sonnets 9–14), the speaker has to pay the consequences of the octave's declaration, "'I, if I perish, perish'" (8: 1). In the sequence's final 'tercet' (sonnets 12–14), the speaker gives up both her career and her lover. Muses and poetic inspiration, the sonnet suggests, are subject to change and death, while doing God's will leads to true and lasting peace.

Rossetti's experiment with gender-role reversal in Petrarchan sonnet convention makes not only a feminist point about a woman writing a man, but also a religious one about a poet writing a muse. If any poet idolizes his or her muse, s / he runs the risk of a broken heart, not because of the inevitability of separation through death, but because of an idolatrous failure of spiritual faith. This is a lesson which Dante learns in the *Purgatorio* when Beatrice chastizes him (*Purgatorio*, 30: 124–9).

Yet Rossetti's sonnet sequence is not unsympathetic to the Petrarchan plight of its speaker. *Monna Innominata* is so successful because its network of allusions allows it to act simultaneously as tribute and critique of both the motivations of its speaker and the poets of the past. While its speaker is silenced, the poem, like the poetry of Dante and Petrarch, still sings. Rossetti's Tractarian philosophy of unity in multiplicity is woven into the contrasting textures of theologies, poetics, and emotions which make up the fabric of the sequence. The language, allusion, ideology, and themes of *Monna Innominata* interlace the various kinds of love which the sequence describes, structurally enacting both the Petrarchan and the Christian 'knot' of love.

4
'A Courteous Tilt in the Strong-Minded Woman Lists': Rossetti, St. Paul, and Women

Imagination and responsibility

One of the most distinguishing marks of Rossetti's authorial maturity is her increasing awareness of her audience. The layout of her early volumes encouraged readers to make connections between devotional and general poems, but it is in the works of middle age that Rossetti's sense of her readership starts to appear as part of the text itself. In *Monna Innominata*, for example, the responsibilities of the poet to her muse and her God animate the conventional narrative of its love story. God is watching in nearly all of Rossetti's poems, but the later works are increasingly conscious of our gaze as well. Occasionally, and startlingly, Rossetti stares right back at us, as in the following entry for 4 December in the devotional prose work, *Time Flies*:

> I once heard an exemplary Christian remark that she had never been accused of a fault without afterwards recognising truth in the accusation.
> And if she, how not I.
> At the least her words should make me cautious not to rebut any charge in anger or in haste.
> And if me, why not you?[1]

(232)

Here, Rossetti herself becomes the parable she describes, and, by extension, so do we. Like the 'I' of Rossetti's poetry, the 'me' of her prose is of course a persona. Yet this devotional persona, adopted to forge a strong link between reader, writer, and the wider Christian community, is more direct than the younger, 'reserved' Rossetti.

In Rossetti's case, what she writes and thinks about the female members of that community is as much a question of audience as it is of subject matter. While certainly enjoyed by both men and women, her devotional prose work was written with a Christian female audience in mind, and much of its content is geared toward the female experience of reading the Bible. For example, *Letter and Spirit* examines the Ten Commandments as they apply to the women of Rossetti's day, while *Time Flies* takes the shape of a commonplace book or a diary, forms which were familiar to women readers. As she grew older, Rossetti's sense of Christian responsibility to her readership increased. In turn, her contemporary reputation as a devotional writer was linked with her gender, and with that of her readers.

The notion of Rossetti as a woman's writer persists in the feminist recovery of Rossetti but her faith, and the faith of her female Christian readership, has not always been considered part of the equation. When her Christian philosophy is studied, it is generally set up in opposition to her artistic aspirations. Although the relationship of faith and artistic imagination was a dominant theme of Rossetti's career, both Victorian and modern critics suggest it was an issue of which she was somewhat unaware. For example, a juxtaposition of a passage from Gosse's 1893 article and Angela Leighton's essay of 1992 shows the persistent critical implication that Rossetti's poetic ability existed separately from her faith.

What is very interesting in her poetry is the union of the fixed religious faith with a hold upon physical beauty and the richer parts of nature which allies her with her brother and their younger friends. She does not shrink from strong delineation of the pleasures of life even when she is denouncing them.[2]

In *The Face of the Deep*, for instance, [Rossetti] piously advises the reader to 'Strip sin bare from voluptuousness of music, fascination of gesture, entrancement of the stage, rapture of poetry, glamour of eloquence, seduction of imaginative emotion' (1892: 399). Yet the more she lists them, the more avid she sounds to imagine all the lovely, deceitful appearances of sin.[3]

Leighton's other conclusion that 'Rossetti was daring, in contradiction of all her opinions, in her imagination' (125) bears a marked resemblance to Gosse's opinion that 'two qualities combined, in spite of their apparent incompatibility, — an austere sweetness coupled with a luscious and sensuous brightness, — to form one side of Miss Rossetti's curious poetic originality' (213). What is at issue in both evaluations is religion. For Rossetti, religious faith and imagination are not so far apart. For the modern critic this gap yawns wide, while for the Victorian, it is bridged by Rossetti's association with the male imagination of the PRB. Where Gosse ignores the subversive implications of this 'apparent incompatibility', Leighton overemphasizes them, giving the upper hand to imagination over religious faith. In fact, the issue of the 'contradiction' between imagination and faith is often at the very center of Rossetti's Christian philosophy. The very sentence quoted by Leighton belongs to a larger meditation on the rigors of maintaining the faithful imagination. This passage is not simply about the contradiction between faith and imagination, but about being able to distinguish between the faithful and the corrupt imagination. 'Study sin, when study it we must, not as a relishing pastime, but as an embittering deterrent', is her advice to contemporary readers. Here, sin must be imagined and studied in order for it to be discovered and stripped bare, as 'bald as in the Ten stern Commandments' (*FD* 399).

The way in which Rossetti battles to understand inconsistencies in the Bible and to relate them to contemporary life shows both a consciousness of the issues and self-consciousness in their treatment. Whereas Gosse's argument demonstrated the Victorian tendency to imply that Rossetti's faith 'distanced her' from 'her involvement in and response to some of the controversial issues of her day',[4] Leighton's modern contention is that Rossetti's religion stands at odds with her secret 'avid' desire for such involvement. Yet the passage Leighton selects recommends open confrontation of the realities of contemporary life. The advice to which Leighton refers is intended, not only for the general reader, but specifically for the Christian female reader. Rossetti is not asking women to abandon their imaginations, but rather to use Christian teachings to differentiate between imagination and dangerous illusion. Far from using faith as a strategy to shut down or circumvent argument, Rossetti uses her faith in combination with her imagination to open up and explore various avenues and identities, particularly for women. What Rossetti advocates here is for women to examine the nature of their own imaginations through a specifically Christian confrontation with the world.

The whole passage from *The Face of the Deep* is about recognizing sin in order to break free from its illusions. It begins by asking readers to imagine themselves as St. John and the angel who leads him to the Whore of Babylon in Revelation 17:1–3.

He who exhibits is an angel, and he who inspects is a saint: yet does this exalted pair betake themselves into "the wilderness," there and not elsewhere to set themselves face to face with an impersonation of abominable wickedness. So likewise did their and our Divine Master do when He deigned to confront Satan. And if the Standard Bearer among ten thousand, and if the flower of His armies did thus, it leaves us an example that we should tread in their steps.

Some innocent souls there are who from cradle to grave remain as it were veiled and cloistered from knowledge of evil. As pearls in their native deep, as flower buds under Alpine snow, they abide unsullied: the lot has fallen unto them in a fair ground. But for most persons contact with evil and consequent knowledge of evil being unavoidable, is clearly so far ordained: they must achieve a more difficult sanctity, touching pitch yet continuing clean, enduring evil communications yet without corruption of good manners.

(FD 399)

Here she tells women to imagine themselves following in the footsteps of angels, saints, and God himself. The task of those 'who ... remain ... cloistered from knowledge of evil' is far less daunting than that of 'most persons' whose 'contact with evil and consequent knowledge of evil' is 'unavoidable'. The 'difficult sanctity' that she describes also recalls Milton's *Areopagitica*:

I cannot praise a fugitive and cloister'd vertue, unexercis'd and unbreath'd, that never sallies out and sees her adversary, but slinks out of the race, where that immortall garland is to be run for, not without dust and heat. Assuredly we bring not innocence into the world, we bring impurity much rather: that which purifies us is tri-all, and triall is by what is contrary.[5]

While Rossetti does not go so far as to withhold praise from those 'veiled and cloistered from knowledge of evil', she maintains Milton's view of the confrontational relationship between mankind and evil. It is next to impossible, she implies, to 'abide unsullied', and so the next best thing is to confront evil head-on.

To each such imperilled soul, Angel and Apostle here set a pattern. If we too would gaze unscathed and undefiled on wickedness, let us not seek for enchantments, but set our face toward the wilderness. Strip sin bare from voluptuousness of music, fascination of gesture, entrancement of the stage, rapture of poetry, glamour of eloquence, seduction of imaginative emotion; strip it of every adornment, let it stand out bald as in the Ten stern Commandments. Study sin, when study it we must, not as a relishing pastime, but as an embittering deterrent. Lavish sympathy on the sinner, never on the sin ...

Wherever the serpent is tolerated there is sure to be dust for his pasture: he finds or he makes a desolate wilderness of what was as the Garden of Eden. Only an illusion, a mirage, can cause a barren desert to appear in our eyes as a city of palaces, an orchard of fruits.[6]

(399)

Read in its fuller context, Rossetti's detailing of sin is not just a subconscious yearning for sin, but also a warning and an enactment of how enchanting sin can appear. Rossetti is more than aware of its attraction, which causes her to caution readers to 'study sin ... not as a relishing pastime, but as an embittering deterrent'. The feminist subversion here is not simply in Rossetti's unconscious desire to dwell on the attractions of sin, but more in her advocation of female appropriation of traditionally male traits and tasks. Faith is what makes these roles available to women. Christian women here are scholars who can learn to distinguish divine reality from satanic illusion — quite an aspiration for the descendants of Eve, the first woman, who failed to make this distinction.

Rossetti and Eve

As Diane D'Amico has noted, Rossetti is both traditional and subversive in the way she interprets Eve as a cautionary tale for women.[7] Following on from D'Amico's conclusion that for Rossetti, Eve's transgression was disobedient rather than sexual, I am interested in how Rossetti's treatment of Eve offers us a meditation on the nature of female intellect. Rossetti's conclusion is ultimately conservative, but her argument is notable for the way in which it uses Christian tradition to re-evaluate Eve.

Despite having previously stated in *The Face of the Deep* that women should aggressively confront and interact with the world in order to discover its truths and illusions, Rossetti presents the opposite argument concerning Eve:

Not till she became wise in her own conceit, disregarding the plain
obvious meaning of words, and theorizing on her own responsibility
as to physical and intellectual results, did she bring sin and death into
the world.

(FD 310)

This seems at first glance a shocking conclusion from a female devotional poet who specializes in 'theorizing' about 'her own responsibility as to physical and intellectual results'. Rossetti's writings on Eve, and
on the role of Victorian Christian women, are characterized by confusion and ambivalence, a fact that has not gone unremarked upon by
feminist critics. However, it makes no more sense to read these contradictions as evidence of a reactionary Rossetti 'buried alive in a coffin of
renunciation'[8] than it does to read them as evidence of the revolutionary Rossetti, piously reiterating dogma to conceal her true feminist
agenda. The truth for Rossetti lies in her analysis of the nature of Eve's
sin, and it is here that knowledge of her religious beliefs, and acceptance
that her faith to her was real and important, can reveal something of
what she thought about women.

The quotation applied to Eve above incorporates Paul's advice in
Romans 11:25: 'For I would not, brethren, that ye should be ignorant of
this mystery, lest ye should be *wise in your own conceits*; that blindness
in part is happened to Israel, until the fulness of the Gentiles be come
in' (emphasis mine).[9] The mystery to which Paul refers is salvation
through Christ, which he compares to the process of grafting 'wild'
olive branches onto 'good' trees.[10] While Rossetti chastizes Eve for drawing her own conclusions about 'physical and intellectual results', the
use of Romans 11:25 lets us know that she is not connecting Eve's sin
with her gender, particularly, but with her human vanity. By linking
Eve's transgressive thoughts to the prospective Roman converts, whom
Paul has to warn against boasting and highmindedness, Rossetti relates
disobedience to the sin of vanity. Paul's phrase is itself of Old Testament
origin, found in Proverbs which describe 'wisdom in conceit' as the
worst kind of foolishness.[11] The reason that such wisdom is (paradoxically) foolish, is revealed in Proverbs 28:11: 'The rich man is wise in his
own conceit; but the poor that hath understanding searcheth him out'
and is drawn on in the New Testament, in 1 Corinthians 1:25: 'the foolishness of God is wiser than men; and the weakness of God is stronger
than men'.

The distinction between wisdom and understanding is one which is
important to Rossetti. Where logic (wisdom) fails in Christianity,

faith (understanding) must take over. Wisdom without faith leads to 'conceit', a false sense of knowledge which puts the soul in danger. Eve was wise, but her vanity about her intellectual ability led to a false understanding, a lack of faith that God must be obeyed. In *Letter and Spirit*, Rossetti again worries about the gulf between human reasoning and divine understanding:

> those who acquire that dangerous thing, a little learning, are more likely to be puffed up by the little they know than ballasted by the much they know not; conceit spurns at reverence and submission, and the undermining of natural piety is too often followed by the repudiation of spiritual loyalty.
>
> (*LS* 68)

At first glance Rossetti's judgment of Eve seems to be drawing a gender-biased conclusion about the intellectual abilities of women, one which stands in direct conflict with her own project. But, if we recognize and trace Rossetti's allusion to Proverbs, Romans, and Corinthians, an argument about the relationship of humanity to knowledge also emerges, which is based not on gender, but on faith. Though a gender-bias against Eve still suggests itself, the idea that Eve's sin was not one of temptation but of intellectual vanity removes Eve's sexuality and her abilities as a temptress from the equation. And though, in the end, Eve's intelligence leads to her expulsion from paradise, for Rossetti to view her confrontation with the serpent as intellectual rather than sexual is a more radical move in her time than it seems to readers today.

Rossetti, in the spirit of the New Testament, anticipates love as a resolution to all the conflicts engendered by the Fall. For example, sonnet 15 of *Later Life* interprets the lesson of Adam and Eve's earthly love as a prefiguration of divine forgiveness.

> Did Adam love his Eve from first to last?
>   I think so; as we love who works us ill,
>   And wounds us to the quick, yet loves us still.
> Love pardons the unpardonable past:
> Love in a dominant embrace holds fast
>   His frailer self, and saves without her will.
>
> (9–14, 2: 144)

Theologically, Rossetti is influenced by the New Testament vision of a God of love and forgiveness. This poem also seems influenced by the final scene of *Paradise Lost*, which ends with an image of the solemn yet loving unity of Adam and Eve.

> Some natural tears they dropp'd, but wip'd them soon;
> The World was all before them, where to choose
> Their place of rest, and Providence their guide:
> They hand in hand with wand'ring steps and slow,
> Through Eden took their solitary way.
>
> (XII: 645–9)

Rossetti elides the issue of responsibility for the Fall by dwelling instead on the forgiveness within the relationship. Their love prefigures the redemption of humanity through Christ:

> To begin with Adam and Eve; one is so accustomed to contemplate the Fall as well-nigh simultaneous in both, that perhaps the subsequent Christ-likeness of Adam, presumably in forgiving and cherishing, certainly in retaining, the wife who had cost him life and all things, may pass unnoticed. That Eve responded to his love and patience we need not doubt. *Nor need we attempt to settle which (if either) committed the greater sin;* Adam's faithful love ... remains in any case.
>
> (*LS* 56–7, emphasis mine)

This supportive and ultimately redemptive love between Adam and Eve ignores Paul's vision of couplehood, wherein salvation is the responsibility of the woman: 'Notwithstanding she shall be saved in childbearing, if they continue in faith and charity and holiness with sobriety' (1 Timothy 2:15). For Rossetti, women's salvation is not predicated on biological destiny, but on spiritual behavior. In *The Face of the Deep* she quotes Galatians 4:27: '"The desolate hath many more children than she which hath an husband"' (*FD* 312).[12] This should not be read as a criticism of motherhood, however, an institution for which Rossetti had much respect. Rather, her point here is that motherhood has nothing to do with biology, and everything to do with spiritual duty.

Rossetti's focus on faithful and loving partnership responds more to the second part of 1 Timothy 2:15, which portrays a couple living 'in faith and charity and holiness with sobriety'. It is the shirking of the responsibilities of male dominance and female submission within the partnership that Rossetti sees as problematic. For example, Adam, as the dominant and stronger partner in the relationship, must accept responsibility for his role in the Fall, as Rossetti suggests in the entry for 15 January in *Time Flies*.

> Adam's initial work of production ... was sin, death, hell, for himself and his posterity.
> Not that he made them in their first beginning: but he ... re-made them for his own behoof. Never had the flame kindled upon him or the smell of fire passed upon him, but for his own free will, choice, and deed.
>
> (13)

The concept of free will holds Adam entirely accountable for his choice, and, significantly, Eve is not mentioned as the cause of his temptation. Yet here again, love is offered as the ultimate redemptive force, in the poem which follows this prose passage, 'Love understands the mystery'.

> Love understands the mystery, whereof
>   We can but spell a surface history:
> Love knows, remembers: let us trust in Love:
>   Love understands the mystery.
>
> Love weighs the event, the long pre-history,
> Measures the depth beneath, the height above,
>   The mystery, with the ante-mystery.
>
> To love and to be grieved befits a dove
>   Silently telling her bead-history:
> Trust all to Love, be patient and approve:
>   Love understands the mystery.
>   (*TF* 13; Crump, II 295)

Written at the intersection where many kinds of salvation meet — spiritual, personal, and intellectual, the poem anticipates a time when all will be reconciled by Love's ultimate authority, God. History is a primary concern of the poem, but here its significance is not secular, but spiritual. This poem shows a Tractarian understanding of biblical history, as it alludes to both Testaments, yet gives precedence to the New

Testament. The New Testament gives us 'event' and 'mystery', while the Old Testament deals with 'long pre-history' and 'the ante-mystery'. However, these are merely 'surface history' — only God can weigh and measure their significance, and reconcile them. Mankind must simply 'be patient' and 'trust' that this reconciliation is possible. Rather than presenting an Old Testament God to be feared, the poem instead emphasizes a New Testament God to be loved, and the 'mystery' of humanity's salvation in Christ. History appears again in the third stanza, but this time it does not refer to biblical but to personal history. The poem contrasts human love's sequential time ('surface history', 'bead-history'), and the eternal, spatial time of divine love. The dove telling 'her bead-history' also refers to human love's expression, the act of prayer, and to the comforts available in memory and ritual. This idea of a redemptive, loving interchange between mankind and God is a feminized version of the Platonic relationship between man and the gods, characterized as

> the power to convey and transport to the gods the things of man and to man the things of god, prayers and sacrifices being the things of men, and directions and answers to prayer the things of god. The supernatural, being a mean between the two, supplements both and combines them into a self-contained whole ... God has no direct contact with man, but all commerce and conversation between gods and men ... is by supernatural means...These supernatural beings are many and various, and Love is one of them.
>
> (Plato, *Symposium*, 202D–203A)

The dove, the shape God's spirit takes when he visits the earth, is made feminine in Rossetti's poem in deference to her female readership.[13] She is not so much trying to suggest a feminine God, but rather to provide a model for an explicitly female interchange with God. She suggests that women's personal histories can be understood in a devotional context, and can be incorporated as part of their spiritual lives through the act of prayer. In this way, human emotions (and here specifically female emotions) can have a part to play in the history of mankind's redemption.

This poem interprets the Old Testament event of the fall through the New Testament in its anticipation of mankind's salvation through Christ. Both 'Love' and 'mystery' operate in a double sense, as Love stands both for the concept and its creator,[14] while the mystery is not just the puzzle of life on earth, but also the paradox of the Trinity.[15]

Biblical analysis reveals a Christian tautology at work in the poem, because if love is God and the mystery is also God, then ultimately, love is love. It is this sense of equivalence and balance that the poem seeks to achieve, both structurally and ideologically. Love is God's gift to man, both figuratively, as a means to understand the mystery of life, and literally, in the form of man's savior, Christ.

The roundel was a favorite form for Rossetti. As Battiscombe notes, Rossetti 'used it frequently in her religious verse although the formal scheme with its repetition of rhyme and phrase seems ill adapted to such [religious] themes'.[16] Upon closer inspection, the 'formal scheme' of the roundel turns out to be very well-suited to Rossetti's theology, particularly in 'Love understands the mystery'. Here, Rossetti uses the roundel form to structurally enact her poem's sense of weight and measure, while the refrain contributes to the poem's reassuring tone. The first stanza's confidence in what love is and what love does is maintained by the roundel's regular iambic pentameter and comforting rhyme scheme (abab). The lulling rhythm is continued in the internal rhyme of the first and third line ('love / whereof', 'us trust'), and the repetition of the word 'Love'. The impression of balance and symmetry conveyed formally in the first stanza is made explicit in the second, where 'Love weighs' and 'Measures', balancing 'the mystery with the ante-mystery'.[17] The deviations from metrical regularity in the second stanza, as well as its three lines as opposed to four, and different rhyme scheme (bab) structurally enact the process of weighing and measuring, as the stanza considers present and past, depth and height, mystery and ante-mystery. The poem is brought back into balance in the third stanza, as the rhyme, meter, internal rhyme ('love / dove, 'Love / approve') and number of lines parallel that of the first stanza.

In 1893, Rossetti adds a Pauline gloss to the poem by titling it, 'Judge nothing before the time' in *Verses*. This is from 1 Corinthians 4:5: 'Therefore judge nothing before the time, until the Lord come, who both will bring to light the hidden things of darkness, and will make manifest the counsels of the hearts: and then shall every man have praise of God'. Not only does Rossetti's new title emphasize the poem's redemptive message of love, but also it recontextualizes Paul's advice to 'my beloved sons' by applying it to women (4:14).

Rossetti and St. Paul

Rossetti's Christian faith always restrains her from taking her biblical meditations to a socially radical conclusion. Because she sets up human relationships as dark reflections of humanity's relation to God, it should be remembered that her theories about women, however forward-thinking they seem, are always ultimately subordinate to and answerable to God's higher authority. However much she hints at a more liberating theology for woman, she perpetually reins in these impulses by reminding readers, and herself, that women's relationships with men must conform to the Pauline model of submission and obedience to the divine will. At the same time, though, she does assert that men too have a responsibility to fulfill their roles as husbands, just as Christ does to his Church.

In her consideration of the tenth commandment,[18] Rossetti visualizes a relationship of equality between men and women inside marriage:

> Although "wife" follows "house" in the Tenth Commandment, we must first of all view her as included equally and indivisibly with her husband in that neighbour whom we must not desire to supplant. The precept is constructed explicitly for men, implicitly for women; were it not so, to covet a neighbour's *husband* would become defensible! Thus obviously she ranks with the man himself, being constituted equally with him an informing presence of a forbidden house. Besides this she takes her place as first, nearest, dearest, most precious, and altogether unique among his possessions: as indeed he ranks among hers. Without ignoring either aspect I think we may feel safe in dwelling chiefly upon the former, when we recollect that marriage expresses to us Christ's ineffable union with His Church ...
>
> (*LS* 190–91)

Here, Rossetti reinterprets an Old Testament commandment through the New Testament, in relating marriage between man and woman to the union of Christ and the Church. This strategy is Tractarian and conservative, but its hypothesis suggests something more socially radical. By reading through Christianity a Jewish law meant to maintain social order as well as the covenant between God and man, she transforms it into an argument for the spiritual and social equality of women with men. There are several hurdles to establishing this position, not the least of which is the fact that the commandment lists the wife along with the husband's other possessions. Rossetti elides this issue by reimagining the commandment as if it were written for women. According to Rossetti, the commandment applies to women by extension, otherwise, she jokes, 'to covet a neighbour's husband would become defensible!' Rossetti ranks the wife 'first' and 'unique among his possessions', but then assigns the husband equal status by ranking him first among the wife's possessions. However, her conclusion draws back from this passage's most powerful statement, as Rossetti reassures readers that 'we may feel safe in dwelling chiefly' on the explicit idea of the wife as the 'nearest and dearest' of her husband's possessions, rather than the implicit idea that he also belongs to her. Yet she also advises readers not to 'ignore' the reciprocity of such a relationship on religious grounds, invoking 'Christ's ineffable union with His Church'. Her New Testament reading politicizes the Old Testament text, making God's injunction to Moses, the liberator of the Jews, relevant to Victorian Christians, and particularly women.

The mutual responsibilities of marriage are addressed again in entries for 9 and 10 July in *Time Flies*, with another comparison of Christ and Church to husband and wife, drawn from St. Paul's Epistle to the Ephesians:

> I have seen too — once indeed I possessed, so I write from memory — a most exquisite shell, composed of two halves, which joined together make up one flawless heart.
>
> Each separate half is beautiful, shaded with darker and lighter rose tints, worked in grooves and curves, and finished with a notched edge. Yet each by itself remains obviously imperfect and purposeless.
>
> Join them together and notch fits into notch; each brings out, proves, achieves, the perfection of the other.
>
> Does such an illustration seem to excel and shame the possibilities of even the highest and purest human love?
>
> Nay, but St. Paul quoted that same mutual human love in illustration of a Love which is not human merely but Divine also: —
>
> "A man ... shall be joined unto his wife, and they two shall be one flesh. This is a great mystery; but I speak concerning Christ and the Church".[19]
>
> (9 July, 131)

> The less symbolizes the greater, the lower the higher.
>
> Our study ... of a shell ... will not entail loss of time ... if it helps us to realize that all reciprocal human love worthy of the name, exhibits a tinge of heaven as well as a warmth and colouring of earth.
>
> That it is so far selfless as to be only one harmonious part of a better whole.
>
> That it is faithful, fitting into nothing except its own other self.
>
> And that unless it sets Christ before us at least as in a glass darkly, it were good for it not to have been born.
>
> (10 July, 132)

Like St. Paul's letter, this passage sees human love as an illustration of divine love, and a symbol of the relationship between Christ and the Church. Rossetti's approach, however, differs from St. Paul's, in that it is more interested in the reciprocity of such an arrangement than in its hierarchy. Rather than engaging with St. Paul's famous diktat, 'Wives, submit yourselves unto your own husbands, as unto the Lord', Rossetti expounds his idea that husband and wife should be one flesh (Ephesians 5:22). She writes of a mutually beneficial relationship, wherein 'each brings out, proves, achieves, the perfection of the other', as do two halves of a shell. The issue of wifely submission is elided by this Platonic image of two half-selves merging into a perfect whole. Whereas St. Paul recommends that a husband *love* his wife, and a wife *reverence* her husband, in imitation of Christ's relationship to the Church, Rossetti highlights instead the 'mutual' and 'reciprocal' elements of this union.[20] Here the wife's reverence for her husband is a symbol of her love for Christ, a way of expressing love for God 'through a glass darkly'. The husband is less a superior than an 'other self', and union with him will result in 'a better whole'. The only opinion Rossetti gives on male dominance within marriage is that 'The less symbolizes the greater, the lower the higher', reminding us that the husband has a superior in God, and that those who are meek and inhabit the lowest place on earth, such as wives, might expect the highest in heaven.

Rossetti addresses this theme, and her dialogue with St. Paul, in an entry for 23 March in *Time Flies*:

In common parlance Strong and Weak are merely relative terms: thus the "strong" of one sentence will be the "weak" of another.

We behold the strong appointed to help the weak: Angels who "excel in strength," men. And equally the weak the strong: woman, "the weaker vessel," man.[21]

This, though it should not inflate any, may fairly buoy us all up. For every human creature may lay claim to strength, or else to weakness: in either case to helpfulness. "We that are strong," writes St. Paul, proceeding to state a day of the strong. *We* who are weak may study the resources of the weak.[22]

(57)

Here, Rossetti rewrites women's 'helpfulness' as a function of partnership, rather than a mark of inferiority. While reinforcing a traditional Christian understanding of gender roles, Rossetti simultaneously makes a case for the uncredited 'feminine' strengths of forbearance, endurance, and support. 'Weak' here is redefined as another kind of strong. Again, without disagreeing with St. Paul, she has turned his opinions about the weakness of women into a testimony to their strength. She destabilizes the meaning of 'Strong' and 'Weak', claiming they are 'merely relative terms', rather than fixed indicators. While stronger angels assist men who are weaker than they, women assist men stronger than themselves. Despite their weakness, women have the strength to perform the same function as creatures stronger than men. This argument stops tantalizingly short of claiming that men are the weaker sex, but it does credit the 'angel in the house' with a kind of intelligence and agency. This is a claim, she hastens to add, intended neither to 'inflate any', nor, by implication, to deflate St. Paul, but to 'buoy us all up'. Again heterosexual union is kept afloat more by mutuality and reciprocity than by observation of a strict hierarchy. An ethic of cooperation is proposed, based on the more traditionally 'feminine' values of caretaking and support. The idea that 'every human creature may lay claim to strength, or else to weakness', suggests that strength is less biological or inherent than it is a matter of will. The final lines of this passage suggest, if they do not directly propose, an interesting parallel. Rossetti addresses women ('*We* who are weak') in terms similar to those St. Paul uses to address men ('We that are strong'). St. Paul, we are told, predicted 'a day of the strong', and though Rossetti hesitates to forecast a 'day of the weak' for women, her advice that they 'study the resources of the weak', implies that such a day may be coming.

In 'A Helpmeet Made for Him' (pub. 1888), Rossetti sees Christianity as liberating women from gender norms, not by denying their traditional roles but by revaluing them.[23]

> Woman was made for man's delight;
>   Charm, O woman, be not afraid!
> His shadow by day, his moon by night,
>   Woman was made.
>
> Her strength with weakness is overlaid;
>   Meek compliances veil her might;
> Him she stays, by whom she is stayed.
>
> World-wide champion of truth and right,
>   Hope in gloom and in danger aid,
> Tender and faithful, ruddy and white,
>   Woman was made.

(2: 169)

Like the metaphor of two halves of a shell in *Time Flies*, this poem assigns equal importance to women and men within a relationship as 'Him she stays, by whom she is stayed'. The power imbalance of strength between men and women suggested by the title is complicated by the assertion that 'her strength with weakness is overlaid' and 'Meek compliances veil her might'. Woman, despite her humble status as 'help-meet', is in fact both crafty and strong, using the appearance of weakness to conceal her strength. This impression is reinforced in line 11, which alludes to the Song of Solomon 5:10, 'My beloved is white and ruddy, the chiefest among ten thousand'. Within the typological inter-pretation of this Old Testament text, 'white and ruddy' are understood as referring to Christ, the bridegroom. Rossetti reassigns these Christ-like physical characteristics to 'woman' in order to stress the power which underlies her submissiveness. Yet the use of passive voice restrains these lines from crediting woman with deliberate strategy — she is only fol-lowing the will of God who 'made' her that way. By concealing an advo-cation of women's agency safely within a Christian context, Rossetti's poem enacts the feminine practice of veiling which it celebrates.

In using a theological, rather than a social or biological argument, Rossetti treads a thin line between disputing and reinforcing women's traditional roles. The poem continues Rossetti's dialogue with St. Paul about the relative strength and weakness of women, not by confrontation or refutation, but by reinterpretation of Christian doctrine. She both agrees and disagrees about women's inferior position by redefining what it means to be weak. Women and men, she seems to suggest, are strong in different ways, whereby the strengths of one complement the weakness of the other so that together, they can 'stay' one another. This idealized vision of male and female partnership re-evaluates Pauline doctrine, placing the emphasis on reciprocal support over rank. At the same time, in Rossetti's conception, woman does not escape her origins in Genesis, where she is made as a 'helpmeet' for man. Woman's championing of 'truth and right' only takes place within the act of service, where the expression of her strength is defined by her supportive roles. 'Woman' in 'A Helpmeet Made For Him', serves a divinely ordained, rather than a socially prescribed function. 'Woman', in serving man, serves God.[24]

By interpreting the writings of St. Paul to argue that women were 'made' strong, and in disseminating that opinion to a largely female audience, Rossetti challenges the established authority of both the clergy and the saint. Again, in an entry for "Whitsuntide: Ember Friday", located in the Appendix of *Time Flies*, she uses St. Paul's writ-ings to argue that holiness is the responsibility, yet not necessarily the exclusive privilege, of apostles and clergy. She begins by quoting 1 Corinthians 15:10.

> "By the grace of God I am what I am: and His grace which was bestowed upon me was not in vain; but I laboured more abundantly than they all: yet not I, but the grace of God which was with me," writes St. Paul, comparing himself with the other Apostles.
>
> Now if it was not "Paul" but "grace" which led that life, performed those deeds, achieved that glory; what valid reason can any man allege, least of all any ordained man, for not living in some sort as St. Paul lived ... True, such an one may be incompetent to preach as he preached, or write as he wrote. But surely not even inspired sermons or epistles were foremost in that chosen vessel's mind when he averred: "To me to live is Christ, and to die is gain" [Philippians 1:21].
>
> (274–5)

Rossetti is keen to stress that the 'glory' of ordained men, as with Paul, comes not from themselves, but from the grace of God. They are servants to God, 'vessels' who carry grace, but do not create it. In this passage such 'grace' is not connected to their gender or position, but to their labors and deeds. The suggestion that 'grace' is not exclusive to ordained men is borne out in the next paragraph.

> A spiritual race, an unearthly fight, self-subdual, Christ-likeness and oneness with Christ, all these went towards making up that blessed life wherein St. Paul made himself all things to all men that he might by all means save some. Amongst these we recognise no miraculous gifts, but legitimate fruits of a grace within the reach of all Christians ...

Here, 'self-subdual' and 'Christ-likeness' are available to 'all Christians'. God's grace, it seems, is not an exclusive privilege of St. Paul, the clergy, or even the male sex, but is legitimately 'within the reach of all Christians'. Rossetti does, however, stop short of suggesting that the ministry itself be available to 'all Christians', simply ending the passage with a prayer for 'all who shall now be ordained to any holy function' (*TF*, 275).

Rossetti and female suffrage

Although the question of women's spiritual equality inspires Rossetti, she is generally more cautious about women's social equality. Anticipating her modern feminist critics, women writers in Rossetti's own time were probably frustrated with the ways in which her High Church beliefs informed her position on gender politics. The Langham Place Circle, a group of writers who, among other activities, contributed to the Portfolio Society, never truly claimed her as one of their own. She corresponded with its members, contributed to their magazine, and was acquainted with Adelaide Proctor, Dora Greenwell, and Jean Ingelow, but never formed permanent attachments, either artistic or personal.[25] Although she did work with fallen women at Highgate, she probably would have seen her involvement as motivated by religion rather than politics. She was more interested in saving women's souls than in liberating her sex politically, and seldom acknowledged a connection between the two activities. The overtly political poem rarely intrudes in Rossetti's body of work, with one or two exceptions, like "'The Iniquity of the Fathers Upon the Children'" (1: 164), and even that gives a Christian perspective on the social inequality brought by illegitimate parentage.

Rossetti is lackluster in her response to suffragism, and generally uninvolved in front-line politics, with the exception of her work, late in life, in the anti-vivisection movement, which again she saw as a religious issue concerning mankind's spiritual duty towards animals. Yet as Mary Arseneau notes, 'While party politics may have left her cold, she was political in the broadest sense'. Arseneau's recent research proves that along with her more well-known work at the Highgate Penitentiary, she was active in petitioning for the abolition of pew rents and in 'her work to protect minors and to raise the age of consent' (35–6). But Rossetti's political opinions would always be guided by religious considerations.

When Augusta Webster, a poet whose work she admired, asked Rossetti in 1878 to lend her voice to the cause of female suffrage, she was resolute in withholding her support, and forthcoming — if not entirely straightforward — as to her reason.[26] Although reasonably well-known, this letter is worth reproducing in full, particularly as it has been excerpted by D'Amico, Palazzo, and Arseneau in three recent major works on Rossetti. While Palazzo reads it as an affirmation that 'In principle ... she accepted woman's right to determine the fate of a nation' (77), D'Amico and Arseneau both agree that the letter is typically Rossettian in that its 'meaning' is notoriously difficult to pin down:

> You express yourself with such cordial openness that I feel encouraged to endeavour also after self-expression — no easy matter sometimes. I write as I am thinking and feeling, but I premise that I have

not even to my own apprehension gone deep into the question; at least, not in the sense in which many who *have* studied it would require depth of me. In one sense I feel as if I had gone deep, for my objection seems to myself a fundamental one underlying the whole structure of female claims.

Does it not appear as if the Bible was based upon an understood unalterable distinction between men and women, their position, duties, privileges? Not arrogating to myself but most earnestly desiring to attain to the character of a humble orthodox Xtian, so it does appear to me; not merely under the Old but also under the New Dispensation. The fact of the Priesthood being exclusively man's, leaves me in no doubt that the highest functions are not in this world open to both sexes: and if not all, then a selection must be made and a line drawn somewhere. — On the other hand if female rights are sure to be overborne for lack of female voting influence, then I confess I feel disposed to shoot ahead of my instructresses, and to assert that female *M.P.'s* are only right and reasonable. Also I take exceptions at the exclusion of married women from the suffrage, — for who so apt as Mothers — all previous arguments allowed for the moment — to protect the interests of themselves and of their off-spring? I do think if anything ever does sweep away the barrier of sex, and make the female not a giantess or a heroine but at once and full grown a hero and a giant, it is that mighty maternal love which makes little birds and little beasts as well as little women matches for very big adversaries.

(Letters, 2: 158)

As the Bible does not contain much in the way of women's rights to representation proportional to their taxation, Rossetti considers what the Bible says in general about the rights and duties of women. The Pauline prohibition of women preachers is invoked: 'Let your women keep silence in the churches: for it is not permitted unto them to speak; but they are commanded to be under obedience, as also saith the law. And if they will learn anything, let them ask their husbands at home: for it is a shame for women to speak in the church' (1 Corinthians 14:34–5). This is reiterated in 1 Timothy 2:11–12: 'Let the woman learn in silence with all subjection. But I suffer not a woman to teach, nor to usurp authority over the man, but to be in silence'.

However, the dramatic shifts in tone and in logic which characterize the rest of this letter challenge William Michael's further assertion that, under his sister's over-scrupulous Christianity, 'Her temperament and character, naturally warm and free, became "a fountain sealed"' (*Memoir* lxviii). The confusion in the letter, the flashes of anger, humor, frustration, and triumph, are, in their expressiveness, more indicative of a fountain running over. Rossetti struggles and fails to resolve the religious, personal, and political issues brought out by the question of female suffrage, but she certainly seems to be enjoying the argument.

The Old Testament and New Testament are employed in Rossetti's defense of her views as an 'orthodox Xtian', yet these same texts are the source of her hope that the segregation of men and women will not be permanent. She writes, 'the highest functions are not *in this world* open to both sexes', reminding Webster of the most important hierarchy of all — the sacred over the secular (emphasis mine). Even so, she does indulge in a rare engagement with the affairs of the world, imagining a time when women are not just voters, but also MPs. Her subsequent defense of married women's right to vote hints at the social, as well as the sentimental, significance of motherhood.[27] Her belief that maternal love could 'sweep away the barrier of sex' is at once traditional and radical. While it locates the source of female power in caregiving rather than independent agency, it also imagines a leadership based on the more 'feminine' value-system of love. Yet, she quickly retreats from this position by defending male dominance on the grounds that, as men make up the nation's fighting force, they deserve to rule.

> Nor do I think it quite inadmissible that men should continue the exclusive national legislators, so long as they do continue the exclusive soldier-representatives of the nation, and engross the whole payment in life and limb for national quarrels. I do not know whether any lady is prepared to adopt the Platonic theory of female regiments, if so, she sets aside this objection: but I am not, so to me it stands.[28]

This wry assessment of the ultimate price of male power lends another element to the fantasy of female power which underlies this letter. While of course this vision is in some ways a parody, and a way of poking fun at suffragism, it also takes pleasure in its subversive imaginings. With mothers as heroes and giants in a realm defended by 'female regiments', Rossetti has gone farther than her 'instructresses' in imagining alternative government, although certainly not in making it happen.

Though Rossetti ultimately decides not to support female suffrage and derides her own knowledge of its issues, she argues with passion, humor, ambiguity, irony, and an artistic self-assertion which challenge her advocation of a passive political stance. Her letter is a critique of Webster's feminism on the paradoxical grounds that it is both too ambitious and too self-effacing. On one hand, she thinks female suffrage may be against Pauline doctrine, and so will not support it, while on the other, she suggests that suffragists' aims are not ambitious enough, and that women should become M.P.s and heroes, and not just voters.

The second letter written to Webster on this issue is more straightforward.

> Many who have thought more and done much more than myself share your views, — and yet they are not mine. I do not think the present social movements tend on the whole to uphold Xtianity, or that the influence of some of our most prominent and gifted women is exerted in that direction: and thus thinking I cannot aim at "women's rights."
>
> Influence and responsibility are such solemn matters that I will not excuse myself to you for abiding by my own convictions: yet in contradicting you I am contradicting one I admire.
>
> (*Letters* 2: 159)

Her concern that those who support women's rights do so primarily for social, rather than Christian reasons, prevents her from lending her support. 'Influence and responsibility' worried Rossetti as an artist, particularly in her later years, as she felt a tremendous obligation to uphold the tenets of Christianity within her writing. She was famously measured and discreet in both action and printed word, not only because she was a private person, but because she took a stance at once humble and arrogant in feeling that she must set a good moral example to her readers. The implication that perhaps Webster is not doing the same is not entirely disguised by Rossetti's praise for 'one I admire'.

Where Rossetti's biblical knowledge clashes with the modern world, she often tries to force the both the world and the letter of God's law to mesh. This strategy works better with Rossetti's more abstract and theoretical explorations of devotion, prayer, poetry, and art, but when applied to contemporary social issues, the cracks in her methodology begin to show. Ultimately, we are left with the bizarre impression than Rossetti is both against and in favor of female suffrage. This contradiction is more skillfully handled in 'A Helpmeet Made For Him', which was sent to Reverend Charles Gutch, editor of church magazine *New and Old*, when he asked for Rossetti to speak out *against* female suffrage. Yet what Rossetti's responses in poetry and prose have in common is their core of resistance, and their interest in toying with expectation. Where Webster hopes to receive her endorsement, Rossetti's first letter is so ambivalent and playful that the poet herself recognizes the need to send another, briefer and clearer response. Where Gutch expects unqualified support for his campaign against female suffrage, Rossetti sends him a poem which, though it conforms to traditional Christian ideas about women's roles, also contains subversive hints of women's secret strengths and intelligence. Neither party, pro or con, really receives a straight answer.

Three years later, on 9 August 1881, Rossetti knowingly alludes to this episode with yet another image of women warriors, in a letter to her brother. Of Webster she remarks, 'Once she and I had a courteous tilt in the strong-minded-woman lists' (*Letters* 2: 293). The playful aspects of her responses to both Webster and Gutch tell us more about Rossetti's view of politics than her view of women. For her, political wrangling is somewhat absurd, as it concerns the things 'in this world', which from an orthodox 'Xtian' perspective, is a transient illusion, subordinate to, and not to be mistaken for the real kingdom of heaven. The more pressing issue, for Rossetti the Anglo-Catholic, is the welfare of the soul. It was not until 1888 that Rossetti committed herself to a stand on women's rights, signing Mary Ward's anti-suffrage petition, a stroke of her pen creating havoc for feminist scholars of the future (*LB* 466).

Rossetti and Old Testament women

In her consideration of contemporary Christian womanhood, Rossetti often turns to the example of female characters of the Old Testament. This choice is both religious and artistic. Anglo-Catholics read Old Testament characters as 'naïve Christians', who, though they lived before Christ, had a pre-Christian sensibility and instinct. Because of this unique status, Old Testament Jewish women were permitted to act in a manner which would be forbidden to the Victorian Christian woman. Furthermore, Old Testament women had comparatively prominent roles in both their stories and their communities, such as Esther who was the active savior of her people and Miriam who was a prophet. In the New Testament, these roles would be entirely taken over by Jesus and his disciples, to whom women reacted, but with whom they seldom interacted. It became commonplace, as Cynthia Scheinberg notes, for female Victorian poets to look to Old Testament women for inspiration.

Because the Hebrew Scriptures offer numerous examples of women acting as prophets, poets and agents of religious history, women of

Christian and Jewish affiliation used those Hebraic women as models for both religious and literary identity. By referring to women like Miriam, Esther, Deborah and Hannah — Jewish women who created poetry, had direct relationships with God, and interacted in the public and political life of their community — Victorian women poets could construct a viable model for the female poet / prophet in Victorian England'.[29]

Rossetti, a poet well-versed in both the Bible and in secular literature, also recognized a good story when she read it. Scheinberg rightly points out the social benefits of Victorian women poets' selection of Hebraic women models in terms of their agency, but it is important also to remember that these were women whose stories were particularly compelling, and tantalizingly open to interpretation. Unlike the apostles and disciples of the New Testament, Old Testament characters do not often tell us what they are feeling and why; this opacity seems designed to stimulate readers, as the long tradition of rabbinical commentary suggests. Rossetti's reasons for choosing Old Testament women are as much creative as they are religious or socially motivated. Furthermore, it was acceptable for female poets to re-animate Old Testament female characters, as Scheinberg observes:

> Women's poetry ... was one of the few places where women could interpret Scripture for themselves in a public forum; because the Biblical women were often understood as prophets and poets in their own right, the discourse of poetry repeatedly intersects with the discourse on Biblical women.
>
> (267)

Rossetti often chooses Old Testament women to explore both what it is like to be a woman, and what a woman ought to be like. Although certain that woman was created as 'a helpmeet' for man, Rossetti does not regard woman's secondary status as an obstacle to examining either woman's internal life, or her relationship to man and to God. Female observance of the hierarchy between men and women is important only insofar as it affects women's relationship with God. This theology is very much invested in the idea of the reversal of earth's hierarchies in heaven, so that the site of Rossetti's politics is relocated to heaven, rather than the world. A politics still emerges, but it is one bound to religious faith. Her worries about female suffragism and female education come as much from theology as from reactionary politics. Rossetti sees the Old Testament conflict between faithful obedience and intellectual freedom as still relevant to women.

Rossetti often returns to the Old Testament as a source for female role models, reading each Old Testament woman through the New Testament according to her project of redemption. She sees Judaism as the precursor to Christianity; Judaism contains lessons for Christians to learn in their quest for heaven. For example, the following passage about the book of Ruth suggests the redemptive power of female love and loyalty:

> the whole Book of Ruth should be studied for the portrait of this humble-minded serviceable saint, whose history illustrates that word of truth, "Before honour is humility". (Prov. xv:33)
>
> If in Ruth we recognize not a simple forestalment but also a vivid type of that Gentile Church which has been grafted into the sacred stock and inherits the promises, from her attitude of reverent and tender protection towards Naomi,[30] we may deduce a lesson for Christians in general; teaching us how we should behave towards that Jewish race which (however fallen) was yet our elder in the Divine favour, and whose God is truly our God.
>
> (*LS* 53–4)

Again, Rossetti uses the Pauline metaphor of grafting, this time specifically to describe the relationship of Christian *women* to their religion. Just as Paul asks the Romans to think of themselves as new Christian branches grafted onto the tree of the Old Testament God, Rossetti posits that 'The Gentile Church', grafted into the 'sacred stock' of Judaism, 'inherits' the covenant between the Old Testament God and the Jewish people. The Tractarian practice of reading the Old Testament as the New Testament's forerunner is a double-edged sword for Rossetti, as the Old Testament, while respected, must always be portrayed as secondary to and dependent on the New Testament. While she idealizes the relationship of both Testaments as Christianity being grafted onto Judaism, in typological practice, such grafting is often more violent and forced than the metaphor suggests.

As much as this passage is about Jews and Christians, it is also specifically about women. For Rossetti the story of Ruth is not only a model for Christian behavior towards Jews, but is also significant as an illustration of redemptive human love. This time, however, it is a story of love between women which she characterizes as holy. In the Book of Ruth, the widowed Moabite Ruth follows her mother-in-law Naomi back to Bethlehem, forsaking her own homeland and family. There, Ruth marries Boaz, and becomes mother to Jesse and great-grandmother to David, to whom the secular lineage of Christ can be traced. Rossetti reads the relationship of Ruth to Naomi as a template for Christian women's behavior to Jewish women, which should be one of 'reverent and tender protection', with a focus on their common God. This passage is made especially relevant to her female readers by Rossetti's identification of the close relationship between Ruth and Naomi as the primary cause of the rise of the house of David, rather than the marriage between Ruth and her husband Boaz, or even the relationship between Ruth and God, who 'gave her conception' (Ruth 4:13). As with Rossetti's approach to Eve and Adam, there is no sense of Ruth as Boaz's temptress. Just as Rossetti reads Eve's transgression as intellectual rather than sexual, she credits Ruth with feminine wisdom rather than sexual prowess.

Female wisdom is again at issue in the full proverb which Rossetti partially quotes: 'The fear of the Lord is in the instruction of wisdom; and before honour is humility'.[31] Ruth's humility toward Naomi and Boaz gained her the 'honour', not only of social and economic improvement via marriage to Boaz, but of being a part of the lineage of Christ. Paul's instruction, 'Be not highminded, but fear' (Romans 11:20), echoes 'The fear of the Lord' in Rossetti's chosen proverb. This passage makes both Old Testament proverb and New Testament instruction explicitly relevant to the experience of women, via the relationship of Ruth to Naomi. For Rossetti, Christian women's earthly humility is evidence of their wisdom, and a precursor to their eventual honor in heaven. Rossetti's readers can learn from studying the story of Ruth as an example of a female spiritual 'history' which 'illustrates that word of truth'. This theme recurs nine years later in *The Face of the Deep*, where Rossetti writes, 'Wisdom ... associates with kindness: to cultivate kindness is to frequent the society of wisdom. A clue especially vouchsafed to us women' (*FD* 405). Female support and kindness are championed by Rossetti as expressive of both Christian virtue and wisdom, and as evidence of intellect behind action. Rossetti's writings about Old Testament women hint at an alternative wisdom tradition, one which is both conventional in its deferral to patriarchal hierarchy, and imaginative in its reinterpretation of sacred texts from a female perspective. She is certainly aware of the possible charges of intellectual arrogance or even blasphemy which might greet this strategy, but is unwilling to give up her project, as she makes apparent in *Letter and Spirit*.

I feel it a solemn thing to write conjectural sketches of Scripture characters; filling up outlines as I fancy, but cannot be certain, may possibly have been the case; making one figure stand for this virtue and another for that vice, attributing motives and colouring conduct. Yet I hope my mistakes will be forgiven me, while I do most earnestly desire every one of my personages to be in truth superior to my sketch.

(LS 158)

The book of Esther provides Rossetti with another 'sketch' of an Old Testament heroine for her to elaborate.[32] As with Ruth, Rossetti is aware that she is using a Jewish woman as an exemplar for Christian behavior.

Vashti we may hesitate to condemn. Esther, in her humble reverent demeanour and prayerful policy towards her husband, modern wives would do well to copy. The force of the example is enhanced by (in this instance) the husband's essential inferiority, by no one more inevitably known or more fully understood than by a wife of the still sacred though enslaved race (Esther i. 10–12, iv. 10–17, v. 1–8, vii. 1–4, viii. 3–6).

(LS 58)

In Esther, the king, misled by a corrupt advisor, plans a mass slaughter of the Jews, the 'enslaved race' to which Rossetti refers. In order to stop him, Esther violates the court protocol that no wife can visit the king without permission, and convinces him to spare her people. Again Rossetti includes references to the biblical texts in order to encourage further independent study. Typically, this passage combines traditional ideology with unconventional thinking. Although Rossetti praises ancient Esther's humility and reverence toward her husband, she advises modern women to follow the queen's example in disobedience and subversion. Rossetti identifies Esther's difference, both sexual and religious, as the source of her knowledge and understanding of her more powerful partner. Humility becomes a 'prayerful policy' with which Esther disguises her intelligence, allowing her to further her agenda under its cover. This ability to turn the weakness of humility into a secret source of strength distinguishes Esther's superiority from 'her husband's essential inferiority'. Rossetti's word choice is significant here, as the terms 'known' and 'understood' also identify Esther's actions with the wisdom of Solomon.[33]

The passage's first sentence seems a non-sequitur, but its ambiguous phrasing ('we *may hesitate* to condemn') suggests that its reasoning may be connected with Rossetti's parable of Esther (emphasis mine). Although Vashti, unlike Esther, was not humble or prayerful but disobedient to the king in not coming when she was summoned, Rossetti does not appear to want to condemn her for this. Yet 'modern wives' should 'copy' Esther, and think twice about Vashti. Rossetti uses Vashti and Esther to illustrate different aspects of disobedience. Both women disobey the king, the first by refusing to come when he commands, the second by coming to him without being commanded. The difference is that Vashti's disobedience is selfish and Esther's is self-sacrificing, as she knowingly risks her position and her life to save her people. Still, modern women 'may hesitate' to condemn Vashti, and instead, like the passage itself, turn their attention toward the more positive, effective, and wise example of Esther. That they should 'hesitate to condemn', suggests that they can also imagine themselves in the place of the king. Rossetti ultimately evades the issue of Esther's defiance by making her look compliant by contrast with Vashti. Her argument seems to be that for women, obedience to God is more compelling than obedience to man. This allows women an element of spiritual, if not always social, choice.

Rossetti's thoughts on Esther eventually lead back to her argument with St. Paul about women's weakness. For her, female weakness can be turned into strength, as the story of Esther shows. Though Esther defies her king, that she does so with humility and with righteousness convinces him to stop the slaughter of the Jews. Nine years after the verdict on Esther's actions in *Letter and Spirit*, Rossetti continues to justify her redefinition of weakness in the New Testament figure of Jesus Christ.

Thus is accomplished one of the Beatitudes: "Blessed are the meek: for they shall inherit the earth" [Matthew 5:5]. Thus Christ in His own adorable Person heads the army of those who "out of weakness were made strong, waxed valiant in fight, turned to flight the armies of the aliens."[34] Thus, "the weakness of God" stands forth as "stronger than men."[35] "Not by might, nor by power, but by My Spirit, saith the Lord of hosts." And thus also by a condescension of grace, Jael, a certain woman (*see* Judges ix. 53), Esther, Judith, become figures illustrative of like truth.

Weakness, however, is not *as* weakness this more than conqueror. Our Redeemer's weakness was rather the triumph of His strength, because to become weak and work mightily through weakness He laid aside His strength and kept it in abeyance. Our weakness, if it is to win a victory, must include a voluntary element; at the least so far as to will in concert with the Divine Will, and never to have recourse to illicit weapons.

(*FD* 409)

Rossetti here expands on her redefinition in *Time Flies* of the Pauline concept of female weakness, by giving examples of Old Testament women who turn their perceived weakness to their advantage 'by a condescension of grace'. Like 'Our Redeemer', the women whom Rossetti names serve God, and in this they are 'wiser than men' because their 'grace' allows them to overcome physical and social disadvantage.

Despite Rossetti's advocation of these women's Christ-like grace, they also exhibit characteristics of the fearsome Old Testament God. The examples of Jael and 'a certain woman' are particularly vivid illustrations of women's strength, not weakness, as both women violently slay their enemies. Jael lures an enemy into her husband's tent, feeds him, and after persuading him to sleep, drives a nail through his ear (Judges 4:17–22). A 'certain woman'[36] never named, beats in her enemy's head with a rock, after which he, on the point of death, begs another man to finish him so that 'men say not of me, A woman slew him' (Judges 9:54). The linking of these women's weakness to the weakness of Christ is problematized by their brutal physical actions. Yet Rossetti is eager to stress that the overcoming of weakness by the Old Testament women she cites is made possible not by their own 'might, nor by power', but 'by a condescension of grace'. Their 'weapons', are not 'illicit', because they are utilized 'in concert with the Divine Will'.

For Rossetti, there is a morality of victory which is its true definition:

> And I think that in these days of women's self-assertion and avowed rivalry with men, I do well to bear in mind that in a contest no stronger proof of superiority can be given on either side than the *not* bringing into action all available force. As yet, I suppose, we women claim no more than equality with our brethren in head and heart: whilst as to physical force, we scout it as unworthy to arbitrate between the opposed camps. Men on their side do not scout physical force, but let it be.
>
> Does either man or woman doubt where superiority resides, when at chess one player discards a pawn in favour of the other?
>
> (*FD* 409–10)

Rossetti brings her argument abruptly up to date with a critique of feminist movements of her time. Here she probably is referring once again to her old argument with Webster about female suffrage. In Rossetti's opinion, women should adopt a politics of passivity in order to uphold a Christ-like standard of behavior. Like Christ, women should 'work mightily through weakness'. While obviously reactionary, this viewpoint also suggests that women aspire, not only to Jael and Esther, but to Christ, and by extension, God himself. She identifies the values of Christ as feminine ones like passivity and mercy rather than the masculine ones of aggression and physical force.[37] This refusal to participate in the contests of men or to adopt the strategies of men registers a kind of female protest about the ways of man's world:

> Society may be personified as a human figure whose right hand is man, whose left woman; in one sense equal, in another sense unequal. The right hand is labourer, acquirer, achiever: the left hand helps, but has little independence, and is more apt at carrying than at executing. The right hand runs the risks, fights the battles: the left hand abides in comparative quiet and safety; except (a material exception) that in the *mutual* relations of the twain it is in some ways far more liable to undergo than to inflict hurt, to be cut (for instance) than to cut.
>
> Rules admit of and are proved by exceptions. There are left-handed people, and there may arise a left-handed society!
>
> (*FD* 410)

Rossetti's political conservatism re-establishes itself with this traditional assessment of gender roles. The same argument is used to refute Webster's support of suffrage. That women do not have a right to political equality because they do not risk themselves in battle is reiterated. Yet Rossetti also admits that this power imbalance can be more dangerous for women, because their passivity makes them more vulnerable to abuse. Her final comment, which at first seems to anticipate social equality between men and women, upon closer inspection only reaffirms male and female roles. The rise of 'a left-handed society' would not overturn gender inequality, but on the contrary would be the exception that 'proved' the 'rules' governing male and female behavior. That the passage is meant to reinforce traditional social roles for men and women is made apparent in the poem which immediately follows.

> Content to come, content to go,
>   Content to wrestle or to race,
> Content to know or not to know,
>   Each in his place;
>
> Lord, grant us grace to love Thee so
>   That glad of heart and glad of face

At last we may sit high or low
   Each in his place:

Where pleasures flow as rivers flow,
   And loss has left no barren trace,
And all that are, are perfect so
   Each in his place.
               (*FD* 410; Crump, 2: 258)

That acceptance rather than rebellion is the poem's goal is immediately apparent from the first stanza's repetition of 'content', as well as its fourth line, 'Each in his place'. The key to this contentment is the 'grace' in the second stanza, which allows humanity to be redeemed through love of God.[38] Its third line echoes Rossetti's lifelong struggle to be content with the 'lowest place', but this poem communicates a sense of acceptance that is missing from many of the poet's earlier treatments of this theme. Although the difficulty of life is acknowledged with images of wrestling and racing, the miracle of heaven, where 'loss has left no barren trace' and 'all are, that are perfect' is offered as a comfort. The spiritual release of heaven is indicated by the movement from the quietly resigned contentment of the first and second stanza to the anticipation of the limitless 'pleasures' of heaven. At the same time, the third stanza evokes the image of loss in the flow of the river, yet this river does not bear our pleasures away; the syntax can even suggest that we have suffered a kind of benign 'loss', which 'has left no barren trace' behind it, as though loss itself were in heaven a sign of plenitude.

The placement of this poem shifts the emphasis of the argument from earth to heaven, and its main issue from social to spiritual equality. For Rossetti, unequal social status has no bearing on women's spiritual merit; in fact, her work consistently anticipates a reversal of fortune for the socially weak and the lowly in heaven. The test of spiritual merit depends on each party's conduct within the confines and limits of earthly existence. This poem is not a call to arms for a left-handed society, but an affirmation of faith in God's plan. At the same time it cannot be one without evoking the other; just as the poem's rivers of pleasure could not exist without recalling loss, or, as Rossetti puts it, 'Rules admit of and are proved by exceptions'.

The theme of faith in 'Content to come, content to go' is further emphasized with its appearance in *Verses* (1892) under the new title, 'Do this, and he doeth it', which refers to a miracle from chapter eight of Matthew, when a centurion asks Jesus to cure his leprous servant.[39] Jesus agrees to visit the sick man, but the centurion says that he has so much faith in Jesus' healing powers that he believes Jesus need 'speak the word only, and my servant shall be healed' (Matthew 8:8). Jesus replies that he has 'not found so great a faith, no, not in Israel', and rewards the centurion's faith by curing his servant from afar (8:10). Contentment stands for faith in Rossetti's poem, as it indicates mankind's willingness to trust, like the centurion, in the mercy of God, and in the efficacy of His plan for humanity. The poem itself bypasses the prose debate about social inequality by stressing the primary importance of the spiritual state of affairs. Ultimately, it is faith, not gender, which will determine everyone's 'place' in heaven.

Despite the parallels drawn between Christ and the feminine in Rossetti's work, woman's place in heaven will be gendered, as she can expect to become Christ's bride. 'As everything human that is masculine is or should be typical of Christ, so all that is feminine of the Church', she writes (434). The figure of the bride is extrapolated from both the Old and New Testaments, so that she symbolizes both the Christian Church and the legacy of her Jewish foremothers. A blend of the female speaker of the Song of Solomon, Esther, Ruth, and the wise virgins of the New Testament, this bride in heaven will, like Rossetti's parable of two halves of a shell, form a perfect union with Christ. The union between Christ and bride will thus also unify the two texts of the Old Testament and New Testament. To stress this point, Rossetti draws up a comprehensive list of Old Testament women whose stories prefigure the coming of Christ. To give a few selected examples: 'As God brought Eve to Adam, so now is He bringing each pure and lovely soul to Christ'; 'As Moses sang and Miriam answered, so will there be "the song of the Lamb," and the responsive adoring song of the Church'; 'As Ruth by untried paths journeyed home to Boaz, so are sweet souls by untried paths journeying home to Christ'; 'As the daughters of Zelophehad were espoused by their near kinsmen, so to blessed souls Christ deigns to say, "My sister, My spouse"[40] (433); 'As Esther excelled Vashti and assumed her forfeited crown, so the Christian vocation at once human and superhuman hath the promise of that which now is, and of that which is to come' (434).

She concludes these comparisons with, 'All this and much more I profess when I say: I believe in the Communion of Saints, and the life everlasting. Amen', including the Old Testament women as saints who also may share in 'life everlasting' (434). Rossetti's list takes up a page and a half, its abundance giving the impression that she has more interest in typological examples of Old Testament women prefiguring the Christian Church than in the struggles of their New Testament counterparts. However, she stops herself abruptly and self-consciously: 'Why then break off our parallel with the galaxy of holy maids and matrons memorialized in the Old Testament, and not carry it further by help of their sister saints in the Gospel?' Break off the parallel she does, 'Because it is so lovely a privilege to have stood really and truly in some direct relation to Christ that it may well take precedence of aught figurative' (434). While Rossetti claims that New Testament women's relation to Christ is closer than 'aught figurative', her list of New Testament women's encounters with Christ is notably brief in comparison with her Old Testament list, taking up only a paragraph. This brevity, along with the cursory tone of the list itself, suggests that Rossetti's devotional imagination is more stimulated by the 'figurative' than the literal. Each New Testament woman's relationship with Christ she outlines sparsely, functionally, and sometimes tautologically, as in the case of Mary: 'There is no title by which to indicate the Blessed Virgin Mary half so august as that of His Mother'. The directness of Christ's relation to each woman dispels the sense of mystery which pervades Rossetti's typological comparisons. To list a few examples: 'To the Woman of Samaria he announced himself as the Messiah'; 'On the Canaanitish Mother He bestowed an unique commendation'; 'Martha and her sister Mary He loved'; 'He set store by the Widow's two mites' (434).

There is less imagination in these sentences, less passion in the conjecture, less poetry in the telling, because Rossetti is being cautious about blasphemy. The 'pre-Christian' status of the Old Testament text leaves the female exegete much more room to maneuver than the Christian New Testament, whose sacred status outweighs that of its predecessor. Again, Cynthia Scheinberg's theory about Christian women's appropriation of Hebraic female identity comes into play. As 'naïve Christians' the Jewish women of the Old Testament are not yet saved, nor can they behave in accordance with the rules of a Christ who does not yet exist. In order to resolve and elide the differences between Old Testament Jews and New Testament Christians, Anglo-Catholicism encourages its followers to draw imaginative, typological comparisons which re-locate Christ in the Old Testament text. This approach appeals to Rossetti because it weds the aims of her writerly sensibility and unshakeable Christian faith. In searching both texts for evidence of a Christian salvation for Old Testament women, Rossetti uses her creativity, intellect, and religious feeling. Her reconstruction of a matrilineal religious history challenges assumptions that Rossetti's religious writing is pious and overscrupulous.

For example, in the following passage, Rossetti uses a radical metaphor of transformation.

Beds of weariness, haunts of starvation, hospital wards, rescue homes, orphanages, leper colonies, fires of martyrdom, in these and such as these did she [the bride] set up mirrors whereby to fashion herself after Christ's likeness; workhouses, prisons (thank God!), the sea, the land, the rocks for a shelter, each and all send up their contingent of saints; palaces, hovels, houselessness, homelessness, again saints; east, west, north, south, still saints.

(FD 436)

The bride does not imitate the female 'saints' of the Bible, but tries 'to fashion herself after *Christ's* likeness' (emphasis mine). 'Mirrors' in which woman is 'to fashion herself' is a metaphor suggestive of a fluidity of gender. The breadth of Rossetti's survey also explores contemporary Christian female identities created and expressed from hospitals to workhouses to palaces. Christ-like behavior provides a model of sainthood for Victorian women not limited by gender, geography, or social circumstance. They can see themselves in the image of a Christ who belongs to both genders.

The passage's image of transformation is a reversal of that which appears in the poem designated for 'Advent Sunday', first printed in the Appendix of *Time Flies*: 'His eyes are as a Dove's, and she's Dove-eyed; / He knows His lovely mirror, sister, Bride' (*TF* ll. 14–15, 254). The Song of Solomon is here used typologically to reflect the relationship of Christ to his Church, which the addition of the mirror implies. That the bride is also Christ's 'mirror' suggests that he sees himself in her, perceives a resemblance in both a physical sense (sister) and a spiritual sense (bride). In *Time Flies*, Christ uses the bride as a mirror in which to know himself, while in *The Face of the Deep*, the bride uses the world as a mirror in which to transform herself to Christ. That Christ can see himself in a woman and a woman can see herself in Christ, and that they regard each other with the same ungendered eyes, anticipates the transformative power of reunion with God. Interestingly, it also suggests that the bride will not be the only one changed by the encounter, but that it will equally affect the bridegroom.[41] Her contention that God's erotic and spiritual claim on her is reciprocal asserts both her poetic and spiritual authority.[42]

Rossetti is aware that the theme of waiting for Christ holds particular danger for women, not socially perhaps, but spiritually. Using the example of the wise virgins, she advocates an active over a passive spirituality. Her own relationship with God she sees in intellectual as well as in emotional terms.

Shadows befit probation, but befit not the promised beatitude. Whilst set in their midst I must thankfully utilize them, yet must not make myself so comfortable in their region as to settle down or to drop asleep. Symbolism affords a fascinating study: wholesome so long as it amounts to aspiration and research; unwholesome when it degenerates into a pastime.

(FD 438)

Rossetti is aware of the danger of typological readings of the Bible, and of becoming too 'comfortable' with her own 'fascinating study'. Her intellectual curiosity must be directed beyond itself if it is not to foster complacency. She sees her project not as a pious pastime, but as spiritual discipline, and encourages her female readers to have similar devotional 'aspiration'. Although the patience of women is construed as socially passive, it is spiritually active, as she asserts in the sonnet which follows.

> Lord, to Thine own grant watchful hearts and eyes;
>> Hearts strung to prayer, awake while eyelids sleep;
>> Eyes patient till the end to watch and weep.
> So will sleep nourish the power to wake and rise
> With Virgins who keep vigil and are wise,
>> To sow among all sowers who shall reap,
>> From out man's deep to call Thy vaster deep,
> And tread the uphill track to Paradise.
> Sweet souls ! so patient that they make no moan,
>> So calm on journey that they seem at rest,
>>> So rapt in prayer that half they dwell in heaven
>>> Thankful for all withheld and all things given;
>> So lit by love that Christ shines manifest
> Transfiguring their aspects to His own.

(FD 439; Crump, 2: 243)

Here, feminine qualities of patience and calm represent active vigilance rather than passive acceptance. Being 'Thankful for all withheld and all things given' is figured, not as second nature to women, but as a grueling spiritual test, a struggle 'uphill'. Women's spiritual journey is shown to be both external and internal, as the octave describes what they do ('keep vigil') and the sestet how they feel ('so patient', 'calm', 'rapt'). Rossetti chooses the sonnet form first to stress that this is a love poem, and secondly to help reflect the movement of its journey from earth to heaven. The sense of the plodding, earthly 'uphill' progression is emphasized in the octave's traditional, regular abba rhyme scheme, then freed in the sestet's rhyme (cde edc) whose formal chiasmus images the mirror it describes. The rhyme of the final three lines of the sestet is a 'transfiguring' of the rhyme of the first three. This final image of transformation, when Christ transfigures 'their aspects to His own' again highlights the reciprocal power of love between Christ and women.[43]

A Pauline anticipation of reunion in heaven is made specific to women in Rossetti's 'bride' poems, which hope for self-knowledge, and a fulfilment which is intellectual, emotional, and spiritual. The distorted reflection provided by the mirror of the earth will be replaced by the unmediated gaze of Christ, so that women will no longer see themselves or Christ through a glass darkly, but face to face. For Rossetti, love between woman and her creator is absolute in its reciprocity, as the limiting social definitions of female roles (lover, sister, spouse) are obliterated by divine reunion, or, as she puts it, 'Where two bodies touch the dividing line is imaginary' (471).

5
Spiritual Autobiography in *Time Flies: A Reading Diary*

The self-imposed silence of *Monna Innominata*'s speaker seems to have had the opposite effect on Rossetti. Its publication in *A Pageant and Other Poems* ushered in a productive period which saw the release of three devotional prose works in five years: *Called to be Saints*, *Letter and Spirit* and *Time Flies*. There is little evidence here of a 'heart pent up, forlorn', but rather an intellect at play. Germaine Greer, not an admirer of Rossetti's devotional work, accuses her of 'profound and perverse self-absorption' that caused her 'to waste her life', adding that 'Her assiduity in frittering her time away was unrelenting'.[1] But Rossetti's publishing record is a strong counterargument. Despite frequent periods of convalencence, Rossetti, like Wordsworth, lived and worked beyond all expectations. 'Frittering her time away' was anathema to Rossetti, both professionally and spiritually. In fact, the use and abuse of time is one of the leading concerns of her penultimate devotional prose work, *Time Flies: A Reading Diary*.

The volume marks the days of the Christian calendar year with poems and prose passages. Halfway between parable and sermon, these 'entries' are very intimate and personal, written in a plain, simple style, yet containing worlds of complexity. Partially inspired by the devotional writings of John Keble and Isaac Williams, *Time Flies* also speaks to and about the experience of religious women. Yet Rossetti is equally interested in interrogating human authority in general, and her own in particular, as a writer and a Christian thinker. She touches on issues which are familiar to twenty-first century society, such as the difficulties that questions of faith pose for the artist — how, she wonders, is it possible to reconcile individual spiritual responsibility with the responsibility to one's community and work?

Mindful of the potential difficulties her own claim to authority might pose, Rossetti's prose volumes tread carefully, yet still press on. Her aspirations as an artist and religious commentator did not escape the attention of contemporary clergymen. Lifelong friend and religious instructor Rev. Henry Burrows endorses her 1874 collection of prayers, *Annus Domini*, with a preface that praises 'their fervour, reverence, and overflowing charity', but cautions that 'all the prayers are addressed to the Second Person in the Blessed Trinity, and are therefore intended only to be used as supplementary to other devotions'.[2]

Over a century later, clergyman Tony Castle echoes Burrows in his 1989 introduction to *The Prayers of Christina Rossetti*:

> Beautiful as these prayers are, I have to confess that I would not use them myself, not as they are written. However I do use them as the starting point, or springboard, for my own daily meditation ... This is as much a source book for meditation as a collection of prayers.[3]

Many of the 'prayers' Castle selects appeared originally as poetic corollaries to the ideas presented in her final prose work, *The Face of the Deep*. An examination of the poems in context reveals that each acts as a transition between prose passages or as a meditation on their finer theological points. Castle is so convinced by his recontextualization of *The Face of the Deep* poems as prayers that he forgets his own role in their appropriation. He is not the only editor to remove the poems from their original context. The first person to do this was Rossetti herself, when she published her final volume, *Verses* (1893), a collection of poetry from *Called to Be Saints*, *Time Flies*, and *The Face of the Deep*. Crump notes that Rossetti added titles to these poems, changed some wording and punctuation, and arranged them in thematic groups such as 'Christ Our All in All', 'Some Feasts and Fasts', and 'Gifts and Graces', to name a few.[4] Every subsequent editor of her selected and complete poems has done the same. The poetry's original context is lost to the twenty-first-century reader, not least because Rossetti's complete prose works have not been published accessibly in their entirety since the early twentieth century. The recent work of D'Amico, Palazzo, and Hassett has been more sensitive to these works' original contexts, leading the way in their recovery. Still, as these authors have acknowledged, this remains a rich field for discovery. Perhaps the fact that the devotional work remains difficult to define formally, as it draws on poetry, prayer, parable, and memoir, has also contributed to its neglect.

Maude (1850), Rossetti's unpublished novella of adolescent religious crisis, seems in retrospect an early experiment in this kind of writing. Consisting of poetry, prose, prayer, and dogma, it has intrigued critics with its ambiguous, and semi-autobiographical treatment of its heroine's

quest for spiritual and artistic fulfillment. Its publishing history and subsequent critical attention are a consequence of both the feminist rehabilitation of her work and the continuing search for biographical clues
embedded in the text. In 1897, three years after her death, William
Michael published *Maude* with a prefatory note, explaining that it 'shows
Christina's mind to have been at that date overburdened with conscien-
tious scruples of an extreme and even wire-drawn kind'.[5] In 1976 it was
rediscovered and published by Crump, who found it 'one of her most
autobiographical compositions; it sheds considerable light on the inner
suffering and intensity of her outwardly uneventful life' (intro, 7). It has
since been published in 1993 by Elaine Showalter as a companion piece
to a Dinah Mulock Craik story, and in the selected prose collections of
Jan Marsh (1994) and David A. Kent (1998). Its availability gives a disproportionate impression of its importance to Rossetti studies, at the
expense of her later devotional writings, and of the life of a writer who
lived for 40 years past its composition. The 'wire-drawn' persona of
Maude had a long way to go to reach the mature and wise persona of
Time Flies, where it is confident enough to present a *Reading Diary* of the
writer's thoughts on art, life, and love, both human and divine.

Time Flies borrows its structure from *The Book of Common Prayer*, providing a devotional prose passage or poem for each day of the Christian
calendar year. The entries also imitate liturgical tradition, as they are
organized by question and response. Nearly every entry in *Time Flies* poses
questions, some of which are rhetorical. However, Rossetti's is a rhetoric
meant to inspire contemplation. Numerous questions are found throughout the book: 'What gift or grace can quite supply the lack of common
sense?' (2 January, *TF* 2); 'Who ever became more like Christ by loving
less?' (10 May, 90); 'What indeed is there of any value, except it foster
love?' (23 June, 119); 'And cannot we, who are so much better than bird
or flower, take courage to trust our Heavenly Father implicitly?' (3
September, 171).

These rhetorical questions draw on the technique of the biblical writers, both in the Old Testament (Psalms and Proverbs) and the Gospels,
and they have a particular affinity with the challenging, questioning
speech of Christ. This spiritual affiliation with Christ, founded on the
concept of divine love, and apprehended both intellectually and emotionally, is confirmed in the first entry of *Time Flies*:

> Mother Church who opens the ecclesiastical year for her children
> with the alarum of Advent, opens for them the civil year with a
> Divine example of self denial.

For whatever Christ did or suffered for us was all, first and last, the loving choice of His own free Will.

(1 January, *TF* 1)

Here Christ provides 'a Divine example of self denial', but also of spiritual self-empowerment through free will. The passage advocates subordination of the self to the wishes of God and the Church, but stresses that this 'loving choice' is an act of will as much as it is one of faith. Furthermore, in self-denial, people have the opportunity to be divine in action, to be like Christ. At the same time, the passage also illustrates Rossetti's powerful, sometimes even willful, way with interpretation. 1 January, the day of this entry, is, as she notes, the Feast of the Circumcision, a rite she parallels with Christ's death: 'He was but eight days old when He shed the first drops of His Blood' (1). Rossetti's logic takes quite a leap is its assumption that Christ, at eight days old, could consciously accede to his circumcision in 'a Divine example of self-denial'.

Time Flies consistently advocates a Christ-like approach to others, and to the world. Old Testament resignation to the will of God gives way to New Testament hope in redemption through Christ. Rossetti's identification with Solomon, so apparent in the poetry of her early and middle years, continues in *Time Flies*, but here it is read through the gospels of Paul. The wisdom and understanding of Ecclesiastes resurface as the Pauline virtues of faith, hope, and charity. *Time Flies* uses the gospels of Paul to advocate the active participation of humanity in the project of its own salvation, and to stress the cooperative nature of the relationship between God and mankind. Ecclesiastes' conception of time as finite and vain is reworked in light of the Pauline notion of eternity. Time becomes humanity's opportunity to redeem itself from its fallen state as the vanity of human life is balanced against the hope of eternity in heaven.

A Pauline emphasis on Christian community inheres in this volume's design, as it is structured around the communal rituals that mark both ordinary and festival days. Rossetti's individual experiences are often related to the wider context of human experience, as her authorial 'I' gives way to the collective 'we'. Personal events inspire Rossetti's meditations on the universal responsibilities of all Christians, while her solitary observations of nature become parables about the duties of Christians to God, the world, and each other. A strong sense of audience shapes every entry of *Time Flies*, as Rossetti struggles to reconcile her private relationship to God and her public obligation to her readership.

Religious authority and spiritual humility

William Michael speculates in his memoir that his sister did not think herself worthy to join an Anglican Sisterhood, while critics such as Jan Marsh and Sharon Smulders identify her refusal to be a bride of man or Christ as a feminist assertion of autonomy. I would like to posit another explanation which draws on elements of both theories. Rossetti may have been trying to escape the passive, confining identity of the nun, and it is equally likely that she thought herself unworthy of being a Bride of Christ.[6] However, choosing not to marry Christ is a decision which paradoxically reveals both humility and arrogance. The search for 'the lowest place' is, after all, a form of competition, a hint of which can be found in her poem of 1863 of the same title. 'Give me the lowest place: or if for me / That lowest place too high, make one more low', she writes (5–6, I 187). The implication is that in heaven, it is the meek who will inherit the earth, and thus the 'lower' one's place is on earth, the higher one's place will be in heaven.[7]

Rossetti is more comfortable conflating poetic and preacherly identities than committing completely to one, as she assumes spiritual responsibility for herself and her readership. Although William Michael's view that her religion was 'far more a thing of the heart than of the mind' (*Memoir*, liv) is an over-simplification, his perception about her struggle to elide difference between literal and biblical truth by at times subordinating her own intellect reveals the paradox at the heart of Rossetti's devotional philosophy. Choosing faith over intellect is, after all, an intellectual choice. Rossetti herself admits this in a letter to fellow poet Margaret Junkin Preston on 27 December 1872: 'It is a most blessed variety from the prevalent tone of the day when one finds distinct Christianity in combination with intellect, & finds it not ashamed to assert itself' (*Letters* 1: 416).[8]

Rossetti had some conception of the power of her intellect, and consequently worried about expressing herself with 'latitude of thought and word' which might lead less intelligent, or less faithful, readers astray. According to William, she felt that to write 'anything for publication is to incur a great spiritual responsibility' (lxvii). Her worries about spiritual responsibility, in combination with her confidence in her own theological understanding, are evident in her letter of 21 June 1878 to Keningale Robert Cook, the editor of *The University Magazine* from which she withdrew on religious grounds:

> Were I of the authoritative sex & thus a born teacher & preacher, I might perhaps advantageously take up a position at once of protest &

of fellowship on your staff: as it is, I think it is as much as I am competent to do to hold my own without either compromise or gratuitous self-assertion. You see whither this conviction cannot but lead me: & to avow it to you, who honour claims of conscience, is so far a pleasure.

It surely needs something more edifying than "a bright poetic angel" to influence those whom you (*not* I) characterize as "publicans & sinners." Moreover if I took into my head that I wore a halo, I think one of the first texts for my study would be S. Mat. 21.31.

(*Letters* 2: 168)

This letter is typical of Rossetti's writing because it simultaneously proves and refutes its main assertion: she writes that she does not have the authority of a preacher and then proceeds to preach with authority. While she acknowledges that her gender disqualifies her from the clergy, she still defends, with biblical exegesis, the "'publicans and sinners'" of the magazine's readership. Matthew 21 is the chapter in which Christ casts out the tradesmen and moneychangers occupying the temple in Jerusalem. When the 'chief priests and the elders' ask him, 'By what authority doest thou these things? and who gave thee this authority?' (21:23), Christ answers with a parable about two sons, the first who initially refused, then assented to his father's request that he work in the vineyard, the other who initially assented, and then refused his father's wish. When Christ asks the elders, 'Whither of them twain did the will of his father?', they reply, 'The first', at which points Christ rebukes them for their own impenitence: 'Verily I say unto you, That the publicans and the harlots go into the kingdom of God before you. / For John came unto you in the way of righteousness and ye believed him not: but the publicans and the harlots believed him: and ye, when ye had seen it, repented not afterwards, that ye might believe him' (Matthew 21:31–2).

With this allusion, Rossetti compares the arrogance of the elders toward Christ in Matthew with what she sees as Cook's condescension toward her religious 'conviction' and 'conscience'. The main reason for her withdrawal from the magazine has to do with its freethinking contributors, but she also takes personal offence at her devotional aspirations being patronized by Cook.[9] Rossetti writes, with a hint of bitterness, that gender (and not ability) prevents her from being a preacher. Yet by drawing attention to the part of the parable in which Christ shows the religious elite to be in error, she suggests that male authority is not unassailable. She may not be a member of the 'authoritative sex', but she is 'competent' enough to 'hold my own' as a devotional thinker. She goes on to prove this by using Cook's own biblical allusion against him ('your words, *not* mine').

Her use of Matthew 21:31 also chastises Cook for condemning people as 'sinners,' in effect suggesting to Cook that 'harlots and sinners' will enter God's kingdom before him. Although his biblical words are used in jest, to her religion is no laughing matter. Rossetti sees Cook's comment not only as blasphemous, but also as an insult to the seriousness of her project as a Christian writer. She feels her intelligence has been insulted by Cook's flippant characterization of her as '"a bright poetic angel"', as she sarcastically suggests that he seek out 'something more edifying'.

Rossetti's conviction in the scope of her own influence betrays the writer's confidence in both her intellect and its expression. Again we are given a sense of paradoxical presumption in claiming 'the lowest place', the aspiration rather to be like Christ than his bride. This familiar Rossetti theme is addressed in a prose passage and its accompanying poem in *Time Flies*. It describes Rossetti's ascent of Mount St. Gotthard, but also the inevitable descent into another kind of 'lowest place' — the grave. During Rossetti's ascent, she comes across 'a garden of forget-me-nots':

> Thus I remember the mountain. But without that flower of memory could I have forgotten it?
>
> Surely not: yet there, not elsewhere, a countless multitude of forget-me-nots made their home.
>
> Such oftentimes seems the principle of allotment ... among the human family. Many persons whose chief gifts taken one by one would suffice to memorialise them, engross not those only but along with them the winning graces which endear. Forget-me-nots enamel the height.
>
> And what shall they do, who display neither loftiness nor loveliness? If "one member be honoured, all the members rejoice with it."[10]
>
> Or, if this standard appears too exalted for frail flesh and blood to attain, then send thought onwards.
>
> The crowning summit of Mount Gotthard abides invested, not with flowers, but with perpetual snow: not with life, but with lifelessness.
>
> In foresight of the grave, whither we all are hastening, is it worth while to envy any?
>
> (14 June, *TF* 113–14)

The referenced verse comes from a 1 Corinthians 12, a chapter which views all humankind as part of one body: 'Now ye are the body of

Christ, and members in particular' (12:27), so that achievement and failure bear collective responsibility. Yet for those of 'frail flesh and blood' who may find it difficult to rejoice in the someone else's achievement, there is comfort in the omitted part of the passage's Corinthians quotation: 'And whether one member suffer, all the members suffer with it' (12:26). The experience of both honor and suffering should be collective, as well as individual. Rossetti pushes this 'thought onwards', suggesting that in the end, all earthly achievement, and non-achievement, is made equally insignificant by humanity's ultimate destination, the grave. Rossetti's parable effectively levels the mountain by comparing the end of its ascent (the 'lifeless' summit) with the end of life (death).

Yet Rossetti's parable hints at the reward for those who aspire to such humility, as do two other verses of 1 Corinthians 12: 'And those members of the body, which we think to be less honourable, upon these we bestow more abundant honour; and our uncomely parts have more abundant comeliness / For our comely parts have no need: but God hath tempered the body together, having given more abundant honour to that part which lacked' (12:23–4). The heavenly inversion of the earthly order is the true summit of spiritual experience, and can be achieved, not only through a lack of envy, but through the practice of humility.

This prose passage's suggestion of the lowest place as an alternative to 'loftiness' and 'loveliness' is taken up by the poem which follows on 15 June:

> The lowest place. Ah, Lord, how steep and high
>   That lowest place whereon a saint shall sit!
> Which of us halting, trembling, pressing nigh,
>   Shall quite attain to it?
>
> Yet, Lord, Thou pressest nigh to hail and grace
>   Some happy soul, it may be still unfit
> For Right Hand or for Left Hand, but whose place
>   Waits there prepared for it.
>
>   (15 June, *TF* 114; Crump, 2: 307–8)

The 'lowest place' comes from Christ's parable in Luke 14:

> When thou art bidden of any man to a wedding, sit not down in the highest room; lest a more honourable man than thou be bidden of him;
>   And he that bade thee and him come and say to thee, Give this man place; and thou begin with shame to take the lowest room.

But when thou art bidden, go and sit down in the lowest room; that when he that bade thee cometh, he may say unto thee, Friend, go up higher: then shalt thou have worship in the presence of them that sit at meat with thee.

For whosoever exalteth himself shall be abased; and he that humbleth himself shall be exalted.

(Luke 14:8–11)

Knowledge of this parable is crucial to understanding Rossetti's worries about artistic and spiritual responsibility. The self-abasement required of a Christian writer both forestalls criticism and prepares her to 'go up higher'. Voluntarily taking the lowest room allows her to avoid the potential 'shame' of being forced to do so. In the second half of Christ's parable, this voluntary submission starts to look very like canny self-assertion as Christ reveals that in the final analysis, humility will be rewarded with exaltation, and arrogance with abasement. This inversion is anticipated in the poem's first stanza: 'how steep and high / That lowest place whereon a saint shall sit!' (1–2). Rossetti tries to bypass the problem of self-exaltation in the quest for the lowest place by suggesting that it is God who 'pressest nigh to hail and grace / Some happy soul' (5–6). Here the lowest place can be sought by mankind, but only achieved by God's will.

In a later entry, *Time Flies* interprets humility as the lesson not only of Luke's book, but of his life:

Setting aside a question easily raised and not easily answered, whether the "Luke" or "Lucas" named three times by St. Paul is or is not this Evangelist, and assuming such identity, we notice how very tenderly he is mentioned as "Luke, the beloved physician:" [Colossians 4:14] and again, with a brevity more expressive than a multitude of words, "Only Luke is with me." [2 Timothy 4:11]

But in St. Luke's Gospel, and in his Book of Acts, his own name occurs not so much as once. In the Gospel it seems impossible to trace him, except perhaps by help of tradition: in the Acts we infer his presence on certain occasions only from his use of the word "we" and its derivatives.

Thus St. Luke illustrates for our edification one of King Solomon's noble Proverbs: "Let another man praise thee, and not thine own mouth; a stranger, and not thine own lips" [Proverbs 27:2].

(18 October, *TF* 201)

In Rossetti's reading, Luke follows the example of Christ, in that both figures are the embodiment of their teachings. Luke acts on the advice

of Christ's typological precursor, Solomon, by advocating and exempli-
fying the humility of Proverb 27:2. He claims the lowest place by *not*
praising himself, and is thus rewarded a higher place by another man's
praise and by posterity. Rossetti places herself in this tradition by trying
to demonstrate humility within this passage. Rossetti reveals her own
struggle between deference and self-assertion, acting as the 'stranger'
who praises Luke, while at the same time cautiously 'setting aside' the
theological question of his appearance in Colossians and Timothy. She
is equivocal about identifying Luke the Evangelist with the Luke mentioned by Paul, but at the same time her exegesis depends entirely on
'assuming such identity'.

While the prose passage about Luke debates a question 'easily raised
and not easily answered', the poem which follows asks a question and
then answers it, if not easily, then with utter confidence:

> How can one man, how can all men,
>   How can we be like St. Paul,
> Like St. John, or like St. Peter,
>   Like the least of all
>   Blessed Saints? for we are small.
>
> Love can make us like St. Peter,
>   Love can make us like St. Paul,
> Love can make us like the blessed
>   Bosom friend of all
> Great St. John, — though we are small.
>
> Love which clings and trusts and worships,
>   Love which rises from a fall,
> Love which teaching glad obedience
>   Labours most of all,
>   Love makes great the great and small.

> (19 October, *TF* 201–2; Crump, 2: 290)

While humility earns mankind high praise in the prose passage, it is
Christ's transformative love that 'makes great the great and small' in the
poem. This idea comes from 1 John 4, a chapter which takes God's love
of humanity, and humanity's responsibility to love one another, as its
theme: 'Beloved, let us love one another: for love is of God; and every
one that loveth is born of God, and knoweth God' (1 John 4:7). Rossetti
tries to be 'Like St. John' with her repeated use of the word 'love' and
her emphasis on its power. Although humility can help Christians to

emulate Luke, love can 'make us like' St. Peter, Paul, John, or 'the least of all / Blessed saints'. Rossetti identifies love as the source of all other Christian virtues, such as trust, worship, and even humility itself ('glad obedience').

Although each named saint is male, the poem's use of 'we' and 'us' suggests that saintly aspirations are not exclusive to men, but inclusive of 'all' who love. By encompassing notions of the individual and the communal Christian in its transition from 'one man' to 'all men' to 'we', the poem further illustrates the prose passage's linking of Luke to Solomon, to Christ, and finally to devotional readers. Rossetti also preserves the humble anonymity she admires in Luke's gospel, following his example in avoiding any direct reference to herself. Her 'presence', like Luke's, is inferred in this poem from her use of 'the word "we" and its derivatives'.

The notion of spiritual responsibility plagues her as an author of devotional prose, as does her own worthiness. On 16 April 1883 she writes to Margaret Henderson, 'That you like "Seek and Find" gratifies me on (I hope) worthier grounds than any personal vanity involved. All the more I ought to feel how grave a responsibility rests on those whose writings far outrun their attainments' (*Letters* 3:112). The 'grave ... responsibility' she feels comes from conviction in her own influential ability as a writer, despite the fact that she is writing beyond her 'attainments'. The ambiguous, self-conscious language in which these statements are couched challenges their humble sentiment.

Rossetti's writing, as well as her life, gives the impression that much of humility's virtue derives from the difficulty mankind encounters in achieving it. Far from being merely appreciated in and of itself, humility in Rossetti's works is valued for its preparation of the Christian individual to learn even greater virtues. 'Patience and humility predispose to faith, hope, charity: and where these are, there is safety', Rossetti writes. (2 September, *TF* 170). The Pauline virtues of faith, hope, and love figure prominently in *Time Flies*, and Rossetti often uses them to interpret both personal experience and biblical text. For example, she uses all three in her re-interpretation of St. Thomas's doubt of Christ, rewriting the episode as a parable promoting the redemptive power of love:

> St. Thomas doubted.
> Scepticism is a degree of unbelief: equally therefore it is a degree of belief. It may be a degree of faith.
> St. Thomas doubted, but simultaneously he loved. Whence it follows that his case was all along hopeful.

If we are spirit-broken by doubts of our own, if we are half heart-broken by a friend's doubts, let us beg faith for our friend and for ourself; only still more urgently let us beg love.

For love is more potent to breed faith than faith to breed love. Because there is no comparison between the two: "God is Love;" and that which God is must rank higher, and show itself mightier than aught which God is not.

Nevertheless, faith also is required of us, and faith overflows with blessings.

"If thou canst believe, all things are possible to him that believeth … Lord, I believe; help Thou mine unbelief."

"Elisha prayed, and said, Lord, I pray Thee, open his eyes, that he may see. And the Lord opened the eyes of the young man; and he saw."

(20 December, *TF* 245)

This passage intimates that because the concept of 'unbelief' cannot exist without a degree of 'belief', then 'doubt' cannot be disentangled from faith. Rossetti's selection from Mark, 'Jesus said unto him, If thou canst believe, all things are possible to him that believeth. / And straightaway the father of the child cried out, and said with tears, Lord, I believe; help thou mine unbelief', emphasizes this connection (9:23–4). These verses are taken from an episode in which Christ drives an evil spirit from a child. Rossetti edits the original quotation so that Christ's words of comfort run into the child's father's words of prayer, its new cadences suggesting the ritual interchange between minister and congregation. Here faith is shown to be an individual act of will (*If thou canst believe*), and is made up, as the father's words suggest, of a degree of belief and unbelief. Paradoxically, the father's request that Christ help his unbelief is itself an act of faith in Christ's legitimacy and ability.

Rossetti reinforces her view with an allusion to an Old Testament episode in which the prophet Elisha's faith protects him from the Syrian army, who are at war with Israel. When Elisha's servant tells him of the Syrian army sent to capture him, Elisha reassures him: 'And Elisha prayed, and said, Lord, I pray thee, open his eyes, that he may see. And the Lord opened the eyes of the young man; and he saw: and, behold, the mountain was full of horses and chariots of fire round about Elisha' (2 Kings 6:17). For Rossetti, God's protection of Elisha is an Old Testament demonstration of the kind of faith that Christ requires of the father in 9 Mark. The 'degree of unbelief' here is provided by the fear of Elisha's servant, who asks, 'Alas, my master! How shall we do?' (2 Kings 6:15), while the 'degree of faith' is shown by Elisha's confidence in God's protection. This episode is given as typological support for the faith demanded of all Christians, with Elisha standing in as an Old Testament Christ-figure who teaches faithfulness to his servant.

Rossetti conflates these episodes with characteristic boldness in order to support her view that Thomas's doubt is redeemable as a degree of faith. As often in her work, an Old Testament text is so penetrated by its typological meaning that it can assume a kind of priority — for the quotation from 2 Kings concludes the passage and seals the argument. Thomas's doubt is mitigated by love, because love outranks other Christian virtues, as Rossetti reminds us with 1 John 4:8, '"God is love"'. Thomas's skepticism here is no more damaging than the questions of Elisha's servant or the confessed unbelief of the father in 9 Mark. Because 'love is more potent to breed faith than faith to breed love', Thomas is rebuked for his doubt, but forgiven for his love. Love, because it is God, can also 'breed' hope, as Rossetti suggests by deeming Thomas's case, 'all along hopeful'. Faith and hope in this passage come by degrees, but love, because it is God, is the most powerful force, capable of engendering both. This passage revisits the conclusion of the 17-year-old Rossetti's poem 'Repining': '"Thou, who for love's sake didst reprove, / "Forgive me, for the sake of love"' (251–2).

Reconciling artistic and spiritual responsibility

Time Flies continues to explore faith, hope, and love, both through biblical parable and personal anecdote. Rossetti uses the first person throughout, addresses her readers directly, and often is anxious and self-conscious about her theology. Because of the author's intimate tone, it is tempting to search *Time Flies* for the autobiographical clues so absent or ambiguous in Rossetti's published poems. However, *Time Flies*, with its nod to the religious writings of Augustine, uses autobiography as a knowing and deliberate strategy to teach Christian lessons, rather than as an opportunity for confession. As in Ecclesiastes, or even in the parables of Christ, the story of the life is intended to be secondary to the lessons of the speaker / writer. Diane D'Amico points out that the poetry of *Time Flies* 'is presented ... as if it were indeed [Rossetti's] own voice, and not a persona distinct from the poet, nevertheless it is a voice that could be interpreted as belonging to every or any human being who seeks God'.[11]

Rossetti's awareness of her responsibility to her Christian readers means that she wants them to approach *Time Flies* critically, as she makes clear in its second entry:

> I am desirous to quote here or there an illustrative story or personal reminiscence: am I competent to do so? I may have misunderstood, I may never have understood, I may have forgotten, in some instances I cannot recall every detail.
>
> Yet my story would point and clench my little essay.
>
> So here once for all I beg my readers to accept such illustrations as no more than I give them for; true or false, accurate or inaccurate, as the case may be. One perhaps embellished if I have the wit to embellish it, another marred by my clumsiness.
>
> All alike written down in the humble wish to help others by such means as I myself have found helpful.
>
> (3 January, 3–4)

As in her letter to Margaret Henderson, Rossetti ends the passage with a humility which is sincere and at the same time not entirely convincing. The purpose of the book may be 'to help others', but such an aspiration is hardly 'humble'. The self-consciousness of the above passage in fact reveals Rossetti's confidence in her own ability, simply because after having questioned her own competence, wit, and motivation, she proceeds with the writing of the book. The answer to her question ('am I competent?') although implicit, is affirmative. Like the Book of Ecclesiastes, *Time Flies* varies between self-assertion and self-abnegation as it struggles to see intellect and faith in harmony. The result of this strategy is that the reader must ask and answer the questions that the author poses, both in relation to the author, and to him / herself.

One of these questions has to do with the relationship of religion and art, an issue which is often at the heart of Rossetti's devotional work in both poetry and prose. Just as she elides factual and theological difference so as to read the Old and New Testaments in agreement, she presents religion and art as mutually reinforcing. Much of *Time Flies* is devoted to proving this belief, as in an entry for 27 January which exemplifies the self-consciousness of the author's project:

> When we so set our hearts on doing well that practically we do nothing, we are paralysed not by humility but by pride. If in such a temper we succeeded in making our light to shine, it would shine not in glorification of our Heavenly Father but of ourselves.

Suppose our duty of the moment is to write: why do we not write? —
Because we cannot summon up anything original, or striking, or pic-
turesque, or eloquent, or brilliant.
  But is a subject set before us? — It is.
  Is it true? — It is.
  Do we understand it? — Up to a certain point we do.
  Is it worthy of meditation? — Yes, and prayerfully.
  Is it worthy of exposition? — Yes, indeed.
  Why then not begin? —
  "From pride and vainglory, Good Lord, deliver us."

(TF 22)

Formally, this passage is remarkable in its blurring of the boundaries
between prose and poetry. Near the end of the entry, the prose turns
into something closer to a poem, indicated by a shift in tone and
increasingly incantatory rhythms. Most of the other entries in *Time Flies*
are either prose passages or poems, and generally, when the two forms
appear under one entry, they are separated by spacing and indentation.
The lack of a space between the prose passage and these last seven lines
maintains a doubt about how exactly it should be read. The separate
lines and long dashes which maintain the balance of the rhythm
between question and response are suggestive of poetry, while the questions and responses themselves echo the formal exchange between minister and congregation during a church service. In the penultimate line,
this format is brought up short against the blank space, for this final
question goes eloquently unanswered; it is followed by the turn to a different and masterful discourse in the last line, transforming the whole
passage into something of a prayer. This conflation of various forms
illustrates the 'meditation' and 'exposition' Rossetti recommends in any
literary attempt at 'glorification of our Heavenly Father'.
  In writing that the subject (Christianity) is 'worthy' of 'meditation'
and 'exposition', Rossetti makes clear that art and religion are not
mutually exclusive, but compatible, in that a religious subject can elevate the form it takes. Here, the subject and its exposition play equally
important roles, both related to the duty of the artist and of the
Christian thinker. For Rossetti, a bad treatment can be redeemed — up
to a point — by a worthy subject, particularly when that subject is a
Christian one. As Diane D'Amico notes in her article about Keble's
influence on Rossetti, 'It seems Rossetti was able to read religious poetry separating the value of the message from the quality of its form'.[12]
Certainly this principle applies to the notion of 'originality'. Being

unable to write because one cannot 'summon up anything original,' represents a failure, not just of the artistic imagination, but of the faithful imagination — a failure brought on by the sins of 'pride and vainglory'.[13] In the Christian view, nothing 'original' exists within humanity's grasp, because God is the origin of all things. But as we shall see, there are limits to the tolerance Rossetti is willing to extend to bad writing, even in a good cause.

Rossetti's exposition of the duties of a dedicated writer, as well as the hybrid form it takes in the passage above, also challenges William Michael's account of his sister's mode of composition as 'entirely of the casual and spontaneous kind ... without her meditating a possible subject' (*Memoir* lxviii–lxix). She gives us further insight into her view of the writing process in an entry for 5 January:

> Can anything be sadder than work left unfinished? Yes: work never begun.
>
> "Well begun is half done," says our English proverb.
>
> Whilst the Italians say: "Il più duro passo è quello della soglia" (The hardest step is at the threshold): and again, "Cosa fatta capo ha" (That which is *done* has a beginning).
>
> True, the final verdict depends on the ending: but neither good nor bad ending can ensue except from some manner of beginning.
>
> I have heard tell of a painter who sought far and wide for an atmosphere wherein to paint. At last he found an available atmosphere in Italy: and returning thither he worked? ... not so: he died.
>
> A bad beginning may be retrieved and a good ending achieved. No beginning, no ending.
>
> It is bad to work loiteringly: it may be worse to loiter instead of beginning to work at all.
>
> (*TF* 4–5)

By not specifying the nature of the 'work' she is discussing, Rossetti allows the word to suggest various meanings. 'Work', in the context of this devotional prose volume, probably refers to the way in which good Christians ought to live their lives, practicing good works of faith, hope, and charity. 'Work' here is also explicitly linked to creative endeavor with the example of the painter. This parable chimes with the book's title, *Time Flies*, in that the painter dies unfulfilled, not because he is talentless, but because he has wasted his time on earth. Here, creative loitering stands in for a kind of spiritual procrastination. This entry, coming as it does near the beginning of the book, shows a self-reflexive awareness as Rossetti takes her first steps over the threshold of her new work. The idea that a 'bad beginning may be retrieved and a good ending achieved', suggests a literary parallel to the Christian redemptive ethic. Literary and spiritual responsibility hang heavy on Rossetti throughout *Time Flies*, which often ponders the role of the writer, her audience, and her God.

In the book's second entry, Rossetti characterizes the Christian writer as a transcriber of the word of God:

> A certain masterly translator has remarked that whatever may or may not constitute a good translation, it cannot consist in turning a good poem into a bad one.[14]
>
> This suggestive remark opens to investigation a world-wide field. Thus, for instance, he (or she) cannot be an efficient Christian who exhibits the religion of love as unlovely.
>
> Christians need a searching self-sifting on this point. They translate God's law into the universal tongue of all mankind: all men of all sorts can read them, and in some sort cannot but read them.
>
> (2 January, *TF* 2)

The Christian writer's spiritual responsibility to his / her readers is at issue here. Translation of God's law is a difficult business, involving knowledge of God on the one hand, and self-knowledge on the other. The imagery of the sieve ('self-sifting') is originally an Old Testament one, generally referring to the process by which God will separate his chosen people from the rest.[15] However, in the New Testament,[16] the Israelites become Christians and the act of sifting is done by Satan.[17] Avoiding the problems raised by Old and New Testament differences between who will be sifted and by whom, Rossetti recommends a third alternative not found in either Book: 'self-sifting.' The idea of self-sifting brings Christianity to the level of the private and the personal. As God sifts nations and Satan sifts people, Rossetti suggests that each Christian sift the good from the bad in him / herself. The concept of self-sifting also seeks to justify the semi-autobiographical interpretative strategy of *Time Flies*. Much of Rossetti's writing worries about sins of vanity and pride, and so the author must find a way to write about herself humbly, to try and sift literary pride from her sense of spiritual mission. The way she decides to reconcile the desire to write with humility is first to write devotionally, and second, to present her project as an example to other Christians.

She tries to protect her writing and theologizing from negative criticism by pointing out that any errors are reflective of the 'self-sifting' imagination and motivated by the 'wish to help others'. However, Rossetti cannot escape the paradox at the heart of her writing, which is that the 'self-sifting' she recommends leads to self-expression as well as divine revelation. No matter how humble her words are, her sentiment is decidedly confident. The words which conclude the third entry in the book are humble, yet their tone is authoritative. Rossetti informs the reader that her 'illustrations' are 'All alike written down in the humble wish to help others by such means as I myself have found helpful' (3 January, 4).

In *Time Flies,* Christianity is as much about writing of the self as it is the writing of God. Translation of God's word, for Rossetti, is not strictly a literal endeavor, but a literary one, involving not just transcription, but interpretation. A 'bad' translation after all, can turn even 'a good poem into a bad one'. 'Scrupulous Christians,' she writes, 'need special self-sifting. They too often resemble translations of the letter in defiance of the spirit: their good poem has become unpoetical' (2). 'Translation' here refers metaphorically to how Christians choose to live by, or not to live by, God's law. However, Rossetti is also writing very self-consciously about the act of interpreting God's word, and wondering about the balance in her own work between spiritual and literary responsibility. These musings about scrupulousness are as much about the good poet as they are about the good person. Over-scrupulous translation cannot reflect the spirit of the word of God, not only because God is ineffable, but also because God's word deserves more respect than to be expressed clumsily. The 'spirit', therefore, must not be translated literally, but poetically, as even form itself is a reflection of the divine.

The third entry continues in this vein as Rossetti writes about 'Scrupulous persons' as 'a much tried and much trying sort of people':

> Sometimes paralysed and sometimes fidgeted by conscientiousness, they are often in the way yet often not at hand.
> The main pity is that they do not amend themselves. Next to this, it is a pity when they gratuitously attempt what under the circumstances they cannot perform.
> Listen to an anecdote or even to a reminiscence from their lips, and you are liable to hear an exercise on possible contingencies: a witticism hangs fire, a heroic example is dwarfed by modifying suggestions. Eloquence stammers in their mouth, the thread even of logic is snapped.

Their aim is to be accurate; a worthy aim: but do they achieve accuracy? Such handling as blunts the pointed and flattens the lofty cannot boast of accuracy.

(3 January, 3)

Here, 'accuracy' has as much to do with the expression of truth as it does with the notional truth itself. Divine truth may be abstract and immutable, but in its concrete treatment by the 'overscrupulous', its power can be sapped or transformed into ineffectual shapes.[18] Just as mankind is a creation of God, without being God, so are mankind's words a reflection of God's truth, without being God's truth.

Rossetti regards scrupulousness as a flaw not only in character, but also a flaw in imagination, in writing. The passage above directly contradicts her brother's famous assertion that she was 'over-scrupulous,' as do in fact, the experimental form, personal anecdotes, musings, questions, and poems which comprise the rest of *Time Flies*. Her theories about poetry, translation, and the act of writing, as well as her call for self-sifting, demonstrate a concern not only with God and the Church, but also with the individual self. She writes that 'These remarks [on scrupulous persons] have, I avow, a direct bearing on my own case' because she intends 'to quote here or there an illustrative story or personal reminiscence'. She hopes that readers 'accept such illustrations,' whether 'true or false, accurate or inaccurate,' or even 'perhaps embellished if I have the wit' (3–4). This very self-conscious writerly introduction betrays the tension between artistic pride and spiritual humility which Rossetti felt as a devotional writer. This latter half of the third entry undergoes a dramatic change in tone as Rossetti worries that, in her attempt to merge autobiographical and devotional genres, she may upset the delicate balance between scrupulousness and creativity.

By criticizing scrupulous writers' 'translations of the letter in defiance of the spirit' in the second entry, Rossetti suggests that meaning is not determined solely by the literal, but also by the literary. This postulation justifies poetic license in devotional writing. Interpretation, both literary and literal, becomes linked to ideas of analogy and reserve, and thus by extension to Christian duty: 'Stars, like Christians, utter their silent voice to all lands and their speechless words to the ends of the world. Christians are called to be like stars, luminous, steadfast, majestic, attractive' (2). The 'silent voice' and 'speechless words' have to do with reserve, with meaning that transcends articulation, while analogically, Christians are linked to stars. Rossetti initially reverses the expected order of such a simile — one would anticipate, 'Christians are like stars', but then switches it back, ('Christians are called to be like stars'), giving a sense of the interlinking and symbiotic bond of nature, mankind, and God. This introduction to the prose volume itself aspires to enact the doctrine of reserve, as it hopes analogically to teach readers to seek and find connections between the translation of God's word and interpretation of His meaning, just as they might read a poem or regard the stars. The force that makes the connection, and its locus, is the human imagination.

The linkage of God's word to poetry is significant because such a union makes Rossetti's project an imaginative one. Because divine meaning is untranslatable literally, it must be divined analogically. Again, meaning is informed by the literal, but completed by the literary. Rossetti justifies creative writing by reading the liberties it takes with truth and accuracy as necessary products of analogy, unavoidable because writing is only a representation, a translation, not meaning itself. In an entry for 14 July, she writes of the literary challenge of describing a friend's antique Greek vases: 'What words can describe their beauty?' (134). Despite her caution, she makes an attempt:

> Placed as they were aloft in my friend's drawing-room, one might stand for sunrise, the other for moonrise.
> *Sunrise* was brilliant as the most gorgeous pheasant; *moonrise* exquisite as the most harmonious pigeon. But, as I said before, words do not describe them: I cannot exaggerate, I can only misrepresent their appearance.
>
> (134–5)

The vases 'might stand for' sunrise and moonrise, or could be 'as' a 'gorgeous pheasant' and a 'harmonious pigeon', but these similes expose more about the gulf between a physical object and its description in language than they communicate about the vases' appearance. Rossetti is frustrated from the start because her 'words do not describe' the vases, but rather 'can only misrepresent their appearance'. Finding herself as a loss to represent their beauty, however, does not prevent Rossetti from appropriating them as symbols in her own parable:

> Well, with these unrivalled vases vivid in my memory, I one day rescued from an English roadside ditch a broken bottle: and it was also oxydised! So, at least, I conclude: for in a minor key it too displayed a variety of iridescent tints, a sort of dull rainbow.
> Now my treasure-trove was nothing to those others: yet could not their excess of beauty annul its private modicum of beauty.

There are, I presume, many more English ditches than Greek Islands, many more modern broken bottles than antique lustrous vases. If it is well for the few to rejoice in sunrise and moonrise, it is no less well for the many to be thankful for dim rainbows.

(135)

Rossetti's study of both 'exquisite' and 'dull' surface gives depth to her comparison. What started as material admiration of rare objects turns into a metaphysical parable about the preciousness of the common and the ordinary. While the comparison is simple, it is far from simplistic. Rossetti begins by abandoning the drawing room for the outdoors. The reader's gaze is directed earthwards, from the vases 'placed aloft' to the bottle in the 'roadside ditch'. The language of comparison is pared down too, as the bottle is not 'brilliant', 'gorgeous', or 'exquisite', but is iridescent 'in a minor key' with its 'dull rainbow'. While the vases' beauty relies upon a certain exclusivity and uniqueness, the bottle's 'private modicum of beauty' lies in its democratic availability. The bottle's 'dim rainbows' are not just an aesthetic feature of the glass, but also an analogic reminder of the covenant between God and Noah. Rossetti's parable about the broken bottle trusts the Christian reader to make the connections between surface and deep meaning, between the 'dim rainbow' and God. It is an illustration of the merits of reserve, both in creative writing and in devotional thought.

Although she is a poet of deliberate reserve (both philosophically and socially), Rossetti is aware of the drawing power of intimacy. She uses anecdotes from her own life as parables to illustrate and reinforce Christian ideology, turning the genre of autobiography into something at once personal and universal. In an entry for 10 April , she gives a personal illustration of the comfort available to every Christian through nature:

One day long ago I sat in a certain garden by a certain ornamental water.

I sat so long and so quietly that a wild garden creature or two made its appearance: a water rat, perhaps, or a water-haunting bird. Few have been my personal experiences of the sort, and this one gratified me.

I was absorbed that afternoon in anxious thought, yet the slight incident pleased me. If by chance people noticed me they may have thought how dull and blank I must be feeling: partly they would have been right, but partly wrong.

Many (I hope) whom we pity as even wretched, may in reality, as
I was at that moment, be conscious of some small secret fount of
pleasure: a bubble, perhaps, yet lit by a dancing rainbow.

I hope so and I think so: for we and all creatures alike are in God's
hand, and God loves us.

(*TF* 69)

As is generally the case with Rossetti, both personal and religious revelation are here governed by reserve. Although readers are given access
to her thought process, the source of Rossetti's anxiety is only hinted at
and never revealed. The location itself is unspecific — 'a certain garden
by a certain ornamental water' — a usage which borrows from the biblical parable ('A certain man', 'A certain king', and so on). This reserve
has to do with both her private nature and with her sense of literary
responsibility. Her parable's universal relevance might be compromised
by too much specific detail, and so Rossetti chooses to appear, not as a
personality that can be identified, but as a figure with whom readers can
identify. Discretion about the causes of her 'anxious thought' maintains
both her personal privacy and her humility.

She begins on a Wordsworthian note, finding personal solace in the
human connection with nature. The appearance of 'a wild garden creature or two' partially redirects Rossetti's 'anxious thought', as she is both
'pleased' and 'gratified' by 'personal experiences of this sort'. It soon
becomes apparent that this particular experience is not only individual,
but also communal. Rossetti's observation of the wildlife makes her
wonder 'if by chance' other people are observing her. In speculating
that 'people may have thought how dull and blank I must be feeling',
she becomes aware of a world larger than her own 'anxious thought', as
she begins to consider her relationship to mankind as well as to nature.
The anxiety and self-consciousness of Rossetti's emotional isolation
marks her reverie as distinctly post-lapsarian, her 'certain garden' a site
of human conflict as well as pleasure.

Though she is 'absorbed in anxious thought', her surroundings bring
her 'pleasure' by reaffirming her connection to the natural and spiritual world. Just as Keats's nightingale frees his poetic imagination,
Rossetti's rainbow liberates her devotional imagination by taking her
out of her 'sole self'. The 'dancing rainbow' in the bubble becomes a
'secret fount of pleasure' because it is a symbol of God's covenant with
Noah: 'I do set my bow in cloud, and it shall be for a token of a
covenant between me and the earth' (Genesis 9:13). Nature here has
provided not only a route to self-examination, but also acts as an

analogue of God. Feelings of anxiety and detachment ('dull and blank') are partially dispelled by the rainbow, as it not only reminds her of God's promise to the fallen earth, but also locates her within a community of 'all creatures alike' loved by their creator.

The importance of God's covenant to both the individual and the Christian community is addressed again in an entry for 29 May:

> A gloomy Christian is like a cloud before the rainbow was vouch-safed.
>
> We all (or almost all) more or less present cloudy aspects, thanks to tempers, griefs, anxieties, disappointments.
>
> But the heavenliest sort of Christian exhibits more bow than cloud, walking the world in a continual thanksgiving; and "a joyful and pleasant thing it is to be thankful."
>
> At unequal distances behind and below him tramp on graduated Christians of every density and tinge: some with full-coloured bows, some with a faint bit of broken bow, some with the merest tint of prismatic colour at a torn edge; all bearing some sign of God's gracious covenant with them.
>
> In this company we fail to trace the gloomy Christian, all cloud, no bow.
>
> But if he really and truly is not traceable high or low among the caravan of pilgrims with their badge of hope, where is he to be sought for on holy ground?
>
> (*TF* 102)

The 'tempers, griefs, anxieties, disappointments' here echo Rossetti's 'anxious thought' in the entry for 10 April, while the appearance of the rainbow again combats gloominess. The rainbow is a symbol of hope, a 'badge' displayed by Christians of their faith in God's protection. Though still presented as a community, Christians here are differentiated by degrees of hope, by their awareness of their personal connection with God. The 'gloomy Christian' who exhibits 'all cloud, no bow', is in danger of being untraceable because s / he has allowed his / her own 'griefs' to overwhelm the remembrance of 'God's gracious covenant'. Rossetti's criticism of 'gloomy' Christians echoes her reservations about 'overscrupulous' ones. Both groups' Christian faith is weakened by the self-absorption at the root of their respective melancholy and pedantry.

William Michael made a point of disagreeing with 'what a great number of critics and readers or half-readers have said before me, that Christina's poetry is "morbid"' (*Memoir* lxviii). Rossetti may well have been trying to challenge this public image by countering her critics with her explicit disapproval of 'gloomy Christians'. The passage's last line, D'Amico notes, 'serves almost as a warning to both Rossetti's readers and herself. Clearly, by the time she published *Time Flies*, she had decided that she must be careful as a poet not to exhibit Christianity to her readers as if it were an unlovely religion of gloom' (*CR* 157).

At the same time, Rossetti defends a certain degree of gloominess as an inevitable part of the human condition, a result of humanity's separation from God. She advocates the exhibition of the rainbow while maintaining a sense of how difficult such a display of hope can be for fallen mankind. It seems likely that Rossetti herself identifies with those 'with a faint bit of broken bow' or 'with the merest hint of prismatic colour at a torn edge'. Her observers in the entry of 10 April who interpreted her 'anxious thought' as only 'dull and blank' were 'partly ... right, but partly wrong', because their evaluation of her public distress was not balanced by the possibility of her private joy. Rossetti's acknowledgement of the personal gradations of thought and feeling that characterize each Christian's display of bow and cloud recalls the significance of 'small secret fount of pleasure' to be found in the bubble's 'dancing rainbow'.

An entry for 7 November, in which Rossetti remembers her sister Maria's death, presents a similarly hopeful study of the relationship between God, nature, the individual, and the community:

> One of the dearest and most saintly persons I ever knew, in foresight of her own approaching funeral, saw nothing attractive in the "hood and hatband" style towards which I evinced some old-fashioned leaning. "Why make everything as hopeless looking as possible?" she argued.
>
> And at a moment which was sad only for us who lost her, all turned out in harmony with her holy hope and joy.
>
> Flowers covered her, loving mourners followed her, hymns were sung at her grave, the November day brightened, and the sun (I vividly remember) made a miniature rainbow in my eyelashes.
>
> I have often thought of that rainbow since.
>
> May all who love enjoy cheerful little rainbows at the funerals of their beloved ones.
>
> (*TF* 213)

Rossetti channels her personal grief into another meditation on the nature of melancholy in general. Her sister's gentle rebuke causes her to re-evaluate her gloomy 'old-fashioned leaning' toward sober funeral clothing. By the end of the passage, she practices the lesson of her sister's hopefulness by finding enjoyment in 'the cheerful little rainbow' which appears in her own tear-stained lashes.

This experience encompasses the individual and the communal in its movement from a private sisterly discussion to the grief of 'all who lost her'. Rossetti's personal comfort in 'the miniature rainbow in my eyelashes' moves her to wish that 'all who love' will experience that same sense of comfort 'at the funerals of their beloved ones'. Solace here is available to Rossetti through both a communal and individual relationship with God and nature. The 'loving mourners' and the 'hymns sung at her grave' provide comfort from the human community, while the rainbow, presumably created by the sun shining on Rossetti's tears, is a divine symbol of private hope in grief, like the rainbow in the bubble from the earlier entry: it converts 'hopeless looking' to hopeful looking. In wishing 'little rainbows' to appear for others, 'at the funerals of their beloved ones', Rossetti places her individual suffering within the context of a Christian community, hoping that 'all' will find solace in their relationship with God.

The poem which follows on 8 November also reminds readers of God's promise to humanity, and of mankind's responsibility for maintaining God's covenant:

> Our heaven must be within ourselves,
>   Our home and heaven the work of faith
> All through this race of life which shelves
>   Downward to death.
>
> So faith shall build the boundary wall,
>   And hope shall plant the secret bower,
> That both may show magnifical
>   With gem and flower.
>
> While over all a dome must spread,
>   And love shall be that dome above;
> And deep foundations must be laid,
>   And these are love.

(TF 213–14; Crump, 2: 315)

The possessive plural 'our' of the first stanza gives the sense of mankind's individual and communal responsibility for its own spiritual fulfillment. As in the preceding prose passage, the bond between God and man provides solace despite the inevitability of death. Here, both mankind and God are the architects of humanity's fate. 'The work of faith' which builds a temporary home on earth will construct a permanent one in heaven. The poem's heaven begins 'within', yet ends without, following the same kind of divine logic which will grant a higher position in heaven to those who occupy the lowest place on earth. Though 'the race of life' 'shelves / Downward to death', death itself is not an end if Christian 'faith' and 'hope' protect mankind from death's permanence with heaven's 'boundary wall' and 'secret bower'. Love, however, is the element needed to bring both faith and hope together, providing the 'deep foundations' and 'dome above'.

The poem expounds the themes of death, faith, and love in the preceding prose passage, taking its cue from the movement in the last prose line from the individual to the universal: 'May all who love enjoy cheerful little rainbows at the funerals of their beloved ones.' It expands Rossetti's parable of private family grief to include the human family, each stanza a more generalized poetic re-phrasing of her dying sister's words, '"Why make everything as hopeless looking as possible?".' The poem tries to reflect the comfort of her sister's faith, while emphasizing the active effort the faithful need to make in order to achieve heaven: 'Our home and heaven the *work* of faith' (emphasis mine). Its advice to readers to find heaven within themselves by persisting in faith, hope, and love, echoes the 'holy hope and joy' shared by Maria Rossetti's mourners. As in the prose passage, death also intrudes in the poem, but the 'boundary wall' of faith, the 'secret bower' of hope, and the 'deep foundations' of love prove stronger than mortality.

Typology

For Rossetti, the Tractarian doctrines of reserve and analogy are transmuted into literary philosophy, as expression itself becomes both a translation *and* a reflection of the sacred message it delivers. The idea that everything on earth can be seen as an analogue of God extends to discourse. Typological interpretation is dependent on the human imagination to bridge the gap between earthly event and sacred meaning. Similarly, the doctrines of analogy and reserve 'see' God in everything, not literally, but literarily, imaginatively. Scrupulous 'translations of the letter in defiance of the spirit' about which Rossetti writes in the first passage of *Time Flies*, are 'unpoetical' because they neglect the human imagination. They therefore do not reflect the spirit of their human creator and cannot hope to reflect the spirit of the ultimate Creator. Translating God's word literally is impossible, but interpreting its meaning literarily is within the scope of human ability.

What is at stake here theologically is the Christian conviction in the unity of the Old Testament and the New. Although the books often disagree with each other in both philosophy and practice, typological interpretation reconciles them. Rossetti's typology is extensive, drawing together not only Old and New Testament themes and events, but also encouraging the reader to find parallels among the entries in *Time Flies*. Despite the pitfalls and vagaries of human translation of the divine, language can also act as a unifying, and ultimately saving, force. In an entry for 18 December, Rossetti reinterprets the story of the Ten Commandments as a parable of cooperation between God and man, discovering redemptive possibilities in fallen language:

> "And the tables were the work of God, and the writing was the writing of God, graven upon the tables ... And the Lord said unto Moses, Hew thee two tables of stone like unto the first: and I will write upon these tables the words that were in the first tables, which thou brakest." — (Ex. xxxii. 16; xxxiv. I.)
>
> Those first tables correspond with Adam, being like himself wholly and exclusively the handiwork of God. The unbroken commandment graven materially on the one, spiritually on the other, added glory to both.
>
> Adam by one sin broke the whole law: offending in one point he became guilty of all.
>
> Then did the Divine sentence as it were take him up and cast him down, breaking him in pieces when it decreed, "Dust thou art, and unto dust shalt thou return."
>
> The second tables, partly of Divine workmanship while partly also of human, correspond with our Lord Jesus Christ, Son of God and Son of Mary. These second tables (so far, I think, as Holy Scripture records) never were broken; but abode intact and sacred, like unto His perfect nature and exhaustive obedience.
>
> Yet as Moses in an access of holy indignation cast the former tables out of his hands and brake them beneath the Mount, so on Mount Calvary "it pleased the Lord to bruise" His sinless Son, not for His own sake, but for the sake of us sinners.
>
> That as in Adam all die, even so in Christ may all be made alive.
>
> (243–44)

By interpreting Old Testament books typologically, Rossetti makes a comparison which forecasts New Testament salvation. When Moses descends from mount Sinai to find his people engaged in idolatrous worship, in his anger he breaks the tablets containing the Ten Commandments. God tells Moses to bring him new tables, upon which he instructs Moses to write 'the words of the covenant' (Exodus 34:28). For Rossetti, the broken tables in Exodus represent God's broken trust in Adam in Genesis, while the second set of tables prefigures the New Testament hope of the redemption of Adam's descendants. The 'first tables correspond with Adam', because like him they are broken and return to dust, while Moses, as the one who breaks them, corresponds with God. Rossetti further implies that both sets of tables stand for Christ. Just as God condemned Adam to mortality for his disobedience, Moses broke the first tables in 'holy indignation' at the sins of Israel. Much later, God would sacrifice Christ 'for the sake of us sinners'.

The second tables have a physical correspondence with Christ in that they are 'partly of Divine workmanship while partly also of human'. Like Christ, these tables endure. Just as the second tables give the Israelites the chance to rectify their sin of idolatry, Christ's obedience to God allows mankind to escape the consequences of Adam's disobedience. The collaborative nature of the relationship between God and mankind affirms a certain faith in humanity's interpretative ability. While 'the finger of God' (Exodus 31:18) writes the first tables, Moses himself brings the second set of tables and writes on them the word of God. The first tables, the exclusive 'work of God' were broken, while the second, the work of God and Moses, 'abode intact and sacred'. What is remarkable about this passage is that it posits collaboration between God and man as the key to salvation. Human and divine cooperation in the Old Testament prefigures the salvation of mankind in the form of a human and divine Christ in the New Testament. This collaboration begins as literary promise (the writing of the tables) which culminates in a literal one (Christ, the word-made-flesh).

The entry which follows on 19 December further emphasizes the cooperative nature of the covenant between God and mankind:

> Again. Those second tables prepared by Moses, written upon, and so completed by God Himself, appear further as a figure of regenerate humanity, recreated by God and Man in unison, even by our Lord Jesus Christ. He puts His Spirit within us, reviving, moulding, beautifying us: He renews in our hearts His perfect law: He feeds us with

His own Body and Blood: He guides us with His counsel, and after that (if so be we persevere) He will receive us with glory.

(244)

The tables themselves are a 'figure of regenerate humanity' not only because they are 'recreated', but because they are recreated 'by God and Man in unison'. Humanity, like the tables broken by Moses, can be revived, moulded, and beautified by God. However, in order for such a renewal to complete, mankind must also play its part, according to 'His counsel'. Christian hearts become like the tables in that they receive the translation of God's 'perfect law', continuing to reflect the cooperative relationship between God and Moses. The spirit and word of God can redeem humanity just as it remade the tables, but the project of salvation still requires man's interpretative capabilities. Rossetti's typological chain of comparison thus contains in its argument a defense of the practice of typology itself.

The structure of *Time Flies* itself encourages typological comparison among its own passages. For example, Rossetti has prepared her readers for her New Testament reinterpretation of Exodus in an earlier entry of June 8:

Nevertheless, although the Manna on six successive days fell within the reach of all, those only who had gathered and stored it on the sixth day of toil, possessed it on the final day of rest.

On that seventh day, any who had it not already laid up could not find it, though they might seek it carefully with tears.

Some who thus sought and found it not, were reproved; and the fault was laid to their own charge.

We Christians in the Sacrament of Christ's Most Blessed Body and Blood, enjoy access to the True Bread from heaven; and to us our loving Lord has said: "This do in remembrance of Me." If in our present day of discipline we neglect thus to lay up Christ in our hearts, and so despise our birthright; on what plea can we lay claim to our blessing, even indissoluble union with Christ, in the day of blessing?

(110)

This passage describes an episode in Exodus 17, wherein the Israelites disobey God and Moses by seeking on the seventh day the manna which God provides for them. God is angered by the people's disobedience, saying, 'How long refuse ye to keep my commandments and my laws?' (Exodus 17:28). While God forbids gathering manna on the seventh day, still 'he giveth you on the sixth day the bread of two days' (17:29). Here, human failure to interpret, trust, understand, and obey God's law causes the people to be reproved. Rossetti sees a lesson for contemporary Christians in the Israelites' behavior, as well as a typological parallel between the gathering of manna and the sacrament of communion. The manna prefigures Christ, 'the True Bread from Heaven', while God's rebuke to the Israelites prefigures his punishment of Christians who 'neglect to lay up Christ in our hearts'.

The passage of December 19 also connects the lessons of the Israelites in Exodus to the duties of modern Christians. That Christ is compared in the June passage to manna from heaven prepares readers for December's comparison of Christ to the tables containing the Ten Commandments. Through typological interpretation, both passages stress the importance of obedience to God, as well as the Christian need to 'persevere' in understanding and accepting the relationship between mankind and God. In all three passages, Rossetti uses the Old Testament story of Exodus as an analogue of the modern Christian's exile from heaven, and a parable of hope for his / her eventual return.

While her theology is heavily reliant on typology, Rossetti is often wary about the compatibility of literary strategy and religious meaning. Although she trusts in God's word, she is aware of the limits of human language. In an entry for 3 February, she commemorates the martyrdom of St. Blaise, comparing him to 'an elevated candle showing light to all the household', because 'tapers and bonfires belonged of yore to the observance of his festival'. Still, she is cautious about her own comparison:

This connexion of fire with St. Blaise is not, it seems, accounted for: the fact however remains certain. A pun on his name of "Blaise" has been suggested as the connecting link, but only to be branded as "absurd" by at least one author of repute. Yet let us hope that this particular pun if baseless is also blameless.

Can a pun profit? Seldom, I fear. Puns and such like are a frivolous crew likely to misbehave unless kept within strict bounds. "Foolish talking" and "jesting," writes St. Paul, "are not convenient." Can the majority of puns be classed as *wise* talking?

(26)

Rossetti's concerns about the dangers of 'foolish talking' reflect an awareness of the vulnerabilities of Christian exegesis. The verse she selects, 'Neither filthiness, nor foolish talking, nor jesting, which are not convenient: but rather giving of thanks', is followed in Ephesians by Paul's further advice: 'Let no man deceive you with vain words: for because of these things cometh the wrath of God upon the children of disobedience' (Ephesians, 5:4, 5:6). Rossetti's distrust of puns harks back to her worries about 'scrupulous persons' and their 'translations of the letter in defiance of the spirit' (2). The interpretation of 'Blaise' as a homonym of 'blaze' is so direct as to go against mankind's mediated understanding of religious mystery, and is therefore disobedient. From a literary perspective, the comparison's blunt inelegance perhaps makes it 'absurd'. When translation becomes this literal, the 'spirit' of the Christian letter suffers. Christian translation ought to take place through indirect apprehension, 'through a glass darkly', in order to reflect mankind's distance from God. Rossetti fears that the passage's pun, which relies not on theology but on wordplay, might make Christian interpretative tradition susceptible to charges of absurdity.

At the same time, Rossetti's desire to be wise and obedient in her interpretation of sacred history competes with her own literary enjoyment of language's quirks. She cautions readers against wordplay, but with a colorful turn of phrase in which words are personified as 'a frivolous crew likely to misbehave'. She not only admits to hoping that the pun about St. Blaise is 'blameless', but also reinforces the comparison by relating St. Blaise to candles and bonfires. This pun, however 'baseless', has merited her further contemplation and inclusion in her book.

Her ambivalence toward wordplay surfaces again in an entry for 13 March:

> Can false etymology ever be of use? I think in one instance it has been of use to me.
>
> "Lent." Good as it is to understand one's own language, I feel neither incited nor helped to observe Lent by being referred to a German root.
>
> But when once (however erroneously) I connect the word with "a loan": that which is lent, that which being lent, not bestowed will someday be withdrawn: then it sounds an alarm in my ears.
>
> Forty chances to be used or abused.
>
> Forty appeals to be responded to or resisted.
>
> Forty battles to be lost or won.
>
> Forty days to be utilized or wasted.
>
> And then the account to be closed, and the result registered.
>
> (*TF* 52)

Here, Rossetti initially treats 'false etymology' with the same skepticism she showed the pun in February's entry. She is wary of her connection of the religious festival of Lent to the secular concept of 'that which is lent' simply because they share the same spelling. Yet despite her parenthetical disclaimer, she proceeds to let her pun, 'however erroneously' direct the passage. The economic metaphor which results spills over into the next entry for 14 March.

> Or again, and yet more solemnly.
> Lent: a loan of forty days: but such a loan as is terminable at the pleasure of the Lender.
> Lent: a loan of unguaranteed duration: the beginning, by God's mercy, ours; the end not assured to us.
> Lent: a period set us wherein specially to prepare for eternity: forty days long at the longest: can forty days be accounted long when eternity is at stake?
>
> (*TF* 52–3)

This correspondence of meaning between 'Lent' and 'lent' fires both her writerly and her religious imagination. Rossetti lets economic double-meanings linger, even in the final sentence, with the words 'accounted' and 'stake'. Unlike the rhetorical question which ended February's passage, 'Can the majority of puns be classified as *wise* talking?', the question which begins March's passage, 'Can false etymology ever be of use?', receives an answer. Rossetti subjects this query to a number of linguistic experiments, using the poet's tools of wordplay and metaphor to prove she can link the two seemingly disparate concepts of 'Lent' and 'lent'. At the same time, Rossetti seeks to protect her punning from St. Paul's charges of 'foolish talking' or 'jesting' by emphasizing the absolute seriousness of what is 'at stake'. Though Rossetti remains reluctant to declare the theological legitimacy of her own interpretation, her hesitancy does not prevent her from making the attempt at exegesis, or from enforcing it with every rhetorical resource at her command. Throughout *Time Flies*, she remains self-conscious yet defensive about interpretative strategy, as in the entry for 23 April: 'Fabrications, blunders, even lies, frequently contain some grain of truth: and though life at the longest cannot be long enough for us to sift all, one occasionally may repay the sifting' (*TF* 78).

Wordplay remains a pervasive literary feature of *Time Flies*, often invoked to aid author's typology. For example, an entry for 18 April uses the Christian association of the sun with the Son of God to guide its exegesis:

> I remember rising early once to see the sun rise.
> I rose too early, and waited wearily and impatiently.
> At length the sun rose.
> At length? Scarcely. The sun kept time, though I kept it not: the sun lagged not because I hurried.
> If the material sun fails not, much more is that supreme "Sun" infallible whereof we read: "Unto you that fear My Name shall the Sun of Righteousness arise."
> Therefore, neither doth our Lord delay His coming, however the Church expectant may reiterate, "Why is His chariot so long in coming? why tarry the wheels of His chariots?"
> "Beloved, be not ignorant of this one thing, that one day is with the Lord as a thousand years, and a thousand years as one day. The Lord is not slack concerning His promise, as some men count slackness; but is longsuffering to usward, not willing that any should perish, but that all should come to repentance."
>
> (*TF* 74)

In this passage, the 'material sun' reminds Rossetti of the Old Testament 'Sun of Righteousness', which in turn prefigures the rising of the New Testament Christ, the son of God. Within this network of allusions, the apocalyptic result of the sun's, and the Son's rising is suggested. While the first quotation, from Malachi 4:2, predicts the healing of mankind through the 'Sun of Righteousness', the preceding verse foretells that mankind will also burn: 'For, behold, the day cometh, that shall burn as an oven; and all the proud, yea, and all that do wickedly, shall be as stubble: and the day that cometh shall burn them up, saith the Lord of hosts, that it shall leave them neither root nor branch' (Malachi 4:1). The tone of Malachi is threatening, meant to inspire respect and fear for God.

Divine punishment is also touched on in the passage's second quotation from Judges, wherein a mother anxiously awaits her son's arrival: 'The mother of Sisera looked out at a window, and cried through the lattice, Why is his chariot so long in coming? why tarry the wheels of his chariots?' (Judges 5:28). Sisera will never come because he has been killed by Jael, and his fate serves as Judges' warning to the 'enemies' of God. The chapter concludes, 'So let all thine enemies perish, O Lord: but let them that love him be as the sun when he goeth forth in his might' (5:31).

Rossetti has chosen this verse from Judges not only to suggest the punishment which will be suffered by God's enemies, but also to make a
point about the difference the true son of God will make to the mortal
world. Whereas Sisera's mother waits in vain for a dead son who will not
come again, the Christian Church is assured by the promise of the New
Testament that God's son, though he died, will return.

The passage's final quotation, from 2 Peter 3:8–9, presents a forgiving
New Testament God, who does not want any one to perish, but rather
to repent. The anticipation of Christ's return in 2 Peter is not without
the darker associations of apocalypse: 'But the day of the Lord will come
as a thief in the night; in which the heavens shall pass away with a great
noise, and the elements shall melt with fervent heat, the earth also and
the works that are therein shall be burned up' (3:10), yet Peter's overall
tone is comforting, confident in Christ's promise of 'new heavens and a
new earth' (3:13). Rather than impatience for the apocalypse, or fear at
its approach, Peter advises humanity to focus on 'what manner of persons ought ye to be in all holy conversation and godliness' (3:11). Here,
Rossetti uses Peter both to substantiate and critique the selected passages from Malachi and Judges. The violent imagery of the Old
Testament God in Malachi is mitigated by the promise of Christ in Peter,
while the act of waiting, so painfully represented in Judges, is reinterpreted as an opportunity for Christian self-examination.

The Sun of Righteousness, the son Sisera, and the Son of God are the
starting point for Rossetti's meditation on the common points of all
three chosen verses, and are used typologically to suggest that the Old
Testament foretells the coming of Christ. Malachi 4:5, for example, foretells the coming of 'Elisha the prophet before the coming of the great
and dreadful day of the Lord', while the agony of Sisera's mother in
Judges forecasts the patience and endurance Christians will have to
exhibit in awaiting the return of God's son. Rossetti's typology is also
inspired by the interrelation of earthly time and heavenly eternity. The
earthly sun is nature's true marker of time against which Rossetti's
human perception of time is measured and found to be flawed, just as
the heavenly Son exists in an eternity which earthly time is inadequate
to measure. The sun 'kept time', while Rossetti 'kept it not', because her
weariness and impatience both wasted time and made it seem longer.
Her impatience has no effect on the sun's rising or setting, because 'the
material sun' operates outside of her perception and regardless of her
wishes. Similarly, the Church's anxiety for Christ's return does not
reflect any delay on Christ's part, but rather its own impatience. The
human perception of time is set against the idea of divine eternity

expressed in Peter, where 'one day with the Lord' is 'as a thousand years'. There is another typological relationship here as 2 Peter 8 is itself a quotation from Psalms: 'For a thousand years in thy sight are but as yesterday when it is past, and as a watch in the night' (90:4).

Time and eternity

A poem for 5 April contrasts mankind's earthly perception of time with the heavenly reality of eternity.

> Heaven's chimes are slow, but sure to strike at last:
>> Earth's sands are slow, but surely dropping through:
>> And much we have to suffer, much to do,
>>> Before the time be past.
>
> Chimes that keep time are neither slow nor fast:
>> Not many are the numbered sands nor few:
>> A time to suffer, and a time to do,
>>> And then the time is past.

(*TF* 65; Crump, 2: 276–7)

Here, Ecclesiastes' philosophy of time is given a redemptive dimension by a Christian conception of eternity. The poem's seventh line, 'A time to suffer, and a time to do', borrows from the third chapter of Ecclesiastes, where there is 'a time to every purpose under the heaven' (3:1). The book's theme of *vanitas*, however, is redirected by the poem's last time, which anticipates an eternity for man. The New Testament promise of salvation through Christ makes time a relative and secondary force. Time measures mankind's suffering, but also limits it, because eventually 'the time is past'. While in the first stanza, time seems 'slow' because mankind has 'much ... to suffer' and 'to do', in the second stanza, resignation to 'much' earthly suffering is offset by the sense of time as finite. Like the sun which 'kept time' in 18 April's passage, the chimes here 'keep time', giving the impression of time as both observed and contained. The human perception of 'many' and 'few' or 'slow' and 'fast' exists only in relation to earthly time. When examined in terms of eternity, these measures become less relevant, as time is 'neither slow nor fast', its sands neither 'many' nor 'few'.

Time Flies is designed to keep the relationship of mankind to time foremost in readers' minds. Not only does the book itself follow the Christian calendar, but its entries also regularly consider and reconsider the implications of humanity's relationship to time. In the entry for 18

September, from which the book takes its title, Rossetti reminds her readers of mankind's responsibility to time:

> Heaven and earth alike are chronometers.
> Heaven marks time in light, by the motion of luminaries.
> Earth marks time in darkness, by the variation of shadows.
> To these chronometers of nature art adds clocks with faces easily decipherable and voices insistently audible.
> Nature and art combine to keep time for us: and yet we wander out of time!
> We misappropriate time, we lose time, we waste time, we kill time.
> We do anything and everything with time, except redeem the time.
> Yet time is short and swift and never returns. Time flies.
>
> (*TF* 180)

Rossetti's meditation draws on Ecclesiastes' study of time and St. Paul's emphasis on eternity, to explore the relation of time to salvation. Ecclesiastes' resignation in the face of mankind's temporary and vain earthly life is read through the New Testament concept of mankind's redemption through Christ. Time is important to man precisely because of the limitations it imposes on his salvation. Ecclesiastes writes that 'For man also knoweth not his own time: as the fishes that are taken in an evil net, and as the birds that are caught in a snare; so are the sons of men snared in an evil time, when it falleth suddenly upon them' (Ecclesiastes, 9:12). This resignation to the force of time is mitigated by Rossetti's allusion to the Pauline alternative, which recommends, 'that ye walk circumspectly, not as fools, but as wise, / Redeeming the time, because the days are evil', (Ephesians 5:15–16). The phrase occurs also in Colossians 4:5, which advises mankind to 'Walk in wisdom toward them that are without, redeeming the time'. Wisdom, a virtue attributed to the writer of Ecclesiastes, takes on New Testament meaning when explicitly linked to mankind's participation in his own salvation. To 'misappropriate', 'lose', 'waste', or 'kill' time is dangerous because humanity ultimately wastes its own chance to save itself from the end of time through Christ.

The passage itself reflects the interaction of nature and art, deciphering in prose the way in which heaven and earth mark time for mankind. The initial personification of earth, heaven, and art gives way to a straightforward description of the relation of mankind to time, while the movement from the complexity of the opening sentences to the simplicity of the final line syntactically reflects the swift flight of time.

The prose itself keeps time with its deliberately measured paragraphs of almost incantatory rhythm. Rossetti uses shifts in form and tone to illustrate different aspects of her Christianized philosophy of time. As with the entry for 27 January, she disrupts this entry's surface by blurring formal distinctions between poetry, prose, sermon, and prayer. A sense of urgency about time's flight is communicated through the passage's brevity and its shift in tone from the speculative to the conclusive. In our conduct time seems to be subject to our agency, our verbs — we do things with it or to it — but ultimately time wrests this agency from us, becoming in the final pared-down sentence its own subject, whose action takes wing and escapes our grasp: 'Time Flies.' In effect, the passage, with its increasingly simple syntax and language, gives us an illustration of language itself running out of time.

6
Imagining Faith: Earth and Heaven in *The Face of the Deep*

The passage of time, or, more precisely, the end of time, is confronted in Rossetti's final devotional prose work, *The Face of the Deep: A Devotional Commentary on the Apocalypse*. Published in 1892, when the author was in her sixties, it contains a prose passage and / or a poem for each chapter and verse of Revelation. More dense, and more challenging a read than *Time Flies*, it is a comprehensive study of the final book of the Bible. 'Believe me,' writes a modern collector, 'it [*The Face of the Deep*] is not a book that one would want to curl up with on a rainy night — or any night for that matter'.[1]

Upon its original release, the book enjoyed a much better reception. My own copy, a third edition of seven, is inscribed by its purchaser, 'To my darling Mother, March, 1897'. *The Face of the Deep* was a commercial success, but this inscription points to its success as a devotional work. The book was one that someone might give to her Victorian 'darling mother' as an appropriate, daughterly offering. At the time of its composition, in fact, Christina Rossetti was old enough to be a grandmother herself. Rossetti never had children, and her spinsterhood has invited readings in terms either of sacrifice (earthly fulfillment vs. spiritual satisfaction) or rebellion (silenced gender conformity vs. vocal poetics). There is also the uncomfortable fact of the poet's productivity, the suggestion being that literary production and physical reproduction are somehow substitutes for one another. Rossetti herself sees this differently, as she explains in *The Face of the Deep*: '"Give me children or else I die,"[2] was a foolish speech: the childless who make themselves nursing mothers of Christ's little ones are the true mothers in Israel' (*FD* 312). This 'speech' was made by the barren woman of another Old Testament couple, Rachel and Jacob, and Rossetti uses it here to suggest alternative possibilities of salvation besides motherhood for Christian women. The kind of nursing to which the poet refers is spiritual rather than physical, the connection still emotional, but also intellectual. Rossetti's rather curt defense of childlessness can't help seeming self-justifying, but that does not mean it has no other motive. Whether personal or not, the statement is forthright enough. Rossetti states that the childless Christian who nurtures 'Christ's little ones' is spiritually superior.

Rossetti is often presented as a poet of resignation where there is a strong argument that she is a poet of acceptance. Although, unlike Rachel, Rossetti chose to remain childless, she suggests that such a choice was predicated on acceptance of personal circumstance. About Eve she writes,

> Eve, the representative woman, received as part of her sentence "desire": the assigned object of her desire being such that satisfaction must depend not on herself but on one stronger than she, who might grant or might deny. Many women attain their heart's desire: many attain it not. Yet are these latter no losers if they exchange desire for aspiration, the corruptible for the incorruptible ...
>
> *(FD* 312)

Her rejection of earthly love relationships is not simply fatalist, because it is predicated partially on choice and is expressed in the language of exchange; desire for aspiration, corruptible for the incorruptible. Nor is her position simply escapist as she balances her wish for heaven with an acceptance (albeit a troubled one) of her place in the world. The restorative exchange of corruptible for incorruptible is outlined in 1 Corinthians 15.

> For this corruptible must put on incorruption, and this mortal must put on immortality.
> So when this corruptible shall have put on incorruption, and this mortal shall have put on immortality, then shall be brought to pass the saying that is written, Death is swallowed up in victory.
> O death, where is thy sting? O grave, where is thy victory?
>
> (1 Corinthians 15:53–55)

This is another example of the way in which Rossetti applies New Testament vocabulary to an Old Testament text, so that Eve becomes a 'representative woman', her relationship to Adam a reflection of women's relationship to Christ, who promises immortality. The salvatory language of the New Testament works retroactively on Eve, providing the possibility of redemption. Yet her desire for Adam need not be interpreted literally by the Christian woman; desire for a mortal husband can be replaced by desire for the immortal Christ.

For Rossetti, immortality in heaven is as much (or more) a reality as life on earth. In *The Face of the Deep* she writes:

> At present and at once all earthly things teach some lesson to the teachable. "For the invisible things of Him from the creation of the world are clearly seen, being understood by the things that are made, even His eternal power and Godhead." And whereas ... accessories in this Inspired Book [the Bible] seem in great measure emblematical rather than actual; I can at least infer thence that every such figure must have an original, every type an antitype. Only a substance can cast a shadow.
>
> (438)

Here, the earth is only a shadow cast by heaven, its purpose to communicate the invisible. However, for Rossetti, the invisible is not linked to the insubstantial. Because heaven is invisible to human eyes, it, as a shadow-caster, is more substantial than the earth, a shadow. Heaven is not an imaginary sanctuary from the problems of the world; it literally, if not physically, exists. For many twenty-first-century readers, heaven is the shadow, and earth the substance, but for Rossetti, heaven is a reality. Decontextualizing heaven as an abstraction in the works of Rossetti, for whatever purpose, reads against the spirit of the poetry.

The daughter who in 1897 inscribed my copy of *The Face of the Deep* to her mother participates in the spirit of Rossetti's devotional work, which was often imagined in terms of a legacy. It parallels Rossetti's own inscription, 'To my mother, for the first time, to her beloved, revered, cherished memory', reminding readers of the close relationship of the personal and the religious in Rossetti's theology. This dedication reminds us that this meditation on the transcendent reality of the divine also confronts a painful material absence. Most of Rossetti's other books were dedicated to her mother while alive, which makes this 'first' dedication to her mother's 'memory' all the more poignant.[3] It also reminds us that the book was published with a specific audience in mind, one whose religious values corresponded to the poet's own, and one for whom the existence of God and the hierarchy of heaven and earth was not at issue. It is crucial to read Rossetti's works with the understanding that for her, and for her Christian audience, heaven was real and earth was not. Or, more precisely, heaven was a reality, and earth its mediated reflection. In order to enter heaven, humanity must first negotiate the earth, or as Rossetti puts it, 'Earth is a race-course, not a goal' (343).

The dogmatic thrust of this sentiment, however, should not be interpreted as a simplistic dismissal of the importance of life on earth. Along with the burden of free will, and knowledge of the distance from the 'goal' of heaven, comes a choice about how to run the 'race-course' of earth. *The Face of the Deep* illustrates this by working to balance Christian dogma with interpretative freedom. *The Face of the Deep* itself must be read, as its title suggests, below its surface of rhetoric and dogma. Rossetti writes of her own work,

> Only should I have readers, let me remind them that what I write professes to be a *surface* study of an unfathomable depth: if it incites any to dive deeper than I attain to, it will so far have accomplished a worthy work. My suggestions do not necessarily amount to beliefs; they may be no more than tentative thoughts compatible with acknowledged ignorance.
>
> (365)

Although the purpose of Rossetti's statement here is to affirm her humility, and to apologize in advance for any religious error, it is also to invite the reader to 'dive deeper' into the text, to draw his / her own conclusions. Her admission that her thoughts and suggestions are 'tentative' opens up a space for disagreement and debate, and advocates a kind of free thinking which modern readers do not associate with Victorian devotional writing, and certainly not with the 'scrupulous' Rossetti.

Contemporary critics recognized the challenges Rossetti's work posed, not only to ways of thinking about religion, but to ways of thinking about poetry as well. Rossetti's insistence on the tentative and speculative in her own work did not prevent it from being appropriated by some of its contemporary readers as a weapon against modern thought: 'In an age when poetry itself has been pressed into the service of doubt and denial, [Rossetti's] is a message to which both mind and heart will be vastly the better for listening'.[4] If such readings flatten Rossetti's probing movements of mind into unreflecting affirmations of dogma, then modern criticism ought not to fall into the same trap. Yet such criticism frequently starts from an opposition (declared or undeclared) to Rossetti's beliefs, and therefore can be in itself another kind of dogma. Colleen Hobbs is partially correct when she writes that for the modern reader, 'the difficulty in accepting Rossetti's contradictions lies in her own failure to see contradictions'.[5] The problem is with Hobbs's use of the term 'failure'. The difficulty critics have in accepting Rossetti's contradiction lies not in her failure to perceive contradiction, but in her unwillingness to be convinced by it. The conception of Rossetti as a poet whose faith blinded her to contradiction began with William Michael's 'Memoir' to her posthumous *Poetical Works*, which condemns what he calls her 'over-scrupulosity'. He writes that his sister's 'over-scrupulosity' is a 'defect ... more befitting for a nunnery than for London streets. It weakens the mind, straitens the temperament and character, chills the impulse and the influence' (*Memoir*, lxvii–lxviii). William Michael's suggestion that Rossetti's temperament was more suitable for a nunnery than the London streets is an odd one because she was a poet neither of the convent nor of the street. Her devotional work inhabits 'the convent threshold', an imaginative space somewhere between the two extremes of the street and the convent, the space, in fact, where contradiction thrives. William Michael continues, however, in the same vein:

> The influence of her work became intense for devout minds of a certain type, and for lovers of poetry in its pure essence; but for a great mass of readers, who might otherwise have been attracted and secured, the material proffered was too uniform and too restricted, and was too seldom concerned with breathing and diurnal actualities — never with rising currents of thought.
>
> (lxviii)

Here Rossetti's subject matter is criticized, not her poetic handling of it. In William Michael's view, the 'pure essence' of poetry may be compatible with a 'uniform' and 'restricted' religious belief, but poetry based on such belief can never have a broad appeal. William Michael therefore worries that Rossetti's work lost a potential audience because it did not concern itself with the earthly, with current issues, ('rising currents of thought') with the body ('breathing', 'diurnal actualities'), with 'the street'. However, Rossetti's religious work was concerned with what she perceived as the restrictions of life on earth, and carries an implicit criticism of what may be restrictive and uniform about the poetry of the earth. Catherine Cantalupo points out that Rossetti's devotional work 'confronted the dominant Romantic aesthetic of nineteenth-century England, especially its emphasis on the primacy of both human imagination and the natural world'.[6] Such a strategy, according to William Michael, may have lost her Victorian readers, and certainly to this day loses her modern readers. In 1906, two years after the publication of William Michael's 'Memoir' in *The Poetical Works*, Virginia Woolf wrote to Violet Dickinson, 'I want to write about Christina Rossetti; so if you can find out what she thought about Christianity and what effect religion had upon her poetry, and will write it on a post card, you will do more for me than if you looked out a train, and bought a new hat.'[7] Her tone is, of course, flippant and somewhat ironic, but Woolf's sentiment nevertheless betrays her consciously 'modern' suspicion of the Victorians. William Michael's summation of his sister's approach to religion would have fulfilled Woolf's expectations, and filled the back of her post card: 'To ponder for herself whether a thing was true or not ceased to be a part of her intellect. The only question was whether or not it conformed to the Bible, as viewed by Anglo-Catholicism' (*Memoir* lxviii). To an extent, William Michael's statement is true. Rossetti did not write devotionally to prove or disprove any aspect of Christianity, but neither was her 'only question' about 'a thing['s]' conformity to the Bible. Rather, her questions had more to do with man's fallen relationship to God, a relationship which is the very reverse of simple and which does not, in any case, necessitate a simple-minded poetic response.

Hobbs observes that Rossetti's devotional work, and the prose in particular, presents such difficulty because it is always 'resisting neat classification'. She speculates that if the devotional poetry within the prose works were considered separately, it would rank with Hopkins, while if the commentary were separate it 'would be shelved with other biblical exegesis'. Hobbs observes that the prose could be also read as a 'female alternative to masculine models' of autobiography, such as Augustine's *Confessions* (410). However, as Hobbs realizes, an attempt to deal only with parts of a whole work undermines the structure of Rossetti's prose works, as it ignores the intertextual and intratextual strategies which themselves are crucial to the poet's understanding of the relationship between the theological and the literary.

While Rossetti's work deals in contradiction and opposition (heaven/earth, man / woman, life / death), it does so via literary strategies of allusion and elision. The inter- and intra-textuality of her texts exist themselves as concrete examples for reconciling the abstract contradictions of heaven and the world. Six volumes of devotional prose challenge the supposition that Rossetti 'failed to see contradictions'. Rossetti is known as a poet of contradictions, of ambivalence and ambiguity, and it is precisely her handling of these issues which ought to intrigue critics of her prose works. The modern critical frustration with these works comes not from Rossetti's refusal to see contradictions, but from her desire to reconcile them. Faith is the ground both of this desire and of the belief that it can be fulfilled — even if only prospectively. In this sense William Michael's exasperation with what seemed to him his sister's *irrational* intransigence misses the point; for Rossetti's faith was not the end of the matter, but the beginning.

> To learn that something in the Christian faith was credible *because it was reasonable* ... went against her. Her attitude of mind was: 'I believe because I am told to believe, and I know that the authority which tells me to believe is the only real authority extant, God.' To press her — 'How do you know that it is God?' would have been no use; the ultimate response could only have come to this — 'My faith is faith; it is not evolved out of argumentation, nor does it seek the aid of that'.
>
> (*Memoir* liv)

The door which is shut here in one direction opens in another. 'Argumentation' and intellectual debate are born out of the desire to resolve earthly and heavenly contradictions. This search for resolution necessarily demands a 'leap of faith' which is not only religious, but also literary, since its medium is language.

Rossetti is aware that her literary work, while in search of divinity, is an earthly pursuit, a fallen art. Yet this art is not inherently sinful because it is provided by God. She writes,

> "I am Alpha and Omega." [Revelation 1:8] — Thus well-nigh at the opening of these mysterious Revelations, we find in this title an instance of symbolical language accommodated to human apprehension; for any literal acceptation of the phrase seems obviously and utterly inadmissible. God condescends to teach us somewhat we can learn, and in a way by which we are capable of learning it. So, doubtless, either literally or figuratively, throughout the entire Book.
>
> Such a consideration encourages us, I think, to pursue our study of the Apocalypse, ignorant as we may be. Bring we patience and prayer to our quest, and assuredly we shall not be sent empty away. The Father of lights may still withhold from us knowledge, but He will not deny us wisdom.
>
> (*FD* 23)

Rossetti invokes God's approval of human attempts to come to terms with divine meaning, as he 'condescends to teach us ... in a way by

which we are capable of learning'. The alphabet itself is 'symbolical language accommodated to human interpretation'. This defense of biblical
interpretation in predicated on the idea that humanity's ability to learn
and study is 'encouraged' by God. Although divine meaning is mediated by human language, mankind has access to the wisdom of God
through figurative, as well as literal attempts at understanding. This
combination of the literal and the figurative lessons which make up 'the
entire Book' also justifies typological interpretation.

Rossetti continues, 'If a letter of the alphabet may be defined as a unit
of language, then under this title "Alpha and Omega" we may adore
God as the sole original Existence, the Unit of Existence, whence are
derived all nations, and kindreds, and people, and tongues'[8] (*FD* 23–4).
This allusion to Revelation is significant because it also evokes the
Tower of Babel (Genesis 11:1–9), the Old Testament story of the disper-
sion of nations, people, and tongues. Here, Rossetti tries to unify the
resultant different nations and languages by pointing to God their common point of origin. She uses New Testament anticipation of reunion to
rework the Old Testament story of dissension into an anticipation of
unity. From a New Testament perspective, the story of Babel marks not
the absolute end of shared language, but acts as a preface to Revelation's
promise of the restoration of a common language. Later in the book
Rossetti makes this link explicit, again quoting Revelation 7:9,

> "All nations, and kindreds, and people, and tongues." — Never, since
> Babel, a unison: no longer, since the first Christian Pentecost, an
> inevitable discord: for ever and ever, a harmony. Babel dissolved the
> primitive unison into discord: Pentecost reduced the prevalent dis-
> cord to contingent harmony, but reclaimed it not into unison.
>
> (231)

Defining God in terms of the alphabet is also a self-justifying metaphorical strategy for Rossetti as a writer. She continues:

> This title [Alpha and Omega] derived from human language seems to
> call especially upon "men confabulant" for grateful homage. As said
> of old the wise son of Sirach: "The Lord hath given me a tongue for
> my reward, and I will praise Him therewith." Or as the sweet
> Psalmist of Israel declared: "I will sing and give praise with the best
> member that I have."
>
> (24)

The passage goes on to describe in fiery terms the potential human misuse
and abuse of language, quoting St. James.[9] Rossetti juxtaposes these two

contradictory passages of the Old and New Testaments in order to create a way of reading them in agreement. She concludes with her hope that 'out of the abundance of our hearts our mouths may speak Thy praise', suggesting that as long as language, 'the tongue', is used in praise of God, it is not 'an unruly evil'. Although language is fallen, it retains a connection to God because He is its source. Language has the ability to redeem itself by praising Him, just as humanity can redeem itself by praising God. In this passage, Rossetti tries to reconcile an apparent contradiction between Old Testament and New Testament views of language, not because she failed to see it, but precisely because she does see it. Whether her attempt is convincing on religious grounds does not have to concern the literary critic: rather, this argument, with its strategies of elision and metaphor, is valuable as a literary attempt to justify the ways in which language *does* communicate. It also provides an insight into the contradiction at the heart of Rossetti's writing process and its goals. Her problem, as a devotional writer, is that she wants to praise God in a fallen language. In order to do this, she must redeem the language, to convince her readers and herself of the unifying legitimacy of her project. Rossetti posits God as the answer to contradiction, and heaven as the place where all contradictions will be resolved. There, differences will cease to matter.

The answer to every question Rossetti asks is God, but she arrives at this answer, not through the assertion of blind faith, but via complex literary strategies involving a combination of two other great contradictory forces: intellect and feeling.

In *The Face of the Deep* Rossetti explicitly addresses the issue of contradiction:

> Multitude no less than Unity characterizes various types of God the Holy Spirit. Water indefinitely divisible, and every portion equivalent in completeness to the whole. Fire kindling unlimited flames, each in like manner complete in itself. Dew made up of innumerable drops: so also rain, and if we may make the distinction, showers. A cloud as a cloud is one, while as raindrops it is a multitude. And as in division each portion is a complete whole devoid of parts, so equally in reunion all portions together form one complete whole similarly devoid of parts: let drops or let flames run together, and there exists no distinction of parts in their uniform volume.
>
> (15)

Here Rossetti creates a democratic space where two seemingly disparate concepts (multitude and unity) not only coexist, but are one and the same. A Tractarian sensibility is at work here, as Rossetti uses examples from nature to illustrate a divine concept. Just as in the case of water, 'every portion [is] equivalent in completeness to the whole', there is no contradiction, no disparity among the 'various types of God'.

Rossetti uses Revelation in particular to justify her philosophy of unity, to suggest that the world's very temporality points to its function. Because the Creation is ordered according to a providential design whose end is known, that end determines the nature of every being or event; each moment of life is a microcosm of the whole.

> The surface of the universe, or to bring my remark within a less unmanageable area, the surface of familiar nature and of society, presents incalculable if not infinite variety. Light stands out against darkness, growth against decay; the contrast of wedding and funeral stares us in the face. Divergences are the order of our day; insomuch that it even has been alleged that no two leaves can be found alike; and I for one am ready to believe it.
>
> Yet the more we think over these diversities ... the more ... we may discern something common underlying all that is individual. To take an instance: at one moment a wedding appears all life, a funeral all death; at another, both are perceived to be equally and at once an end and a beginning.
>
> A step further, and I recognize that during this probational period not some influences only, but all influences as they touch us become our trials, tests, temptations; assayed by which we stand or fall, we are found wanting or not wanting, as genuinely as will be the case with us in the last tremendous Day of account.
>
> (118–19)

This passage communicates its message about the difficulty of unified vision in a fallen world by gradually narrowing its focus from the generalized to the individual. Rossetti uses a visual metaphor to postulate that seeing the common aspect of two small leaves is no less challenging than comprehending the unity of the universe. Rossetti begins with an image of 'the surface of the universe', which she admits, is 'an unmanageable area'. She then focuses on 'the surface of familiar nature and society', still an area too varied to manage, necessitating further specific descriptions based on contrast: light / darkness, growth / decay, wedding / funeral. Still, such surfaces are too vast, and thus her focus further narrows to 'two leaves', which, though their surfaces are small, still display 'incalculable variety'. Yet even as her focus narrows, her thought process becomes more expansive.

Function serves as the unifying principle of Rossetti's vision: all earth's influences are humanity's 'trials, tests, temptations' by which its entrance into heaven is judged. Rossetti arrives at a fairly orthodox conclusion not by weak assertion but by an imaginative and rhetorical process which binds the individual into the collective: 'I for one' belongs equally to 'the order of our day'. The divergences in this passage, with its ever-decreasing focus that suddenly opens wide enough to accommodate 'the last tremendous Day of account', keep the reader off balance. 'Divergences are the order of our day', Rossetti writes, but this phrase has a double meaning. It means that divergences are ordinary and expected, but it also means that divergences give order to our day. Although divergences seem unrelated, they are united by purpose, as they all are the 'trials, tests, temptations' which order our day. This wordplay encourages readers, structurally and rhetorically, to 'think', to 'discern' to 'perceive' order in 'all influences'. For Rossetti, the world is a type to the antitype of heaven, and so its contradictions can best be understood through imaginative re-ordering, through arrangement.

Rossetti's is very much a poetics of arrangement, and her prose expands upon this model. The information, voices, and texts she assimilates, and the self-reflexive way in which she re-assimilates her own work points to a kind of order through anti-order, a mirror image of the way she seeks anti-types through types. In the passage above, she discusses how weddings can be seen as 'all life' and funerals 'all death', then challenges this perception, not by inversion, but by integration: '*both* are perceived to be at once an end and a beginning'. In the same way, Rossetti writes death as not an end of life, but as its antitype, because life becomes integrated into death. She writes that 'this present life is the first stage of [the] future', and that 'strength, beauty, dignity ... may be added; but added only to what we are, never to what we are not. What we essentially are in this world, that we shall be in the other: what here we absolutely are not, we shall not be there' (105). Here, humanity is a type of its divine antitype, a post-lapsarian, incomplete version of man in the 'first stage' of his / her future. After death, no radical transformation of humanity's character will take place; rather its existing attributes will be added to, so that 'what we essentially are' remains. The political and social arrangement of heaven will be earth's inverse (the meek shall inherit the earth, and so on), but on an individual basis heaven will be earth's extension.

Rossetti's own devotional prose is preoccupied with arrangement. *Time Flies* is organized by the Christian Calendar, *Letter and Spirit* (1883) is guided by the Ten Commandments, and *The Face of the Deep* is sequentially ordered by each chapter and verse of Revelation. Yet within these ordered structures are many digressions and 'divergences', which draw attention to those contrasts between light and dark, growth and decay, which make up the very fabric of lived experience. Additionally, the somewhat fractured structure of the prose serves the purpose of illustrating the problems of fallen language, of the inability of the mediated to express fully the original. The structure of Rossetti's prose resists dogmatism because it is halting, unstable, and unsure in its project to give order to the earth's 'divergences' and contradictions.

Rossetti's devotional work, if mentioned critically, is often discussed in terms of the poet's biography, but it serves a literary function as well. The prose is most notable for the way in which it overtly instructs readers how to read Christianity, and implicitly how to read Christina Rossetti. As Arseneau and Marsh comment,

> while William Michael's tendency to arrange Rossetti's poems chronologically probably fueled the biographical/amatory approach that has so dominated Rossetti criticism in the past, what the original volume structures reveal is a poet whose aim is not self-revelation but rather the guidance of the reader's response to her work, an observation which is supported by evidence found in the devotional pieces.[10]

The prefatory note to *The Face of the Deep* reveals the book's instructive purpose, as Rossetti invites the reader to go below the surface of the text: 'If thou canst dive, bring up pearls. If thou canst not dive, collect amber' (7). This introductory sentence is mysterious and abrupt, its metaphor hovering on the page without a clear referent. Such ambiguity allows it to have at least a double reference: to the primary text of Revelation and to Rossetti's secondary text about Revelation. This parable is about reading, the kind that takes place both above and below the surface. Bringing up pearls requires a dive below the face of the deep, while collecting amber takes place on the surface of the earth. While pearl diving is privileged, amber collecting is still seen as a valuable pursuit. 'Though I fail to identify Paradisiacal "bdellium," I still may hope to search out beauties of the "onyx stone", Rossetti continues, strengthening the association between paradise and the pearl, and earth and amber.[11]

In order to 'collect' knowledge and understanding, readers should regard earthly objects (amber, onyx, texts) as metaphorical lessons, as earthly translations of heavenly objects. The text enacts its own metaphor of reading below the surface by secretly providing the identity of 'bdellium' in its first sentence. Yet Rossetti is careful not to discourage less exegetical kinds of readings: if readers do not recognize the 'Paradisiacal "bdellium"' they 'still may hope to search out beauties' of recognizable, earthly onyx. Diving below the surface of the text through theology and exegesis is recommended, but not essential for understanding. Or rather, understanding is not as essential as the thought process itself. 'It is nobler to believe than to understand', Rossetti writes (46). Belief in God is a noble act because it involves a faith in the unseen, the imagined and the imaginative.

Later, in reference to the Ethiopian Eunuch,[12] Rossetti, echoing the language of her prefatory note, affirms her faith in readerly potential:

> it already was his in a measure to enjoy, respond to, improve, even before his father in God [Philip] preached Christ unto him. What could he do before that moment? He could study and pray, he could cherish hope, exercise love, feel after Him Whom as yet he could not intelligently find.
>
> So much at least we all can do who read, or who hear, this Book of Revelations: thus claiming, and by God's bounty inheriting, the covenanted blessing of such readers and hearers.
>
> (12)

Here, feeling is as important as knowing, praying to God as important as finding Him. Just as those who cannot identify paradisiacal bdellium can still 'hope' to explore earthly onyx stone, the Eunuch, before his conversion, can still 'cherish hope' to 'improve' spiritually. If readers accept guidance (John's in Revelation and Rossetti's in her commentary on Revelation) as the Ethiopian did, those who may not always understand what they read can still 'feel after Him Whom as yet' they cannot 'intelligently find'.

Following the example of Philip and John, Rossetti wants to guide her readers through Revelation, to instruct them on how to understand what they read, using both the Biblical text and her own text. As Arseneau and Marsh point out, 'The pattern of reading an early section in light of a later one is central to much of Rossetti's practice in her devotional prose, for her approach to the Bible is markedly typological' (21). Rossetti's 'pattern of writing' is itself a literary enactment of the typological way in which she believes the Bible ought to be read. The work acts as both instruction and example, a kind of literary proof in which the mutually reinforcing capabilities of practicing and preaching

are demonstrated. Robert Kachur notes that the Apocalypse was of particular interest to Rossetti because it contains not only 'allegorical
images which can be decoded', but also 'divine poetry which provides
endless opportunities for increasingly intimate, mystical encounters
with God Himself'.[13] Rossetti's devotional 'problem' is to maintain
divine mystery while engaged in a project of exegetical decoding.

The book's mixture of poetry and prose is a literary solution to this theological dilemma. This is made clear in the first page of the book when
the prefatory note identifies the lesson of Revelation as patience, then
illustrates the lesson of patience with a poem, 'O, ye who love today'. Its
appearance in the prefatory note is significant because beginnings are
important to Rossetti. In *Time Flies* she writes that 'The hardest step is at
the threshold' and 'That which is *done* has a beginning (*TF* 4).

The importance of beginnings is not at all inconsistent with the
themes of *The Face of the Deep* because, though the book deals with the
end of life on earth, it is the beginning of life in heaven, what Rossetti
calls 'the endless end, the end which is the final beginning' (*FD* 383).
We should expect powerful imaginings of the end at the beginning of
the book, and this is exactly what we get — perhaps more than we bar-
gained for:

> A dear saint — I speak under correction of the Judgment of the
> Great Day, yet think not then to have my word corrected — this dear
> person once pointed out to me Patience as our lesson in the Book of
> Revelations.
>
> Following the clue thus afforded me, I seek and hope to find
> Patience in this Book of awful import. Patience, at the least: and along
> with that grace whatever treasures beside God may vouchsafe me.
>
> (7)

The 'dear saint' is probably her sister Maria, who also appears as 'One of
the dearest and most saintly persons I ever knew' in *Time Flies* (213).
The source of Rossetti's 'clue' for the 'lesson' of Revelation here is not a
canonized saint, but a private one. In turn — in one of her most daring
rhetorical gestures — she affirms the validity of her private judgment of
salvation. The 'end' of her sister's life has been gained by anticipation,
by the power of 'my word'.

The sorrowful notes of hope and grace in the prefatory note, together
with its assumption of authority in language, echo in the book's first
poem, which takes patience as its theme. The metaphor on which it
turns is one of light and darkness. The poem advocates not only an

earthly understanding of the necessity of darkness to perceive light, but also a spiritual understanding about the divine function of metaphor itself. As Kachur writes about High Church teachings, 'it is poetic language, rather than literal language, which comes closest to communicating divine realities which transcend earthly experience' (3). The Bible is Rossetti's lexicon of divine language while metaphor is its earthly vehicle, as poetic language itself becomes a metaphor for how humanity understands the divine.

> O, ye who love to-day,
> Turn away
> From Patience with her silver ray:
> For Patience shows a twilight face,
> Like a half-lighted moon
> When daylight dies apace.
>
> But ye who love to-morrow,
> Beg or borrow
> To-day some bitterness of sorrow :
> For Patience shows a lustrous face
> In depth of night her noon;
> Then to her sun gives place.
>
> (*FD* 7; Crump, 2: 248–9)

Like the prose portion of the prefatory note, the poem addresses the reader both directly and indirectly. The poem's first line can be read simultaneously as a description of the state of being of those 'who love to-day' and as an order for them. This sense of double meaning persists in the treatment of today and tomorrow. 'To-day' and 'to-morrow' rely on their literal definition and on the poetic understanding of the concept of time which they represent. Those who love to-day love both in the present and love the present itself, while those who love to-morrow love both in the future and love the future itself. Each stanza describes the condition of loving to-day and to-morrow, but the implicit subject 'you' of their second lines is suggestive of command. The doubleness of the syntax strengthens the poet's authority: she both sees things as they are, and 'orders' them in language.

The poem's complexity is maintained through imagery and ideology as well as being enacted in its structure. Patience itself is a metaphor for mediated vision; it recognizes the 'sorrow' of reflected light, yet acknowledges that this same sorrow is necessary to anticipate the arrival of direct

light. Rossetti creates patience as an inverted world whose noon is in the
depth of night, and whose sorrow is the joy of anticipation. The first
stanza represents the earthly world, the world of the present, where light
is associated with day, and darkness night. The second stanza represents
an inverted world seen through 'supernaturalized' eyes, a world concen-
trated on the future, where the light that is perceived through darkness
foretells the coming 'sun'. The movements of sun and moon in the first
stanza also have to do with an earthly concept of time coming to an end
which is death, while the second locates time within the eternal 'tomorrow', which is life after death, when the sun (an allusion to the Son of
God) will come again. This second stanza is consistent with Rossetti's
desire, expressed in *Time Flies*, to 'redeem the time' by concentrating on
the eternal, rather than the temporal, by making earth 'the race-course',
not 'the goal'. The second stanza's view of time is further articulated in
a later prose passage:

> What is time? It is not subtracted from eternity, which if diminished
> would fall short of being eternal: neither is it substituted awhile for
> eternity, which thus would assume both end and beginning: neither
> is it simultaneous with eternity, because it is in Him Who inhabiteth
> eternity (not time) that we ourselves day by day live and move and
> have our being. Perhaps I shall not mislead my own thoughts by
> defining to myself time as that condition or aspect of eternity which
> consists with the possibility of probation.
>
> (FD 278)

Trying to conceive of eternity by thinking about time is an impossibility because time is an experience of the fallen, 'a condition or aspect of
eternity'. If such indeed be time', Rossetti writes, 'then in part I understand how at length there shall be time no longer' (278). Time is not an
illusion, but a *subordinate* reality, dependent on the absolute reality of
eternity. Time is only 'a condition or aspect of eternity', because it is only
a representation, a fallen understanding of eternity, which those who
have patience realize. Those in the inverted world of the poem who 'love
to-morrow', choose to love not time, but eternity, not the contingent, but
the absolute. The central paradox of the poem (depth of night=noon),
points to the greater paradox at the heart of the poem; that what humanity sees is appearance, but what humanity feels is reality. Just as those
'who love to-day' in the first stanza have to imagine the daylight dying
away (this event does not actually take place in the poem), so do those in
the second stanza who 'love to-morrow' have to imagine the coming sun

in darkness. The first instance is an image of warning, the second of redemption, but both are equally dependent on 'supernaturalized vision', on imagining what is not there in a concrete sense. The poem's imagined events, daylight dying or the sun rising, are the basis of its argument, reaffirming its paradoxical belief in the reality of the abstract.

Rossetti also writes that 'no break will occur between time and eternity', confirming that, although humanity's perception of time is based on a false representation of divine time (eternity), time and eternity are not mutually exclusive. Time cannot be subtracted from, substituted for, or simultaneous with eternity, because it is not a separate dimension. The richness of this deeply paradoxical approach to time and eternity is illustrated in the structure of the poem, when a break occurs between the first and second stanzas (earthly time and divine time), yet they remain linked by rhyme scheme (aaabcb). The poem accepts our human inability to understand fully the design of Providence — hence the need for patience — yet affirms our ability to explore the boundaries of our condition. Humanity's fallen logic is the cause of its 'bitterness', but Rossetti suggests that humanity's 'sorrow' at its inability to experience directly the divine proves that its connection to the divine still exists. This connection is made through the world, through things like the moon and the sun which represent divine presence / absence, and which seek to illustrate unknowable concepts like eternity. The idea of the unknowable is ever present in the poem, with its paradoxes of night and day, its abrupt, jerky syntax, disorienting rhyme scheme, and the delayed gratification of its imagined arrival of the sun. The deliberately complex structure and paradoxical ideology of 'O, ye who love today' requires patience (the very virtue it advocates) of its reader, making it a self-consciously appropriate prefatory poem for a book whose mission is to inspire its readers 'to seek and hope to find Patience'.

Rossetti uses the Tractarian strategy of communicating divine reality through poetic language, yet this is not to suggest that her program, in this poem and in the larger text of *The Face of The Deep*, leaves literal language behind. Tractarian writers such as Newman and, most notably, Keble, did not leave literal language behind either; their belief in dogma was too insistent for their writing to abandon literalism. Rossetti, however, does not try to assert the authority of the literal didactically. Rather, she challenges the authority of *both* poetic and literal language by focusing attention on the ambiguities created by their intersection. The resultant ambiguity is itself a metaphor for the fallen human condition, for how humanity lives in and tries to understand a world both separate from and deeply connected to God. This literary approach is writ large over the text of *The Face of the Deep*, whose combined earthly prose and poetry interacts with divine biblical text.

Newman was fond of saying that the heart is reached not by reason but by dogma, but Rossetti's poem certainly resists this idea. 'O, ye who love to-day', works as an exercise in patience, but also in free will, because it presents readers with choices. The poem's disorienting lack of purely dogmatic language and consequent resistance to resolution means that readers can choose whether to identify with the lovers of to-day or to-morrow, whether or not to have patience for tomorrow and for the poem itself. Choice is one of patience's most important characteristics, as Rossetti makes clear when she writes that patience is not available 'unless our own free will co-operate with God's pre-disposing grace' (26). The pre-apocalyptic world of *The Face of the Deep* is both troubled and comforted by the idea of free will, as the concept can allow for both understanding and misinterpretation. 'O, ye who love to-day' is a poem troubled by the attraction to and possibility of rejecting patience and living for today, in a way that the more dogmatic works of the Tractarians, like Keble, are not.

Didacticism is too direct for Rossetti's theology. Since mankind inhabits a fallen world, it must be represented by a fallen word. The word that just repeats itself to assert its authority ignores free will, ignores the mediated, the interpretative. Word and understanding can both mean the same thing, but only in heaven can this concept fully be realized. Rossetti's departure from dogmatic language is not only a theological choice, but a poetic one as well.

In her personal life, perhaps she was more dogmatic, as William Michael notes in his 'Memoir'. However, contemplation and meditation, not necessarily resolution, is the goal of Rossetti's devotional work, which is why it is a mistake to say that she 'fails to see contradiction'. What she is doing is redirecting the human impulse to conclude and resolve (after all, for Rossetti, resolution and unity can only take place in heaven). Life on earth is not a mystery to be solved, but a lesson to be absorbed. The human quest should not be for absolute answers (answers are for God), but for wisdom. She warns against 'scrutinizing any text of Holy Scripture as if it were a puzzle or a riddle'. She also does not want to '[make] guesses at what is withheld from me'. Rather, she recommends '[turning] intellectual poverty into voluntary spiritual poverty' in order to 'transmute ignorance into wisdom' (350). By reading contradiction as a symptom of man's fallen state she tries to render it powerless as an argument against her theology. Contemplation may create questions and inconsistencies, but does not have the arrogance to 'make guesses' or solve puzzles. Ignorance can be transmuted into a kind of wisdom through self-knowledge, and knowledge of the self in relation to God. Contemplation, for Rossetti, is both the search for wisdom and wisdom itself.

Christ is a sympathetic figure for Rossetti because he is fully human *and* divine, the embodiment of earthly and heavenly contradiction, and the embodiment of its resolution. Rossetti writes of Christ as the saints' 'pattern and text-book of patience; because He bore contradiction of sinners, so did they; because He, when He was reviled, reviled not again, neither did they; because He prayed for His enemies, they likewise prayed for theirs' (116). Rossetti sees Christ as both teacher and the embodiment of his teachings. He did not create a heavenly / earthly stalemate by reacting to human contradiction with further contradiction, but rather taught through parable and example. This responsive approach would appeal to a religious thinker like Rossetti, because, while still mindful of humanity's inferiority, it shows an empathetic respect for human intelligence and imagination. She praises Christ's 'veritable and accessible Humanity which He assumed, which can be touched with a feeling of our infirmities' (36).

Following the example of Christ, *The Face of the Deep* tries itself to be both pattern and textbook, which is why its exegesis can be, as Harrison puts it, 'elaborate (and sometimes strained)'.[14] This elaborate and strained quality should interest biographical critics because it reveals so much about Rossetti's literary aspirations and practices. As a self-appointed translator of the word of God, Rossetti is as self-conscious about her confidence in her ability as she is about her responsibility as a Christian woman writer:

> St. Paul has written: "Let the woman learn in silence with all subjection. But I suffer not a woman to teach." Yet elsewhere he wrote: "I call to remembrance the unfeigned faith ... which dwelt first in thy grandmother Lois, and thy mother Eunice."
>
> (*FD* 195)

Here Rossetti has taken issue with a contradiction within the Bible, not to challenge divine edict, but to highlight human error. By juxtaposing two quotations from St. Paul, she uses his own words to subvert his argument. She continues that:

> To expound prophecy lies of course beyond my power, and not within my wish. But the symbolic forms of prophecy being set before all

eyes, must be so set for some purpose: to investigate them may not make us wise as serpents; yet ought by promoting faith, fear, hope, love, to aid in making us harmless as doves.

(195)

Rossetti implies that her investigation of scripture and its relation to the world is in some way divinely ordained. She tries to distance her project from any association with Eve's quest for knowledge, appealing to a different motivation. Whereas Eve sought wisdom for personal gain, Rossetti's investigation is for the purposes of promoting Christianity. She quotes Habbakuk 2:2 in her defense: '"Write the vision, and make it plain upon tables, that he may run that readeth it": — God, helping us, we all great and small can and will run' (195).

On 1 January 1881, she writes to Dante Gabriel of 'one's own responsibility in use of an influential talent', and states, 'I dont't [*sic*] think harm will accrue from my S.P.C.K. books even to my standing: if it did, I should still be glad to throw my grains of dust into the religious scale' (*Letters* 2: 257). Rossetti is working on the assumption that she can 'bring up pearls' from beneath the face of the deep, an assumption which troubles her because of its possible association with the sin of pride. Even at the end of her life, 40 years after she composed *Maude*, Rossetti is still trying to reconcile her religious feeling with her desire to write. Bracketed cautions, in which she makes clear that '[I write under correction: I repudiate my own thoughts if erroneous]', are scattered throughout the text (*FD* 125). However, such disclaimers paradoxically reinforce Rossetti's authority. In acknowledging the possibility of error, she forestalls criticism. This strategy is assertive because it implies that her thoughts, even if erroneous, are worth expressing, and, by implication, worth reading. The confidence of her exegesis, as well as the physical reality of the text, belies the submissiveness of her disclaimers. Even the disclaimers' structure, brief and bracketed, suggests a reluctant afterthought. As Westerholm observes, 'having gained a readership with her disclaimers of authority, Rossetti engaged in ... serious and scholarly biblical interpretation, assuming a man's role according to the standards of the time'.[15] According to Hobbs, 'Rossetti's resolute self-deprecation results in the generation of "power out of holiness": an authority, arising from devout self-discipline, that revises religious models from a female perspective' (Hobbs, 416).

Rossetti takes advantage of the slippage between what her text *does* and what it *says* it's doing, not only to preempt criticism for taking a masculine role, but also to preempt self-censure. The self-consciousness of her devotional writings comes not only from a wish to avoid social offence, but devotional offence as well. Her prose is concerned not only about assuming a man's role, but also about Man's role in general in devotional self-expression. Self-expression, she is painfully aware, can be at cross-purposes with Christian mission.

Her prose manages to be both self-effacing and insistently self-justifying, expressing what Harrison calls her 'irrepressible belief in the power of God's Word and the value of renouncing the nonspiritual satisfactions of this world in favor of imitating Christ by mediating God's Word through her own verbal art' (101). The word of God, and her words' relationship to it, preoccupies her prose. In *The Face of the Deep* she discusses the word of God via a meditation on the Epistle of the Hebrews:

> "The word of God is quick, and powerful, and sharper than any two-edged sword, piercing even to the dividing asunder of soul and spirit, and of the joints and marrow, and is a discerner of the thoughts and intents of the heart."
>
> Four points I note: life, keenness, in the weapon; depth, subtilty, in the wound. That which probes and sunders me will never of its own proper nature slay me; for life it is, not death, that thus cleaves its way into my heart of hearts. It will do its work exquisitely, for it is sharp; and thoroughly by reason of the might and skill of Him Who wields it. It may not spare for my crying; nevertheless not a hair of my head need perish, and dear is my blood in His sight Who smites me.
>
> No mere surface work can possibly be this saving work of which the text speaks: a religion without depth is not Christ's religion.
>
> (37)

The image of God's word as a sword with which He 'probes and sunders' to '[discern] the thoughts and intents of the heart' is frightening and aggressive. The suggestion that God's word literally can '[cleave] its way into' a human 'heart of hearts' gives a violent immediacy to language. On Judgment Day, the word will no longer be mediated through the world, but will exist simultaneously as signifier and signified. Just as human souls will be liberated, so too will language itself. Rossetti is reminding readers here that for God, word and action are the same, and that language released from mediation is a dangerous thing.

In writing that 'mere surface work' cannot be 'this saving work of which the text *speaks*', (emphasis mine) Rossetti is not only making a theological point about the literal power of God's word, but is also presenting a literary justification of her devotional project. In *The Face of the Deep*, Rossetti reconciles artistic creativity and religion through the idea of unity of purpose. Artistic talent, if used for the promotion of Christianity, can be divorced from ego and pride. She quotes Revelation 1:19, 'Write the things which thou hast seen, and the things which are, and the things which shall be hereafter'. Rossetti adapts this quotation to her own purposes by decontextualizing it slightly, interpreting it typologically by placing it in relation, not only to John as an apostle, but to herself as a writer:

> "Write" — not any ecstasy of thy love even in this moment of reunion. "Write" — little for the indulgence of thine own heart, unless it be meat and drink to thee to do the Will of Him that sendeth thee, and to finish His work. "Write" that which shall glorify God, edify the Church, bear witness against the world. John the beloved and the true lover could endure this word: if it seems cold and disappointing to us, it seems so because we have not yet the mind of St. John; much less the mind of Christ.
>
> (45)

With a characteristic blend of self-assurance and humility, Rossetti tries to rescue writing from its earthly associations by imbuing it with holy purpose. Though she cautions against vain writing for 'the indulgence of thine own heart', she implies that her writing is the will of God, and that her project is 'to finish His work'. Though one sentence advocates writing 'against the world', the next states that if the *word* 'seems cold and disappointing to us', it is only because we do not have the mind of John or Christ (emphasis mine). This passage tries so earnestly to reconcile its contradictions (Christian humility / artistic pride, the world / heaven, the world / the word) that it succeeds in creating more questions than providing answers. As self-oblating as the passage tries to be, ultimately it is asserting that its author has the mind of John or Christ, and that her book is doing God's work.

Words in the absence of God are words without meaning, are all surface and no depth. The word of God, unlike the word of man, has immediate agency, has power to make a world over the face of the deep. Human language, if it is to participate in this power, must do so through the medium of belief. Without God, both mankind and human language will be emptied of significance. Existence without meaning is true death, as Rossetti implies in her short poem, 'As froth on the face of the deep'. She introduces it by recalling Genesis 1:3, 'Say once again, yea, say again and again, Let there be light: and there shall be light'. The speaker here, however, is not Old Testament Jehovah, but Christ, and Rossetti is asking him to 'call Thy dead out of darkness of death into the light of life'. That the speaker should be Christ is significant here because Christ is the link between earth and heaven, between Man and God. The difference between his calling for light and the Old Testament God's original calling for light is that God's purpose was creative where Christ's is redemptive. The poem which follows is not 'against the world', but rather against the world divorced from God, against a surface-world:

> As froth on the face of the deep,
>   As foam on the crest of the sea,
> As dreams at the waking of sleep,
>   As gourd of a day and a night,
> As harvest that no man shall reap,
>   As vintage that never shall be,
> Is hope if it cling not aright,
>   O my God unto Thee.

(FD 88; Crump, 2: 264)

Just as the biblical face of the deep was void without the spirit of God, so too is everything in the world empty of lasting significance if it is not connected to God. Ephemerality here is characterized not by its link to the earth, but by its disconnection from the divine. This is an important distinction, as Rossetti's earth is not an inherently 'surface' thing. Because it is connected with the divine, 'earth holds heaven in the bud' (185). The earth is divinity's mediated way of communicating with man, and it is man's failure to perceive this connection, his / her tendency to read only the world's surface, which is corrupting. In this poem, failure to perceive metaphor equals death; literal death, the death of the imagination, and spiritual death. The only way for man, for language, and for imagination to escape death is through connection to God.

The importance of metaphor is emphasized structurally through the interaction of similes within the poem. The word 'as', at the beginning of each line creates a pileup of unresolved imagery. Each individual simile links two things (froth / deep, foam / sea, dreams / waking) within each line, but the syntax resists resolution, every 'as' leading only to the next 'as'. The similes are connected to each other within the poem, but their common referent is held back until the final line which connects all with God. This sense of false or delayed resolution enacts the poem's theme of the fruitlessness of a search for meaning in the absence of God.

To help the reader understand the surface, Rossetti makes him / her aware of its connection with depth, both literally and literarily. Froth, foam, dreams, gourd, harvest, and vintage are linked thematically by their temporality, structurally by their placement, and linguistically by the word 'as' which precedes them, and 'hope', their final referent.[16] The significance of these things is determined by their arrangement, by their relation to their surroundings within both the world as God created it and the world of the poem. When the images move from the earthly to the abstract (from froth to hope), it seems at first that the promised resolution of the extended simile has been delivered. However, 'hope' is still an earthly practice, and if it does not 'cling to' God, it is as ephemeral as 'froth'. The poetic imagery itself remains bounded by the world, by the cycle of life and death, until it is released through connection to God.[17]

Rossetti's earthly examples of surface and depth relation suggest that exploring connections between things on earth cannot keep meaning itself from acting as 'froth on the face of the deep'. There is a Tractarian agenda at work here in the analogical treatment of nature, and in the poem's literary ambition; to reclaim poetry itself as sanctified. Rossetti presents metaphor in poetry as spiritually instructive, operating on the assumption that readers who perceive connections in the world the poem represents will be able then to make those connections in their own world. This view is at once exclusive and inclusive, as Rossetti tries to reconcile love of the earth with longing for God, and more importantly, poetic aspiration with Christian duty.

The prose passage immediately following this poem explores further the connection between the literary and the divine, quoting from the Revised Version, Revelation 3:2, "I have found no works of thine fulfilled before My God." Rossetti writes that this 'suggests works left incomplete even according to the standard of human completeness; beginnings broken off short, starts without careers, wishes instead of resolves, repentances still to be repented of' (*FD* 88). Rossetti's interpretation of this sentence is dependent on a double meaning in 'works' and in 'before'. 'Works' refers to human endeavors, but Rossetti discusses such works in language also suggestive of literary endeavor; 'beginnings broken off short', and 'starts without careers'. Just as the hope described in the first seven lines of her poem cannot be fulfilled without God, so too are human works unfulfilled 'before' (in front of) and 'before' (prior to, without) God.[18] Examination of the self and of the world exclusive of God results in literal and literary death. Before the poem, Rossetti writes,

We, every one of us, must at this moment be either dead or alive. Let us put it at the worst, and postulate that we are dead: what shall we do that we may come again to our border, and return into the land of the living? Sardis[19] was bidden "strengthen those things which remain, that are ready to die": whence it follows: This do, and thou shalt live. And what if gazing within we discern nothing remaining; nothing even so far alive as to be ready to die? We still can lift up our eyes and look without ...

(87–8)

Here death is equated with not looking, with ceasing to gaze within and without for evidence of the divine. Examination of the self and the world and how both relate to God is a redemptive act, according to Rossetti, and she goes on to illustrate this idea poetically in 'As froth on the face of the deep'. This passage not only wants to redeem humanity, but human expression as well, and acts as a justification for the existence of poetry. The poem itself becomes evidence of life, an attempt to 'strengthen those things which remain' in the world by linking them to God.

After the poem, Rossetti writes of Lot's wife, 'the son in the Parable', and the 'leafy but figless' fruit tree, refiguring them to defend self-examination. 'We look out of ourselves at these and such as these. God help us to look into ourselves, lest all the while we be such as they and know it not' (89). In losing their sense of community, of their place in the world and of their closeness to God, these figures, like the people of Sardis, lost themselves. Humanity must both look within and without in order to perceive itself and its sanctified relationship to God, just as Rossetti's poem looks within itself and without in order to have its meaning redeemed by God in its final line. Such perception must happen through metaphor because of the ineffability of God. Rossetti realizes that metaphor, as a fallen form of understanding, is frustrating for humanity. Helena Michie writes that Rossetti '[claimed] for metaphorical language a doubled distance from the origin, the signified, the authoritative truth', and that 'written language, twice removed from its referent' is seen to be 'further fallen'.[20] This sense of doubled distance from God is frustrating and painful for humanity, and is the sorrow inherent in Rossetti's understanding of patience. A few lines before 'As froth' she writes: 'If the light that is in us be as darkness that must be felt, let us work and walk by the light that is without us; until the day dawn, and the day-star arise in our hearts' (88). This sentence recalls Rossetti's treatment of patience in her prefatory note, in which perception is reliant on the patient contemplation of contrast.

The 'light that is without us' has a double-meaning which turns on the word 'without', which can mean both 'outside' and 'not with'. God is 'the light' without man, and the world stands 'without' (outside) man as the signifier of His absence. The biggest imaginative hurdle for man is relating to a God whom he is 'without' on earth. This pained sense of separation, the knowledge of the Fall, creates the darkness in man, a darkness defined by an absence of light. This is a darkness doubled because, unlike the darkness upon the face of the deep (the uncreated world) in Genesis, man's darkness is not one of ignorance, but of knowledge. Because of his Old Testament origins in Paradise, and the New Testament arrival / departure of Christ, man perceives darkness as an indication, not that God has never been, but that He has left. This absence, felt by contrast and expressed as darkness, can also be used to humanity's advantage. Because 'darkness reveals more luminaries than does the day', darkness in man provides the contrast necessary to perceive the light of God in the world (116). Because fallen man achieves devotional experience through contrast, through metaphor, s / he needs darkness within to perceive the light without.

Rossetti locates darkness in humanity and light in God, who expresses Himself through the mediated reality of the world. The world is not inherently corrupt; rather it is man's perception of the world, his / her fallen imagination, which can be corrosive.

> What is the world? Wherein resides its harmfulness, snare, pollution? Left to itself it is neither harmful, ensnaring, nor polluting. It becomes all this as the passive agent, passive vehicle if I may so call it, of the devil, man's outside tempter, and of the flesh, man's inside tempter. There is no inherent evil in cedar and vermilion ... nay, nor in sumptuous fare, in down, silk, apes, ivory, or peacocks. St. Peter himself objects not to hair, gold, apparel, but to women's misuse of them. An alabaster box of precious ointment becomes good or bad simply according to the use it is put to. Through envy of the devil death came into the world, and man hath sought out many inventions; but the heavens and the earth, and all the host of them when made and finished were beheld to be "very good."
>
> (333)

Later in the passage she concludes, 'the world is a stage, the flesh an actor, the devil prompter and scene-shifter'. Here, the world as a metaphor is made vulnerable to misinterpretation through its 'doubled distance from the origin', (as the world is to heaven, a stage is to the world). The world is the subject, the 'passive vehicle', whose meaning can be misinterpreted, polluted by man's fallen imagination. The temptation to misread or ignore the lessons of the world comes from both the inside, the flesh, and the outside, the devil. The world's vulnerability to the force of man's free will and the devil's manipulation renders it a passive setting where good and evil will play out; a stage. This metaphor of the stage should not be read as a criticism of art, but as a criticism of misinterpretation. 'Christ exchanged heaven for earth to enable man to exchange earth for heaven. Hast Thou done that for me, and will I not do this for Thee?' Rossetti writes, lamenting man's tendency to prefer the mediated to the real (333). Rossetti's vision faults neither world nor stage for 'harmfulness' and 'pollution', but man's 'inventions'.

Rossetti balances this view of man's harmful inventions with the use of a parable praising women's inventiveness. Accounts of the 'alabaster box of precious ointment'[21] appear in Matthew, Mark, and Luke, and Rossetti uses elements of all three. In Luke 7, a woman sinner anoints Christ: '[she] stood at his feet behind him weeping, and began to wash his feet with tears, and did wipe them with the hairs of her head, and kissed his feet, and anointed them with ointment' (Luke 7:37). When Simon is taken aback that Christ allows himself to be touched by a sinner, Christ chastises him.

> Thou gavest me no kiss: but this woman since the time I came in hath not ceased to kiss my feet.
> My head with oil thou didst not anoint: but this woman hath anointed my feet with ointment.
> Wherefore I say unto thee, Her sins, which are many, are forgiven; for she loved much: but to whom little is forgiven, the same loveth little ...
> And he said to the woman, Thy faith hath saved thee; go in peace.
> (Luke 7:45–7, 50)

In this case, the woman's use of precious ointment to express love for Christ is rewarded with forgiveness of her sins. The explicit connection of human love with divine forgiveness is an exclusive feature of the expanded story in Luke. In Matthew and Mark, the disciples' objection to the woman's actions is not based on her sinful status, but on her waste of expensive ointment which they think should be sold and the proceeds given to the poor. Christ then points out that the woman 'hath wrought a good work upon me', and so 'Wheresoever this gospel shall be preached in the whole world, there shall also this, that this woman hath done, be told for a memorial of her' (Matthew 26:10, 13). In Luke, however, the story becomes about how divine forgiveness is proportional to human love. The woman, in doing all she can for Christ, is honored in Matthew and Mark and forgiven in Luke.

Also, in Rossetti's hands, these different versions become a parable about the dangers of human misinterpretation. By concentrating on the material value of the ointment, rather than on the spiritual value of the woman's gesture, the disciples in Matthew and Mark are distracted from their own duties to Christ. Simon too neglects his obligations to Christ by thinking that the woman's 'good work' is negated by her sin. Rossetti's passage continues, 'Lord Christ ... give us grace never to judge our neighbour rashly, whilst one by one we ourselves endeavour to learn and perform Thy will' (*FD* 333). She implies that Simon has learned his lesson with her allusion to Peter, who 'objects not to hair, gold, apparel, but to women's misuse of them'.[22] Rossetti constructs an anti-materialist critique with her juxtaposition of Christ's words in Luke and Peter's advice to wives. However, her argument stresses that 'there is no inherent evil' in material goods, only 'good' or 'bad' use of them.

The emphasis in *The Face of the Deep* on the pitfalls of human misinterpretation and misuse of divine doctrine reinforces the author's concerns in *Time Flies* about 'translations of the letter in defiance of the spirit' (*TF* 2). The idea of the world as a translation means that it is made vulnerable to misinterpretation by man, not that it is inherently corrupt. At the same time, mankind is equally capable of interpreting the lessons of the earth correctly, and determining his / her relationship with the earth. 'Man is a microcosm:', Rossetti writes; 'a microcosm may be either a miniature heaven or a miniature hell' (349). Humanity's essential make-up, the fact that it is 'designed in some sort and in miniature to become like [God]', gives it as much potential for joy as it does for sorrow, and for goodness as well as evil (105). Because humanity must experience God through the medium of the world, earth is in the paradoxical position of obstacle and gateway, and it is this duality which concerns Rossetti:

> But that word *the world* is frequently used to denote a great portion of the human race. How little must I love the world? How much may I love it? — Love it to the fulness of thy heart's desire, so thou love it with self-sacrifice; for thus to love it is after the Mind of God, the Pattern of Christ ...
>
> (332)

Loving the world, which this passage also connects to loving 'the word', is not necessarily a sin, but can be in fact a demonstration of faith, an imitation of Christ.

The Face of the Deep complicates the 'renunciatory aesthetic' with which Rossetti is often credited. 'Dreadful were it simply to be shut up with self in the darkness of a grave-like solitude', she writes (550). Following the divine precedent set by Christ, each Christian must first engage with the world in order to transcend it. Rossetti's exegesis of Revelation consistently stresses that humanity's place in heaven is determined by its relationship to the things and the people of the earth. She reads Revelation as a book which, rather than condemning or renouncing the world, teaches mankind to redeem the earth and itself. Ultimately, 'our perfection there has to be developed out of our imperfection here' (185). Though it is temporary, the earth is not inherently evil or corrupting because it 'holds heaven in the bud'.

Notes

Introduction

1. 'But if I were bringing a case against God [Christina Rossetti] is one of the first witnesses I should call ... First she starved herself of love, which meant also life; then of poetry in deference to what she thought religion demanded'. *Virginia Woolf Diaries*, vol. 1 1915–19, ed. A. O. Bell (London: Hogarth Press, 1977), p. 178.
2. Virginia Woolf, *The Common Reader, Second Series* (London: Hogarth Press, 1932), p. 242.
3. Germaine Greer, *Slip-Shod Sibyls: Recognition, Rejection, and the Woman Poet* (London: Viking, 1995), p. 359.
4. Betty S. Flowers, introduction to *The Complete Poems*, ed. R. W. Crump (London: Penguin, 2001), xlvii.
5. WMR identifies 'one serious flaw' in his sister's 'admirable character — she was by far over-scrupulous' (*Memoir* lxviii).
6. WMR, preface to *New Poems by Christina Rossetti, Hitherto Unpublished or Uncollected* (London: Macmillan 1900), p. xii.
7. Lynda Palazzo, *Christina Rossetti's Feminist Theology* (Basingstoke: Palgrave, 2002), p. 23.
8. Colleen Hobbs, 'A View from "The Lowest Place": Christina Rossetti's Devotional Prose', *Victorian Poetry* 32 (autumn-winter 1994) 409.
9. Robert M. Kachur, 'Repositioning the Female Christian Reader: Christina Rossetti as Tractarian Hermeneut in *The Face of the Deep*', *Victorian Poetry* 35, no. 2 (summer 1997) 1.
10. Stuart Curran, 'The Lyric Voice of Christina Rossetti', *Victorian Poetry* 9 (autumn 1971) 298.
11. *The Penguin Book of Victorian Verse*, ed. Daniel Karlin (London: Penguin, 1998). This evaluation is clear from the table of contents, and has been confirmed to me by the editor.
12. Gosse, Edmund. 'Christina Rossetti', *The Century Magazine* 46 (June 1893) 216.
13. Mary F. Sandars, introduction to *The Life of Christina Rossetti* (London: Hutchinson, 1930), p. 15.

14. Jerome McGann, 'The Religious Poetry of Christina Rossetti', *The Beauty of Inflections: Literary Investigations In Historical Method and Theory* (Oxford: Clarendon, 1985) p. 210.
15. Linda E. Marshall, 'Mysteries Beyond Angels in Christina Rossetti's *From House to Home*' in *Women's Poetry, Late Romantic to Late Victorian*, eds. Isobel Armstrong and Virginia Blain (London: Macmillan, 1999), p. 313.
16. Mary Arseneau, introduction to *Recovering Christina Rossetti: Female Community and Incarnational Poetics* (Basingstoke: Palgrave, 2004), p. 3.
17. Christina Rossetti, *Maude: Prose and Verse*, edited with an introduction by R. W. Crump, including a 'Prefatory Note' by William Michael Rossetti (Hamden, Archon Books, 1976), p. 31.
18. *VDP*, 203.

1 'Real Things Unseen': The tractarian influence

1. Jerome J. McGann, introduction to *ACR*, p. 8.
2. F. M. L. Thompson, *The Rise of Respectable Society: A Social History of Victorian Britain,1830–1900* (London: Fontana Press, 1988), pp. 251, 252.
3. Tom Paulin, 'The cadence in the song: George Herbert and the greatness of Christina Rossetti', *Times Literary Supplement*, (January 18, 2002) 3.
4. Lynda Palazzo, *Christina Rossetti's Feminist Theology* (Basingstoke: Palgrave, 2002), p. 2.
5. Mary Arseneau, introduction to *Recovering Christina Rossetti: Female Community and Incarnational Poetics* (Basingstoke: Palgrave, 2004), p. 2.
6. See Diane D'Amico's article, 'Christina Rossetti's Christian Year: Comfort for "the weary heart"', *The Victorian Newsletter*, 71–2 (fall 1987) 36–42.
7. John Keble, 'Mysticism as applied to the Works of Nature, and generally to the external World', *Tracts for the Times* (Oxford: Clarendon Press, 1877), vol. 6, p. 143. Quoted in *VDP*, p. 54.
8. John Henry Newman, *Apologia pro Vita Sua* (London: Penguin, 1994), p. 37.
9. Herbert Sussman, *Fact Into Figure: Typology in Carlyle, Ruskin, and the Pre-Raphaelite Brotherhood*, (Columbus: Ohio State University Press, 1979), p. 9.
10. This belief relates to the Old Testament God who appeared often as a cloud or a voice, but never took corporeal form.
11. Isaac Williams, *Selections from the Writings of Isaac Williams* (London: Rivingtons, 1890), pp. 217–18.
12. The phrase, 'consider the lilies' is found in both Matthew 6:28 and Luke 12:27.
13. The word 'single', in a biblical context, means 'sound, healthy, free of defect', *The Combined Bible Dictionary and Concordance* (London: Marshall Pickering, 1990), p. 392
14. The lily occurs often in the Song of Solomon, a book read typically as 'the narrative of Solomon's love which prefigures the love of Christ for the Church'. *The Combined Bible Dictionary and Concordance*, p. 398.
15. 'Spin' here refers to drawing out and twisting into thread. *The Combined Bible Dictionary and Concordance*, p. 401.
16. 'And upon the top of the pillars was lily work'; 'the brim thereof was wrought like the brim of a cup, with flowers of lilies', 1 Kings 7:22, 26.

17. 'I counsel thee to keep the king's commandment, and that in regard of the oath of God', Ecclesiastes 8:2.
18. Isaac Williams, *Sermons on the Characters of the Old Testament* (London: Rivingtons, 1860), p. 214.
19. 'lo, I have given thee a wise and an understanding heart; so that there was none like thee before thee, neither after thee shall any arise like unto thee', 1 Kings 3:12.
20. 'And I have also given thee that which thou hast not asked, both riches and honour', 1 Kings 3:13.
21. Their connection is reinforced with the placement of the poem, which appeared originally within the text of *The Face of the Deep*. The poem follows a prose passage exhorting mankind to be alert and watchful for Christ's return so that 'he shall abide in eternal fellowship with Christ' (*FD* 391). That '"Consider the Lilies of the Field"' follows this sentence is typological-ly significant, because the poem explicitly links the prose idea of fellowship with Christ to Solomon.
22. Isaac Williams, *Thoughts on the Study of the Holy Gospels* (London: Rivingtons, 1876), p. 6.

2 'Decayed Branches from a Strong Stem': Rossetti's Keatsian heritage

1. G. B. Tennyson notes that the Tractarian response to nature was different from Wordsworth's, because 'It is not enough to be responsive to nature's beauties as things in themselves, or even as vague pointers to a higher power'. The Tractarian view of nature relied upon a specifically 'Christian understanding of nature as an analogue of God and a Christian understand-ing of sin as an impediment to seeing God clearly through nature'. *VDP*, 98.
2. It was Polidori's father, Gaetano, who privately printed his granddaughter Rossetti's first volume of poetry, *Verses* (1847).
3. William Michael's assertion is very dubious here, as Wordsworth's influence was inescapable in this period.
4. Mackenzie Bell, *Christina Rossetti: A Biographical and Critical Study* (London: Hurst and Blackett Limited, 1898), p. 13.
5. For a discussion of the Pre-Raphaelite Brotherhood's role in the artistic and commercial rehabilitation of Keats in nineteenth-century art, see Sarah Wooton's essay, 'Ghastly Visualities: Keats and Victorian Art,' in *The Influence and Anxiety of the British Romantics*, ed. Sharon Ruston (Lewiston: Edwin Mellen Press, 1999), pp. 159–80.
6. George H. Ford, *Keats and the Victorians: A Study of his Influence and Rise to Fame, 1821–1895.* (London: Archdon Books, 1962), p. 107–8. Christina Rossetti is only mentioned once in this book.
7. It was a view shared by Oscar Wilde who wrote of Keats as the 'the forerun-ner of the Pre-Raphaelite school'. Quotation taken from Susan J. Wolfson, 'Feminizing Keats', *Critical Essays on John Keats*, ed. Hermione De Almeida (Mass: W. W. Norton and Co., 1990), p. 336.
8. Introduction to *Keats: The Critical Heritage*, ed. G. M. Matthews (London: Routledge and Kegan Paul, 1971), p. 31.

9. J. B. Bullen, *The Pre-Raphaelite Body: Fear and Desire in Painting, Poetry, and Criticism* (Oxford: Clarendon Press, 1998), p. 7.
10. Ruskin's pamphlet, *Pre-Raphaelitism*, is in *The Complete Works of John Ruskin*, ed. E. T. Cook and Alexander Wedderburn, vol. 13 (London: George Allen, 1904), p. 358.
11. Jerome Bump, 'Christina Rossetti and the Pre-Raphaelite Brotherhood', in *ACR*, p. 339.
12. John Ruskin to Dante Gabriel Rossetti, 24 January, 1861, *Letters of Dante Gabriel Rossetti*, ed. Oswald Doughty and John Robert Wahl, vol. 2 (Oxford: The Clarendon Press, 1965), p. 391.
13. James W. Hood, introduction to *Divining Desire: Tennyson and the Poetics of Transcendence* (Aldershot: Ashgate, 2000), p. 8.
14. William Michael's notes on 'Repining' tellingly specify that the original title of the poem was '*An Argument*', and that it was 'very considerably longer' in manuscript form (*The Poetical Works*, p. 460).
15. Barbara Fass, 'Christina Rossetti and St. Agnes' Eve', *Victorian Poetry* (spring, 1976) 33.
16. Lynda Palazzo, *Christina Rossetti's Feminist Theology*, p. 4.
17. Thomas Parnell, 'The Hermit', *Collected Poems of Thomas Parnell*, ed. Claude Rawson and F. P. Lock (Delaware: University of Delaware Press, 1989), l. 23.
18. For more on DGR and Keats, see Chapter 3 of Sarah Wooton, *Consuming Keats: Nineteenth-Century Representations in Art and Literature* (Basingstoke: Palgrave, 2006), pp 78–106.
19. Keats differentiates his own poetic talent from Byron's in his letter to George and Georgiana Keats of 20 September 1819: 'You speak of Lord Byron and me — There is a great difference between us. He describes what he sees — I describe what I imagine — Mine is the hardest task' (*JK Letters*, vol. 2: 200).
20. Hönnighausen, Gisela, 'Emblematic Tendencies in the Works of Christina Rossetti', *Victorian Poetry* 10 (1972) 4.
21. The manuscript poem contains two additional stanzas about a young girl who, though she appeared healthy, has died. (manuscript notes, *Complete Poems*, 242).
22. Antony H. Harrison, *Christina Rossetti In Context* (Brighton: The Harvester Press, 1988), p. 9.
23. D'Amico, *CR* 32.
24. 'For all flesh is as grass, and all the glory of man as the flower of grass. The grass withereth, and the flower thereof falleth away', 1 Peter 1:24.
25. See Ruth 4: 13–22.
26. Keats famously coined the term '*Negative Capability*' to define a quality present in 'a man of achievement, especially in literature', and as a state in which 'a man is capable of being in uncertainties, mysteries, doubts, without any irritable reaching after fact and reason' (To George and Thomas Keats, 27 (?) December 1817. *JK Letters*, vol. 1: 193).
27. DGR, sonnet 4 'On Keats' from 'Five English Poets', *Dante Gabriel Rossetti: Collected Writings* (London: J.M. Dent, 1999), p. 425.
28. Susan J. Wolfson, "Feminizing Keats," *Critical Essays on John Keats*, p. 321.
29. Susan J. Wolfson, "Keats and Gender Criticism," *The Persistence of Poetry: Bicentennial Essays on Keats*. eds. Robert M. Ryan and Ronald A. Sharp (Amherst: University of Massachusetts Press, 1998), p. 89.

30. Susan J. Wolfson, "Keats Enters History: Autopsy, *Adonais*, and the Fame of Keats", *Keats and History*, ed. Nicholas Roe (Cambridge: Cambridge University Press, 1995), p. 31.
31. Elizabeth Barrett Browning to Mary Russell Mitford, 26 October 1841, quoted in Susan J. Wolfson, 'Keats Enters History: Autopsy, *Adonias* and the Fame of Keats', p. 19.
32. P. B. Shelley, Preface to 'Adonais', *Shelley's Poetry and Prose*, ed. Donald R. Heiman and Sharon B. Powers (New York: W. W. Norton and Company, 1977), p. 391.
33. 'And that which fell among thorns are they, which, when they have heard, go forth, and are choked with cares and riches and pleasures of this life, and bring no fruit to perfection' (Luke 8:14).
34. Rossetti's use of the word 'goodly' suggests a further Keatsian link. His sonnet, 'On First Looking Into Chapman's Homer' begins, 'Much have I travell'd in the realms of gold, / And many goodly states and kingdoms seen' (*KCP*, ll. 1–2, 34). Keats's awareness of his own literary inheritance is shown in his appreciation of Homer, and of Chapman's translation which '[speaks] out loud and bold' (line 8).
35. Sarah Wootton, *Consuming Keats*, p. 27.
36. Catherine Musello Cantalupo, 'The Devotional Poet and the Rejection of Romantic Nature' in *ACR*, p. 285.
37. 'Three Stages' 1 was written on 14 February 1848. 'Three Stages' 2 was written on 18 April 1849. 'Three Stages' 3 was written on 25 July 1854. They were first published together in *Verses* (1896).
38. 'And now Lord, what wait I for? my hope is in thee' (Psalms 39:7). 'I wait for the Lord, my soul doth wait, and in his word do I hope' (Psalms 130:5).
39. In *New Poems* (1896), this line reads, 'Till my heart dreamed, and maybe wandered too', as it does in the original 1854 manuscript. Crump, *Complete Poems*, 'Textual Notes', vol. 3: 451, note 22.

3 'Great Love and Long Study': Dante, Petrarch, and *Monna Innominata*

1. A notable exception is William Whitla's detailed structural critique, 'Questioning the Convention: Christina Rossetti's Sonnet Sequence "*Monna Innominata*"' in *ACR*, pp. 82–131.
2. CGR to The Firm, 24 November 1886. *The Rossetti Macmillan Letters*, ed. Lona Mosk Packer (Berkeley: University of California Press, 1963), p. 154. Packer notes that in this letter Rossetti crossed out 'the reader' and replaced it with 'the editor'. See note 3, p. 154 in this edition of the letters.
3. For more on this subject, see Marguerite Mills Chiarenza, *The Divine Comedy: Tracing God's Art* (Boston: Twayne Publishers, 1989), p. 11.
4. *Dante: The Critical Heritage 1314 (?)–1870*, ed. Michael Caesar (London: Routledge, 1989), p. 66.
5. Thomas Carlyle, Lecture 3: 'The Hero As Poet', 12 May 1840, *On Heroes, Hero-Worship, and the Heroic In History: Six Lectures*, reported with emendations and additions (London: James Fraser, 1841), p. 149.
6. John Keats to George and Thomas Keats, 21 December 1817, *JK Letters*, vol 1, 192.

7. S. T. Coleridge, 'Lecture on Dante', *Coleridge's Miscellaneous Criticism*, ed. Thomas Middleton Raysor (London: Constable and Co., Ltd., 1936), p. 152.
8. Steve Ellis, *Dante and English Poetry: Shelley to T. S. Eliot* (Cambridge: Cambridge University Press, 1983), p. 107.
9. John Keats to George and Georgiana Keats, 16 April 1819, *JK Letters*, vol. 2: 91. The text of the verse lines cited below is from this letter; Keats originally drafted the poem on the fly-leaf of his copy of Cary's *Dante* (1814); see *KCP* pp. 245–6.
10. DGR, 'Dante At Verona', *Dante Gabriel Rossetti: Collected Writings*, ed. Jan Marsh. (London: J. M. Dent, 1999), ll. 415–20.
11. CGR, "Dante: The Poet Illustrated Out of the Poem", *The Century Illustrated Monthly Magazine* 27, (February 1884) 572.
12. For a recent discussion of the importance of Dante to the Rossetti family, see Chapter 6 of Mary Arseneau, *Recovering Rossetti*, pp. 163–90.
13. The source of these quotations is *Inferno*, 1: 83.
14. John Keats to Benjamin Bailey, 22 November 1817, *JK Letters*, vol. 1: 184.
15. 'The Imagination may be compared to Adam's dream — he awoke and found it truth', John Keats to Benjamin Bailey, 22 November 1817, *JK Letters*, vol. 1: 185.
16. CGR, "Dante, An English Classic", *Churchman's Shilling Magazine and Family Treasury* 2, (1867) 200.
17. *VDP* 80.
18. Rossetti had been a friend of Hueffer's wife Cathy (daughter of Ford Madox Brown) since childhood. Her sister Lucy married William Michael. Jan Marsh's biography identifies Hueffer's book as a source for *Monna Innominata*.
19. Francis Hueffer, *The Troubadours* (London: Chatto and Windus, 1878), p. 272.
20. Lord Byron, 'Don Juan', (1821) *The Complete Poetical Works*, ed. Jerome J. McGann, vol. 5 (Oxford: Clarendon Press, 1986), canto 3:8.
21. Charles Cayley, *Dante's Divine Comedy*, 3 vols. (London: Longman, Brown, Green and Longmans, 1853). All quotations from the *Divine Comedy* in this discussion are taken from Charles Cayley's translation. Having begun studying Italian under Gabriele Rossetti in 1847, Cayley became Christina Rossetti's close personal friend, though she rejected his proposal of marriage. She became his literary executor after his death. She admired his translation of Dante privately, and promoted it publicly in her article 'Dante, An English Classic', and annotated Cayley's Dante volumes for a second edition (never published). She also uses his translation in her devotional prose work, *Time Flies*. The Italian quotations themselves are taken from the text of Rossetti's *Monna Innominata*. For a fascinating study of Rossetti's relationship with Cayley, see Kamilla Denman and Sarah Smith, "Christina Rossetti's Copy of C. B. Cayley's *Divine Comedy*", Victorian Poetry (vol. 32 1994) 315–36.
22. The Petrarchan epigraphs in Italian are taken from the text of Rossetti's *Monna Innominata*. All English translations of Petrarch's *Canzoniere* are taken from Charles Cayley's translation, *The Sonnets and Stanzas of Petrarch* (London: Longmans, Green and Co., 1879). Cayley's translation includes new titles for some of Petrarch's poems. These titles are reproduced in my

references. Where Cayley gives no title, I have reproduced the numbers he ascribes to each poem.

23. That Rossetti is aware of the problems of such an approach is revealed in her narrator's frustration at her inability to remember the event: 'If only I could recollect it, such / A day of days!'

24. Rossetti notes the relevance of this poetic invocation to contemporary poetry in her article on Dante: 'My first quotation (Paradise, canto I), consisting of an invocation of the Spirit of Poetry, befits both Dante and his translator [Cayley], while, as it were, striking one dominant note of our study ...' CGR, 'Dante. The Poet Illustrated Out of the Poem', *The Century*, 567.

25. In the *Book of Esther*, king Ahasueras is persuaded by his advisor Haman to carry out a slaughter of the Jews. One of his wives, Esther, also a Jew, risks death in violating the law and approaching the king to plead for her people. She gains the king's favor, and he stops the planned genocide, allowing the Jews to avenge themselves on their enemies.

26. The phrase is used in the same way in Genesis 10:18: 'And the Arvadite, and the Zemarite, and Hamathite: and afterward were the families of Canaanites spread abroad'; and Zechariah 2:6: 'flee from the land of the north, saith the Lord: for I have spread you abroad as the four winds of the heaven; saith the Lord' (Zechariah 2:6).

27. Matthew 10:16, 'Behold, I send you forth as sheep in the midst of wolves: be ye therefore wise as serpents, and harmless as doves'.

28. Esther 8:3, 'And Esther spake yet again before the king, and fell down at his feet, and besought him with tears to put away the mischief of Haman the Agagite, and his device that he had devised against the Jews'.

29. Genesis 32:28, 'And he said, Thy name shall be called no more Jacob, but Israel: for as a prince hast thou power with God and with men, and hast prevailed'.

30. This passage is also a link to the Petrarchan quotation of sonnet 4: 'Take flight all thought and things that it contains / And therein love alone with you remains' (canzone 9, 44–5).

31. '"No injury was done me," he replied, / "If One, that taketh whom he lists and when, / This passage to me often has denied. / His will becomes the righteous will of men', *Purgatorio* 2: 94–7.

32. This is perhaps Rossetti's response to sonnet 43, the most famous of the *Sonnets from the Portuguese*, 'How do I love thee? Let me count the ways' (Elizabeth Barrett Browning, *Selected Poems*, ed. Colin Graham [London: J. M. Dent, 1996], line 1, 231).

4 'A Courteous Tilt in the Strong-Minded Woman Lists': Rossetti, St. Paul, and women

1. This passage recalls the poet's younger self with its allusion to lines 115–16 of 'The Lowest Room': 'Why should not you, why should not I / Attain heroic strength?' (1: 200) The speaker of these lines is modeled on Rossetti's sister Maria, who is also the 'exemplary Christian' of this passage.

2. Gosse, Edmund, "Christina Rossetti", *The Century Magazine* 46 (June 1893) 214.

3. Angela Leighton, *Victorian Women Poets: Writing Against the Heart* (London: Harvester, 1992), p. 135.
4. Introduction to D'Amico *CR*, p. 16.
5. John Milton, *Selected Prose*, ed. C. A. Patrides (Middlesex: Penguin Books, 1974), 213.
6. The imagery in this last paragraph of the mirage of an orchard concealing a 'barren desert' recalls another Miltonic passage, the devil's banquet in *Paradise Lost*, when the fruit turns to ashes in the mouths of Satan's followers. See book X, ll. 547–72.
7. See Diane D'Amico, 'Christina Rossetti's "Helpmeet"', *The Victorian Newsletter* (spring 1994) 25–8; and Chapter 5 of *Faith, Gender and Time*.
8. Sandra M Gilbert and Susan Gubar, *The Madwoman in the Attic* (New Haven: Yale University Press, 1979), p. 575.
9. This advice is repeated in Romans 12:16: 'Be not wise in your own conceits'.
10. Romans 11:17–21: 'And if some of the branches be broken off, and thou, being a wild olive tree, wert graffed in among them, and with them partakest of the root and fatness of the olive tree; / Boast not against the branches. But if thou boast, thou bearest not the root, but the root thee. / Thou wilt say then, The branches were broken off, that I might be graffed in. / Well; because of unbelief they were broken off, and thou standest by faith. Be not highminded, but fear'.
11. Proverbs 26:5, 12, 16: 'Answer a fool according to his folly, lest he be wise in his own conceit'; 'Seest thou a man wise in his own conceit? there is more hope of a fool than of him'; 'The sluggard is wiser in his own conceit than seven men that can render a reason'.
12. The complete verse from Galatians reads, 'For it is written, Rejoice, thou barren that bearest not; break forth and cry, thou that travailest not: for the desolate hath many more children than she which hath an husband' (4:27).
13. Matthew 3:16: 'And Jesus, when he was baptized, went up straightway out of the water: and, lo, the heavens were opened unto him, and he saw the Spirit of God descending like a dove, and lighting upon him'.
14. 1 John 4:8: 'He that loveth not knoweth not God; for God is love'.
15. Ephesians 3: 3–4, 9: 'How that by revelation he made known unto me the mystery; (as I wrote afore in few words, / Whereby, when ye read, ye may understand my knowledge in the mystery of Christ)'; 'And to make all men see what is the fellowship of the mystery, which from the beginning of the world hath been hid in God, who created all things by Jesus Christ'.
16. Georgina Battiscombe, *Christina Rossetti: A Divided Life* (London: Constable, 1981), p. 183.
17. The biblical significance of weights and measures relates to Proverbs 20:10: 'Divers weights and divers measures, both of them are alike an abomination to the Lord' and 20:23: 'Divers weights are an abomination unto the Lord; and a false balance is not good'.
18. Exodus 20:17: 'Thou shalt not covet thy neighbour's house, thou shalt not covet they neighbour's wife, nor his manservant, nor his maidservant, nor his ox, nor his ass, nor any thing that is thy neighbour's'.
19. Ephesians 5:31–32: 'For this cause shall a man leave his father and mother, and shall be joined unto his wife, and they two shall be one flesh. This is a great mystery, but I speak concerning Christ and the church'.

20. Ephesians 5:33: 'Nevertheless let every one of you in particular so love his wife even as himself; and the wife see that she reverence her husband'.

21. I Peter 3:7: 'Likewise, ye husbands, dwell with them according to knowledge, giving honour unto the wife, as unto the weaker vessel, and as being heirs together of the grace of life; that your prayers not be hindered'.

22. Romans 15:1: 'We then that are strong ought to bear the infirmities of the weak, and not to please ourselves'.

23. Genesis 2:18: 'And the Lord God said, It is not good that man should be alone; I will make him an help meet for him'.

24. Diane D'Amico notes that the Anglican definition of the word 'helpmeet' is not limited to women within marriage, and also includes women who serve society and God. D'Amico concludes, therefore, that 'Rossetti is not celebrating human love and marriage, but rather the status women can achieve through love of Christ' (Diane D'Amico, 'Christina Rossetti's Helpmeet,' *The Victorian Newsletter* [spring 1994]: 27). However, Rossetti's theology is generally inclusive of various identities for women, and it is likely that this model of female service, while primarily aimed at pleasing God, also encompasses the earthly relationships between men and women.

25. Lynda Palazzo raises the possibility that Rossetti may have kept her distance from this group because she 'did not have the firm social or financial backing which many suffragists enjoyed. She had to court the goodwill of publishers and had to tread warily to avoid offending her brother William, on whose kindness she and her mother depended' (33).

26. Jan Marsh tells us that Rossetti's letter was in response to Webster's argument in her column in the 1878 *Examiner* that 'women householders bore an equal burden of taxation and had an equal right to representation. If the state allowed single and widowed women to live independently ... it must accept the notion of Eve without an Adam and grant her equal citizenship' (*LB* 465).

27. 'For tactical reasons the bill had drawbacks, not the least being that under its provisions married women such as Mrs. Webster herself would still be denied the vote. Some women therefore objected to the bill as seeming to cast a slur on wives and mothers ...' (*LB* 465).

28. Rossetti here refers to Chapter 7 of Plato's *Republic*, wherein it is proposed that women 'take part in warfare and whatever else guarding the community involves' (trans. Robin Waterfield, [Oxford: Oxford University Press, 1993], 169).

29. Cynthia Scheinberg, '"Measure to yourself a prophet's place": Biblical Heroines, Jewish Difference and Women's Poetry', in *Women's Poetry, Late Romantic to Late Victorian: Gender and Genre, 1830–1900*, eds. Isobel Armstrong and Virginia Blain (London: Macmillan, 1999), 265.

30. Ruth 1:16: 'for whither thou goest I will go; and where thou lodgest, I will lodge: thy people shall be my people, and thy God my God'.

31. Rossetti rarely includes chapter and verse citation within her prose, and this specific reference here suggests that she wanted her readers to study this proverb in full.

32. For more on Rossetti and Esther, see the discussion of sonnet 8 of *Monna Innominata* in Chapter 3 of this book.

33. 1 Kings 3:9: 'Give therefore thy servant an understanding heart to judge thy people, that I may discern between good and bad'.
34. Hebrews 11:34: 'Quenched the violence of fire, escaped the edge of the sword, out of weakness were made strong, waxed valiant in fight, turned to flight the armies of aliens'.
35. 1 Corinthians 1:25: 'Because the foolishness of God is wiser than men; and the weakness of God is stronger than men'.
36. Judges 9:53: 'And a certain woman cast a piece of millstone upon Abimelech's head, and all to brake his skull'.
37. Diane D'Amico writes that 'Rossetti's willingness to see the feminine in Christ sets her in opposition to the more popular "muscular Christianity" of her day, reminding us again that although conservative politically, Rossetti was often, for her time, radical in her religious thought' (*CR* 141).
38. Later Rossetti writes, 'We exercise by nature the instinct of inequality: by grace only can we acquire the intuition of equality' (*FD* 501).
39. Matthew 8:9: 'For I am a man under authority, having soldiers under me: and I say to this man, Go, and he goeth; and to another, Come, and he cometh; and to my servant, Do this, and he doeth it'.
40. Song of Solomon 5:1: 'I am come into my garden, my sister, my spouse'.
41. This portrayal of reciprocal love between Christ and women is not new to Rossetti's work. The conclusion of her 1857 poem, 'The Heart Knoweth Its Own Bitterness' looks forward to heaven as a place where 'There God shall join and no man part, / I full of Christ and Christ of me' (55–6, 3: 265).
42. Of 'The Heart Knoweth Its Own Bitterness', William Michael writes, 'Few things written by Christina contain more of her innermost self than this' (notes to *The Poetical Works*, 472).
43. The gender specificity of this poem is given a new twist in *Verses* where it is published under the title 'Vigil of St. Bartholomew'. This title, in effect, explicitly makes the poem relevant both to men and women, and further suggests that Bartholomew acted after the example of the wise virgins, emulating their feminine virtues of calm and patient vigilance.

5 Spiritual autobiography in *Time Flies: A Reading Diary*

1. Germaine Greer, *Slip-Shod Sibyls: Recognition, Rejection, and the Woman Poet* (London: Viking, 1995), p. 369.
2. Rev. H. W. Burrows, preface to Christina Rossetti, *Annus Domini: A Prayer for Each Day of the Year, Founded on a Text of Holy Scripture* (Oxford: James Parker, 1874).
3. Tony Castle, introduction to *The Prayers of Christina Rossetti* (London: Marshall Pickering, 1989) p. 8. Castle mentions *Annus Domini, Seek and Find*, and *Called to be Saints* as 'the best remembered' works, p. 10
4. Rebecca Crump, introduction to *The Complete Poems*, vol. 2: 14.
5. WMR, 'Prefatory Note' to *Maude: A Story For Girls* in Christina Rossetti, *Maude: Prose and Verse*, ed. with an introduction by R. W. Crump (Hamden: Archon Books, 1976) p. 80.
6. Rossetti wrote of her feelings on Sisterhoods to Caroline Gemmer, a fellow writer known under the pseudonym Gerda Fay, on 27 June 1884: '[I] went

thro' a sort of romantic impression on the subject like many young people. No, I feel no drawing in that direction: really, of the two, I might perhaps have less unadaptedness in some ways to the hermit life. But I suppose the niche really suited to me is the humble family nook I occupy; nor am I hankering after a loftier. Nor, I think, I may truly say, did I ever wish to devote myself at any period of my prolonged life. It was my dear sister who had the pious, devotional, absorbed temperament' (*Letters* 3: 196).

7. In her discussion of St. Hilary, who left to become a bishop, Rossetti's sympathies are with the wife, for whom she anticipates a divine reversal of fortune: 'Wherefore of her I am free to think as of one "unknown and yet well known:" on earth of less dignified name than her husband and daughter, in Paradise, it may well be of equal account. For many are they of whom the world is both "not worthy" and ignorant. Moreover it is written: "Many that are first shall be last; and the last shall be first"' (13 January, *TF* 12).

8. Preston was an American poet who had sent Rossetti a copy of her book of poetry, *Old Song and New* (1870).

9. In a previous letter on 14 June 1878, she had warned Cook of the seriousness of her beliefs: 'I never could be at my ease or happy in literary company with persons who look down upon what I look up to. I have not *played* at Xtianity, & therefore I cannot play at unbelief' (*Letters* 2: 167).

10. 1 Corinthians 12:26.

11. D'Amico, *CR*, p. 160.

12. Diane D'Amico, 'Christina Rossetti's *Christian Year*: Comfort for "the weary heart"', *The Victorian Newsletter* 72 (fall 1987) 41.

13. Rossetti here alludes to Ecclesiastes' idea that 'there is no new thing under the sun,' (Ecclesiastes 1:9) and that 'all is vanity' (1:2). In Ecclesiastes, 'The preacher sought to find out acceptable words: and that which was written was upright, even words of truth' (12:10). So, too, does Rossetti ask of her subject, 'is it true?' However, Rossetti ignores parts of the book inconsistent with her thesis, such as the warning that 'The words of the wise are as goads, and as nails ...' (12–11) and that 'of making many books there is no end; and much study is a weariness of the flesh' (12:12).

14. The 'masterly translator' to whom she refers is Dante Gabriel Rossetti, according to the annotations made by the author in a copy of the book at the University of Texas at Austin. ('Notes' to *Selected Prose of Christina Rossetti*, eds. David A. Kent and P. G. Stanwood [London: Macmillan, 1998], note 175, p. 392).

15. Amos 9:9, 'I will sift the house of Israel among all nations, like as corn is sifted in a sieve'; Isaiah 30:28, 'And his breath ... shall ... sift the nations with the sieve of vanity'.

16. Luke 22:31, 'Satan hath desired to have you, that he may sift you as wheat'.

17. In a July 27 entry for *Time Flies*, Rossetti uses Satan's desire to sift Christians as a proof that Christians are inherently good: 'We are certified as good seed by Satan's desiring permission to sift us' (*TF* 143).

18. In *Letter and Spirit* (1883), the book which precedes *Time Flies*, this recognition of the problems inherent in human attempts to translate divine truth is taken to an extreme which comes close to despair. 'To modify by a boundless license of imagination the Voice of Revelation ... falls within the range of human faculties. And thus may not light be thrown on that mass of bewildering error ...

which at every turn meeting us as man's invention, is after all a more or less close travestie of truth? So like in detail, so unlike as a whole, to the truth it simulates, that alternately we incline to ask: If so much is known without immediate revelation, wherefore reveal? If truth pervades such errors, if such errors can be grafted upon truth, is truth itself distinguishable, or is it worth distinguishing?' (*LS* 10–11).

6 Imagining Faith: Earth and Heaven in *The Face of the Deep*

1. Frederick E. Maser, *Christina Rossetti in the Maser Collection*, with essays by Mary Louise Jarden and Frederick E. Maser, foreward by James Tanis (Bryn Mawr College Library, 1991), p. 20.
2. Genesis 31:10. This is said by Rachel, Jacob's barren first wife, about her childless state. She has her husband take her maid to wife, then claims the maid's child as her own.
3. *Called to Be Saints* was dedicated to Maria Rossetti, and the poems of *Sing-Song* 'dedicated without permission to the baby who suggested them'.
4. A. Smellie, 'Christina Rossetti and Her Message', *Wesleyan Methodist Magazine* 118 (1885) 203–6, quoted in *Christina Rossetti: Critical Perspectives, 1862–1982*, ed. Edna Kotin Charles (London: Associated University Press, 1985), p. 23.
5. Colleen Hobbs, 'A View from "The Lowest Place": Christina Rossetti's Devotional Prose', *Victorian Poetry* 32 (autumn-winter, 1994) 411.
6. Catherine Musello Cantalupo, 'Christina Rossetti: The Devotional Poet and the Rejection of Romantic Nature', in *ACR*, p. 275.
7. *The Letters of Virginia Woolf*, vol. 1, 1888–1912, ed. Nigel Nicholson (New York: Harcourt, Brace, Jovanovich, 1975), p. 258.
8. 'After this I beheld, and lo, a great multitude, which no man could number, of all nations, and kindreds, and people, and tongues, stood before the Throne, and before the Lamb, clothed with white robes, and palms in their hands', (Revelation 7:9).
9. 'the tongue is a little member, and boasteth great things. Behold, how great a matter a little fire kindleth! / And the tongue is a fire, a world of iniquity: so is the tongue among our members, that it defileth the whole body, and setteth on fire the course of nature; and it is set on fire of hell' (James 3:5–6); 'the tongue can no man tame; it is an unruly evil, full of deadly poison', (3:8).
10. Mary Arseneau and Jan Marsh, 'Intertextuality and Intratextuality: The Full Text of Christina Rossetti's "Harmony on First Corinthians XIII" Rediscovered', *The Victorian Newsletter* 88 (fall 1995) 20.
11. According to Eastons Bible Dictionary, bdellium 'designates a product of the land of Havilah and ... was probably an aromatic gum like balsam ... Others think the word denotes 'pearls or some precious stone'. Biblical amber is not the fossilized resin we know today, but a compound of silver and gold, or possibly brass. (www.crosswalk.com) Both bdellium and onyx stone originally appear in Eden in Genesis 2:12, 'And the gold of that land is good: there is bdellium and onyx stone'.

12. The Ethiopian Eunuch was converted to Christianity by Philip the evangelist. The Eunuch is reading Isaiah and Philip asks him, 'Understandest thou what thou readest?' (Acts 8:30) and he replies, 'How can I, except some man should guide me?' (8:31).

13. Robert M. Kachur, 'Repositioning the Female Christian Reader: Christina Rossetti as Tractarian Hermeneut in *The Face of the Deep*', *Victorian Poetry* 35, no. 2 (summer 1997) 3.

14. Antony Harrison, *Christina Rossetti in Context*, p. 101.

15. Joel Westerholm, '"I Magnify Mine Office": Christina Rossetti's Authoritative Voice in her Devotional Prose', *Victorian Newsletter* 84 (fall 1993) 14.

16. In addition, the first three images are (so to speak) 'simple', while the last three have a biblical inflection: the 'gourd of a day and a night' alludes to Jonah 4:4–11, while the 'harvest' and 'vintage' are familiar images of judgment and salvation in the New Testament, including Revelation itself (for example, 14:15–20).

17. There is a similar treatment of the theme of hope in *Time Flies* when Rossetti writes, 'Hope, like the rainbow, can be evoked out of clouds and gloom to supply a bridge between earth and heaven: but can only be evoked by the sun-like love of God' (*TF* 279).

18. Rossetti's use of the Revised Version here, instead of the Authorized Version, underscores the idea that human works cannot be fulfilled or complete during the time of humanity's separation from God.

19. Sardis is one of the seven Asiatic churches judged in Revelation 3:1–6. Rossetti here is using Sardis as a metaphor for all humanity.

20. Helen Michie, *The Flesh Made World: Female Figures and Women's Bodies* (Oxford: Oxford University Press, 1990), p. 87.

21. 'And behold, a woman in the city, which was a sinner, when she knew that Jesus sat at meat in the Pharisee's house, brought an alabaster box of ointment' (Luke 7:37).

22. 'While adorning let it not be that outward adorning of plaiting the hair, and of wearing of gold, or of putting on of apparel' (1 Peter 3:3).

Selected Bibliography

Alighieri, Dante. *Dante's Divine Comedy, Translated in the Original Ternary Rhyme*. Translated by Charles Bagot Cayley. 3 Vols. London: Longman, Brown, Green, and Longmans, 1851.

Armstrong, Isobel. *Victorian Poetry: Poetry, poetics, and politics*. London: Routledge, 1993.

_____ and Virginia Blain, eds. *Women's Poetry, Late Romantic to Late Victorian: Gender and Genre, 1830–1900*. London: Macmillan, 1999.

Arseneau, Mary. *Recovering Christina Rossetti: Female Community and Incarnational Poetics*. Basingstoke: Palgrave, 2004.

_____ and Antony H. Harrison, Lorraine Janzen Kooistra, eds. *The Culture of Christina Rossetti: Female Poets and Victorian Contexts*. Athens: Ohio University Press, 1999.

Battiscombe, Georgina. *Christina Rossetti: A Divided Life*. London: Constable, 1981.

Bell, Mackenzie. *Christina Rossetti: A Biographical and Critical Study*. London: Hurst and Blackett, Ltd., 1898.

Bible, Authorised King James Version. London: Collins Clear-Type Press, 1957.

Bowra, C. M. *The Romantic Imagination*. London: Oxford University Press, 1950.

Browning, Elizabeth Barrett. *Selected Poems*. Edited by Colin Graham. London: J. M Dent, 1996.

Buchanan, Robert. *The Fleshly School of Poetry and Other Phenomena of the Day*. London: Strahan, 1872.

Bullen, J. B. *The Pre-Raphaelite Body: Fear and Desire in Painting, Poetry, and Criticism*. Oxford: Clarendon Press, 1998.

Bump, Jerome. 'Christina Rossetti and the Pre-Raphaelite Brotherhood'. In *The Achievement of Christina Rossetti*, ed. David A. Kent, 302–45. Ithaca: Cornell University Press, 1987.

Byron, George Gordon Lord. *The Complete Poetical Works*, Vol. 5. Edited by Jerome J. McGann. Oxford: Clarendon Press, 1993.

The Cambridge Companion to Feminist Theology. Edited by Susan Frank Parsons. Cambridge: Cambridge University Press, 2002.

Cantalupo, Catherine Musello. 'The Devotional Poet and the Rejection of Romantic Nature'. In *The Achievement of Christina Rossetti*, ed. David A. Kent, 274–300. Ithaca: Cornell University Press, 1987.

Carlyle, Thomas. *On Heroes, Hero-Worship, and the Heroic In History: Six Lectures, reported with emendations and additions*. London: James Fraser, 1841.

Castle, Tony. *The Prayers of Christina Rossetti*. London: Marshall Pickering, 1989.

Charles, Edna Kotin, ed. *Christina Rossetti: Critical Perspectives, 1862–1982*. London: Associated University Presses, 1985.

Codell, Julie F. 'Painting Keats: Pre-Raphaelite Artists Between Social Transgressions and Painterly Conventions'. *Victorian Poetry* 33 (1995): 341–369.

Coleridge, S. T. *Coleridge's Miscellaneous Criticism*. Edited by Thomas Middleton Raysor. London: Constable & Co., 1936.

The Combined Bible Dictionary and Concordance. London: Marshall Pickering, 1990.

Curran, Stuart. 'The Lyric Voice of Christina Rossetti'. *Victorian Poetry* 9 (autumn 1971): 287–99.

D'Amico, Diane. 'Christina Rossetti's "Helpmeet"'. *The Victorian Newsletter* (spring 1994): 25–8.

_____. 'Christina Rossetti's Christian Year: Comfort for "the weary heart"'. *The Victorian Newsletter*, 72 (fall 1987): 36–42.

_____. *Christina Rossetti: Faith, Gender, and Time*. Baton Rouge: Louisiana State University Press, 1999.

Dante: The Critical Heritage 1314(?)–1870. Edited by Michael Caesar. London: Routledge, 1989.

Denman, Kamilla and Sarah Smith. 'Christina Rossetti's Copy of C. B. Cayley's *Divine Comedy*'. *Victorian Poetry* 32 (1994): 315–37.

Doughty, Oswald. *Dante Gabriel Rossetti: A Victorian Romantic*. London: Frederick Muller, 1949.

Ellis, Steve. *Dante and English Poetry: Shelley to T. S. Eliot*. Cambridge: Cambridge University Press, 1983.

Fass, Barbara. 'Christina Rossetti and St. Agnes' Eve'. *Victorian Poetry* 14, no. 1 (spring, 1976): 33–46.

Ford, George H. *Keats and the Victorians: A Study of his Influence and Rise to Fame, 1821–1895*. New Haven: Yale University Press, 1944.

Gill, Stephen. *Wordsworth and the Victorians*. Oxford: Clarendon Press, 1998.

Gilbert, Sandra M. and Susan Gubar. *The Madwoman in the Attic*. New Haven: Yale University Press, 1979.

Girouard, Mark. *The Return to Camelot: Chivalry and the English Gentleman*. New Haven: Yale University Press, 1981.

Gosse, Edmund. 'Christina Rossetti'. *The Century Magazine* 46 (June 1893): 211–17.

Greer, Germaine. *Slip-Shod Sibyls: Recognition, Rejection, and the Woman Poet*. London: Viking, 1995.

Harrison, Antony H. *Christina Rossetti in Context*. Brighton: The Harvester Press, 1988.

_____. *Victorian Poets and the Politics of Culture: Discourse and Ideology*. Charlottesville: University Press of Virginia, 1998.

_____. *Victorian Poets and Romantic Poems: Intertextuality and Ideology*. Charlottesville: University Press of Virginia, 1990.

Hobbs, Colleen. 'A View from "The Lowest Place": Christina Rossetti's Devotional Prose'. *Victorian Poetry* 32 (autumn-winter 1994): 409–28.

Honnighausen, Gisela. 'Emblematic Tendencies in the Works of Christina Rossetti'. *Victorian Poetry* 10 (spring 1972): 1–15.

Hood, James W. *Divining Desire: Tennyson and the Poetics of Transcendence*. Aldershot: Ashgate, 2000.

Hueffer, Frances. *The Troubadours: A History of Provençal Life and Literature in the Middle Ages*. London: Chatto and Windus, 1878.

Jarden, Mary Louise and Frederick E. Maser. *Christina Rossetti in the Master Collection, With Essays by Mary Louise Jarden & Frederick E. Maser*, foreword by James Tanis. Bryn Mawr College Library, 1991.

Jones, Kathleen. *Learning Not to be First: The Life of Christina Rossetti*. Gloucestershire: Oxford: Oxford University Press, 1992.

212 Selected Bibliography

Jump, John D., ed. *Tennyson: The Critical Heritage*. London: Routledge & Kegan Paul, 1967.

Kachur, Robert M. 'Repositioning the Female Christian Reader: Christina Rossetti as Tractarian Hermeneut in *The Face of the Deep*'. *Victorian Poetry* 35, no. 22 (summer 1997): 1–17.

Keats, John. *Complete Poems*. Edited by Jack Stillinger. London: Belknap Press, 1982.

_____. *The Letters of John Keats*. Edited by Hyder Edward Rollins. 2 Vols. Cambridge: Cambridge University Press, 1958.

Keble, John. *Tracts for the Times*. Oxford: Clarendon Press, 1877.

Kent, David A., ed. *The Achievement of Christina Rossetti*. With an introduction by Jerome J. McGann. Ithaca: Cornell University Press, 1987.

Kidd, James. 'You'll Pardon me for Being Jocular: *La Belle Dame Sans Merci* and Keats's Light Verse'. In *The Influence and Anxiety of the British Romantics*, ed. Sharon Ruston, 109–37. Lewiston: The Edwin Mellen Press, 1999.

Knoepflmacher, U. C., 'Avenging Alice: Christina Rossetti and Lewis Carroll'. *Nineteenth Century Literature* 41 (1986): 299–28.

_____ and G. B. Tennyson, eds. *Nature and the Victorian Imagination*. Berkeley: University of California Press, 1977.

The Language and Sentiment of Flowers. Compiled and Edited by L. V. London: Frederick Warne and Co., 1866.

Leighton, Angela. *Victorian Women Poets: Writing Against the Heart*. Hertfordshire: Harvester Wheatsheaf, 1992.

_____. '"When I am Dead, my Dearest": The Secret of Christina Rossetti'. *Modern Philology* 87 (1990): 373–88.

Lootens, Tricia. *Lost Saints: Silence, Gender and Victorian Literary Canonization*. Charlottesville: University Press of Virginia, 1996.

Lucas, F. L. *Ten Victorian Poets*. Cambridge: Cambridge University Press, 1940.

Marsh, Jan. *Christina Rossetti: A Literary Biography*. London: Jonathan Cape, 1994.

_____ , ed. *Christina Rossetti: Poems and Prose*. London: J. M Dent, 1994.

_____ . *Dante Gabriel Rossetti: Painter and Poet*. London: Weidenfeld and Nicholson, 1999.

_____. *Pre-Raphaelite Sisterhood*. London: Quartet Books, 1985.

Marshall, Linda E. 'Mysteries Beyond Angels in Christina Rossetti's *From House to Home*'. In *Women's Poetry, Late Romantic to Late Victorian, Gender and Genre, 1830–1900*, eds. Isobel Armstrong and Virginia Blain, 313–24. London: Macmillan, 1999.

Matthews, G. M., ed. *Keats: The Critical Heritage*. London: Routledge and Kegan Paul, 1971.

Mayberry, Katherine. *Christina Rossetti and the Poetry of Discovery*. Baton Rouge: Louisiana State University Press, 1989.

McGann, Jerome J. 'Christina Rossetti's Poems: A New Edition and a Revaluation'. In *The Beauty of Inflections: Literary Investigations in Historical Method and Theory*. Oxford: Clarendon Press, 1985.

_____. 'The Religious Poetry of Christina Rossetti'. In *The Beauty of Inflections: Literary Investigations in Historical Method and Theory*. Oxford: Clarendon Press, 1985.

Milbank, Alison. *Dante and The Victorians*. Manchester: Manchester University Press, 1998.

Milnes, Richard Monckton, ed. *Life, Letters, and Literary Remains of John Keats*. 2 Vols. London: Edward Moxon, 1848.

Milton, John. *Paradise Lost*. Edited by Christopher Ricks. Harmondsworth: Penguin Books, 1989.

———. *Selected Prose*. Edited by C. A. Patrides. Harmondsworth: Penguin Books, 1974.

Motion, Andrew. *Keats*. London: Faber, 1997.

Newman, John Henry. *Apologia Pro Via Sua*. 1864; London: Penguin, 1994.

Nineteenth-Century Women Poets: An Oxford Anthology. Edited by Isobel Armstrong and Joseph Bristow with Cath Sharrock. Oxford: Clarendon Press, 1996.

Packer, Lona Mosk. *Christina Rossetti*. Berkeley: Cambridge University Press, 1963.

Palazzo, Lynda. *Christina Rossetti's Feminist Theology*. Basingstoke: Palgrave, 2002.

———. 'The Prose Works of Christina Rossetti'. Ph.D. dissertation, University of Durham, 1992.

Parnell, Thomas. *Collected Poems of Thomas Parnell*. Edited by Claude Rawson and F. P. Lock. Delaware: University of Delaware Press, 1989.

Paulin, Tom, 'The Cadence in the Song: George Herbert and the Greatness of Christina Rossetti'. *Times Literary Supplement*, January 18, 2002: 3–4.

Petrarca, Francesco. *The Sonnets and Stanzas of Petrarch*. Translated by Charles Bagot Cayley. London: Longmans, Green, and Co., 1879.

Philips, Henry. *Floral Emblems*. London: Saunders and Otley, 1825.

Pite, Ralph. *The Circle of Our Vision: Dante's Presence in English Romantic Poetry*. Oxford: Clarendon Press, 1994.

Plato. *Republic*. Translated by Robin Waterfield. Oxford: Oxford University Press, 1993.

Pre-Raphaelitism: A Collection of Critical Essays. Edited with an introduction by James Sambrook. Chicago: University of Chicago Press, 1974.

Prestige, Leonard. *Pusey*. London: Mowbray, 1982.

Prickett, Steven. *Victorian Fantasy*. Bloomington: Indiana University Press, 1989.

Proctor, Ellen A. *A Brief Memoir of Christina Rossetti with a Preface by William Michael Rossetti*. London: SPCK, 1896.

Roe, Nicholas, ed. *Keats and History*. Cambridge: Cambridge University Press, 1995.

Rosenblum, Dolores. *Christina Rossetti: The Poetry of Endurance*. Carbondale: Southern Illinois University Press, 1986.

Rossetti, Christina. *Annus Domini: A Prayer for Each Day of the Year, Founded on a Text of Holy Scripture*. Oxford: James Parker, 1874.

———. *The Complete Poems of Christina Rossetti*. Edited by R. W. Crump. 3 Vols. Baton Rouge: Louisiana State University, 1979.

———. *The Complete Poems*. Edited by R. W. Crump with notes and introduction by Betty S. Flowers. London: Penguin, 2001.

———. 'Dante, An English Classic'. *Churchman's Shilling Magazine and Family Treasury* 2 (1867): 200–5.

———. 'Dante. The Poet Illustrated Out of the Poem'. *The Century Illustrated Monthly Magazine* 27 (February 1884): 566–73.

———. *The Face of the Deep: A Devotional Commentary on the Apocalypse*. London: SPCK, 1892.

_____. *Letter and Spirit: Notes on the Commandments*. London: SPCK, 1883.

_____. *The Letters of Christina Rossetti*. Edited by Antony H. Harrison. 4 Vols. Charlottesville: University Press of Virginia, 1997.

_____. *Maude: Prose and Verse*. Edited with an introduction by R. W. Crump, including a 'Prefatory Note' by William Michael Rossetti. Hamden, Conn.: Archon Books, 1976.

_____. *Seek and Find: A Double Series of Short Studies of the Benedicte*. London: SPCK, 1879.

_____. *Selected Prose of Christina Rossetti*. Edited by David A. Kent and P. G. Stanwood. London: Macmillan, 1998.

_____. *Time Flies: A Reading Diary*. London: SPCK, 1885.

Rossetti, Dante Gabriel. *Dante Gabriel Rossetti: Collected Writings*. Edited by Jan Marsh. London: J. M. Dent, 1999.

_____. *Letters of Dante Gabriel Rossetti*. Edited by Oswald Doughty and John Robert Wall. 4 Vols. Oxford: Clarendon Press, 1965.

Rossetti, William Michael, ed. *Dante Gabriel Rossetti: His Family Letters with a Memoir by William Michael Rossetti*. London: Ellis and Elvey, 1895.

_____, ed. *The Family Letters of Christina Georgina Rossetti, With Some Supplementary Letters and Appendices*. London: Brown, Langham, 1908.

_____, ed. *New Poems by Christina Rossetti, Hitherto Unpublished or Uncollected*. With a preface by William Michael Rossetti. London: Macmillan, 1900.

_____, ed. *The Poetical Works of Christina Georgina Rossetti*. With memoir and notes by William Michael Rossetti. London: Macmillan and Co., Limited, 1904.

_____, ed. *Præraphaelite Diaries and Letters*. London: Hurst and Blackett Limited, 1900.

_____, ed. *The P.R.B. Journal: William Michael Rossetti's Diary of the Pre-Raphaelite Brotherhood 1849–1853, Together With Other Pre-Raphaelite Documents*. Edited with introduction and notes by William E. Fredeman. Oxford: The Clarendon Press, 1975.

Ruskin, John. *The Complete Works of John Ruskin*. Edited by E. T. Cook and Alexander Wedderburn. Vol. 13. London: George Allen, 1904.

_____. *Modern Painters*. 3 Vols. Sunnyside: George Allen, 1888.

Sandars, Mary F. *The Life of Christina Rossetti*. London: Hutchinson, 1930.

Scheinberg, Cynthia. '"Measure to yourself a prophet's place": Biblical Heroines, Jewish Difference and Women's Poetry'. In *Women's Poetry, Late Romantic to Late Victorian: Gender and Genre, 1830–1900*, eds. Isobel Armstrong and Virginia Blain, 263–91. London: Macmillan, 1999.

Shaw, David W. Review of *Christina Rossetti: The Poetry of Endurance*, by Dolores Rosenblum. *Nineteenth Century Literature* 42, no. 2 (Sept. 1987): 387–9.

Shelley, Percy Bysshe. *Shelley's Poetry and Prose*. Edited by Donald R. Heiman and Sharon B. Powers. New York: W. W. Norton and Company, 1977.

Smulders, Sharon. *Christina Rossetti Revisited*. New York: Twayne, 1996.

Spear, Jeffrey L. *Dreams of an English Eden: Ruskin and His Tradition in Social Criticism*. New York: Columbia University Press, 1984.

Stein, Richard L. *The Ritual of Interpretation: The Fine Arts as Literature in Ruskin, Rossetti, and Pater*. Cambridge: Harvard University Press, 1975.

Stevenson, Catherine Barnes. 'How It Struck a Contemporary: Tennyson's "Lancelot and Elaine" and Pre-Raphaelite Art'. *Victorian Newsletter*, no. 60 (fall 1981): 8–12.

Sussman, Herbert L. *Fact Into Figure: Typology in Carlyle, Ruskin, and the Pre-Raphaelite Brotherhood*. Columbus: Ohio State University Press, 1979.

Symons, Arthur. *Studies in Strange Souls*. London: Charles J. Sawyer, 1929.

Tennyson, Alfred. *The Poems of Tennyson*, 2nd edn. Edited by Christopher Ricks. 3 Vols. London: Longman, 1987.

Tennyson, G. B. *Victorian Devotional Poetry: The Tractarian Mode*. Cambridge and London: Harvard University Press, 1981.

Thompson, F. M. L., *The Rise of Respectable Society: A Social History of Victorian Britain, 1830–1900*. London: Fontana Press, 1988.

Tracts for the Times. By members of the University of Oxford. Vol. 3, 1835–36. London: Rivingtons, 1836.

Victorian Women Poets: An Anthology. Edited by Angela Leighton and Margaret Reynolds. Oxford: Blackwell, 1995.

Victorian Women Poets: A New Annotated Anthology. Edited by Virginia Blain. Harlow: Pearson Education Limited, 2001.

Weintraub, Stanley. *Four Rossettis: A Victorian Biography*. London: W. H. Allen, 1978.

Westerholm, Joel. "'I Magnify Mine Office": Christina Rossetti's Devotional Prose'. *Victorian Newsletter* 84 (fall 1993): 11–17.

Whitla, William. 'Questioning the Convention: Christina Rossetti's Sonnet Sequence, "Monna Innominata"'. In *The Achievement of Christina Rossetti*, ed. David A.Kent, 82–131. Ithaca: Cornell University Press, 1987.

Williams, Isaac. *The Altar; or, Meditations in Verse on the Great Christian Sacrifice*. London: Joseph Masters, 1849.

_____. *Sermons on the Characters of the Old Testament*, 2nd edn. London: Rivingtons, 1860.

_____. *Selections From the Writings of Isaac Williams*. London: Rivingtons, 1890.

_____. *Thoughts on the Study of the Holy Gospels*. London: Rivingtons, 1876.

Wolfson, Susan J. 'Keats Enters History: Autopsy, *Adonais*, and the Fame of Keats'. In *Keats and History*, ed. Nicholas Roe, 17–45. Cambridge: Cambridge University Press, 1995.

_____. 'Keats and Gender Criticism'. In *The Persistence of Poetry: Bicentennial Essays on Keats*, eds. Robert M. Ryan and Ronald A Sharp, 88–108. Amherst: University of Massachusetts Press, 1998.

_____. 'Feminizing Keats'. In *Critical Essays on John Keats*, ed. Hermione De Almeida, 317–56. Massachusetts: W. W. Norton and Co., 1990.

Woolf, Virginia. 'I Am Christina Rossetti'. *The Common Reader, Second Series*. London: Hogarth Press, 1932.

_____. *The Letters of Virginia Woolf*. Edited by Nigel Nicholson. Vol. 1, 1888–1912. New York: Harcourt, Brace, Jovanovich, 1975.

Wootton, Sarah. *Consuming Keats: Nineteenth Century Representations in Art and Literature*. Basingstoke: Palgrave, 2006.

_____. 'Ghastly Visualities: Keats and Victorian Art'. In *The Influence and Anxiety of the British Romantics*, ed. Sharon Ruston, 159–80. Lewiston: The Edwin Mellen Press, 1999.

Index

'a certain woman', 122
Adam, 102–04, 157–58
analogy, 14, 17, 22, 66, 149–50, 151, 156, 191
Anglican Sisterhood, 135
Anglo-Catholicism, 10, 11, 12, 30, 173
  see also Oxford Movement
Apologia, 13
Arseneau, Mary, 2, 3, 5, 11, 179, 180, 202 n. 12

Babel, 175
Barrett-Browning, Elizabeth, 49, 68, 203 n. 32
Bell, Mackenzie, 31
Boaz, 49, 120
Bullen, J.M., 33
Bump, Jerome, 33, 34
Burrows, Rev. Hen, 132
Byron, 31, 68, 200 n. 19

Cambridge Apostles, 32
Cantalupo, Maria, 53, 172
Carlyle, Thomas, 32–3
Castle, Tony, 132
Cayley, Charles, 202 n. 21, 22
Chatterton, Thomas, 42
Christ, 20, 49, 54,133–4, 166, 190
  and the bride, 126, 128, 130
  as muse, 7, 186
  and Solomon, 21–2, 23–4, 28–9, 199 n. 21
  and typology, 157–60, 163–4
  and women, 108–9, 111, 112, 124, 126–30, 174–5
The Christian Year, 12
Coleridge, S.T., 31, 42, 60
Colossians, 166
Cook, Robert Keningale, 135–7
1 Corinthians, 101, 106, 111, 114, 137–8, 168, 205 n. 35
Crump, Rebecca, 133
Curran, Stuart, 4

D'Amico, Diane, 2, 45, 143, 145, 154, 205 n. 24, 206 n. 37
Dante Alighieri, 10
  and Beatrice, 61, 62, 86–7
  Cayley translations of, 202 n. 21
  Inferno, 76
  and Keats, 61–2
  Paradiso, 75, 86, 91, 93
  Purgatorio, 70, 71, 73, 78, 80, 84, 85, 87, 89
  and Romantics, 60–1, 63
  Christina Rossetti essays on, 63–4, 65, 66
  and DGR, 61–2
  and Gabriele Rossetti, 61
  and Victorians, 60–2
David, 83

Ecclesiastes, 20–4, 27, 28, 74, 134, 165, 166, 199 n. 17, 207 n. 13
Elisha, 142–3
Ellis, Steve, 61, 62
Ephesians, 78, 161, 108, 166, 204 n. 15, 19
Esther, 82–4, 121–2, 203 n. 25, 28
Ethiopian Eunuch, 180
Eve, 100–1, 102–4, 169, 187
Exodus, 157, 158, 159, 160, 204 n. 18

Fass, Barbara, 39, 41, 42
Flowers, Betty S., 1

Galatians, 103
Genesis, 83, 152, 189, 203 n. 26, 29, 205 n. 23
The Germ, 33, 34, 42, 52, 53
Gilbert, Sandra, 5
Gosse, Edmund 4, 97–8
Greenwell, Dora, 113
Greer, Germaine, 1, 2, 5, 131
Gubar, Susan, 5
Gutch, Reverend Charles, 116–17